How to Acquire $1 Million in Income Real Estate in One Year Using Borrowed Money in Your Free Time

Movtivated
Sellers

Divorce Probate

Foreclosure - Bankruptcy

Property Vacant

    Eviction Owner
            Moving or

Reo → Banks Living out
    Foreclosure of State
    Inventory

Money Sources

Other Peoples Money Private
                   Lender
       OR
               Rehabs
    Cash Lenders → Whole
                    saler

CT. Homes
LLC . Com

How to Acquire $1 Million in Income Real Estate in One Year Using Borrowed Money in Your Free Time

TYLER G. HICKS

WILEY

John Wiley & Sons, Inc.

Published by John Wiley & Sons, Inc., Hoboken, New Jersey.
Published simultaneously in Canada.

For general information on our other products and services or for technical support, please contact our Customer Care Department within the United States at (800) 762-2974, outside the United States at (317) 572-3993 or fax (317) 572-4002.

Wiley also publishes its books in a variety of electronic formats. Some content that appears in print may not be available in electronic books. For more information about Wiley products, visit our web site at www.wiley.com.

Library of Congress Cataloging-in-Publication Data:
Hicks, Tyler Gregory
   How to acquire $1 million in income real estate in one year using borrowed money in your free time / Tyler G. Hicks.
     p.   cm.
   Includes index.
ISBN-13 978-0-471-75169-4 (pbk.)
ISBN-10 0-471-75169-3 (pbk.)
    1. Real estate investment.   I. Title: How to acquire one million dollars in income real estate in one year using borrowed money in your free time.   II. Title.
HD1382.5.H52   2006
332.63'24—dc22

                        2005038006

Printed in the United States of America.

10 9 8 7 6 5 4 3 2 1

For my youngest son,
Steven David,
with many thanks for assembling the nearly
one thousand real estate lenders
presented in this book.

Contents

PREFACE

Start Here to Learn— How You Can Acquire $1 Million in Income Real Estate in One Year Using Borrowed Money in Your Free Time

What This Book Will Do for You

Do you want to acquire $1 million, or more, of income real estate in one year, or less, using borrowed money, in your free time? If you do, this book shows you exactly how to get that much, or more, income real estate in one year, or less! Using this book you can build your wealth in real estate, even though your credit may not be the best.

How can I say you can do this? Well, a number of readers of my entrepreneurial real estate books tell me, via postal letters, e-mails, faxes, and telephone calls, that they've done just that. To prove to you that readers have written these letters, I reproduce key sections of the actual letters in this book. And you're invited to examine the actual letters in my office in New York City at a time that's convenient to you during normal business hours. All I ask is that you give me a week's notice so we can arrange comfortable desk and seating space for you. Now, let's get back to the book you're reading.

So, do you need the money to buy, renovate, flip, rent out, or develop income real estate in your free time to reach your million-dollar goal in one year? If you do, this book answers that question! It shows you how, and where, you can acquire $1 million, or more, in income real estate assets in one year, or less, using borrowed money. Even if you have poor, or no, credit, or no cash!

Based on my long experience in lending money for many types of income and residential real estate, I show you exactly how to present your money need so you improve your chances of getting your funding quickly, and easily. And, good friend, I give you the specific types of lenders (with name, address, telephone number, fax number, and web site name) to whom you can apply for your loan.

Further, this book gives you more than 700 lenders you can access on the Internet. Using the Internet can save you hours in the Loan Application process. Also, this book gives you some 45 Private Lenders for your income real estate projects. And we provide 50 plus State Lenders for single-family and multifamily homes. Some of these lenders furnish 100 percent financing for your approved real estate projects. For those readers with less than perfect credit we provide data on more than 10 subprime lenders that might help you. No other real estate book we know of provides this many selected lenders, along with details of how to obtain the funding you seek for your income real estate.

Or, if you'd prefer to use venture capital for your real estate wealth-building deals, I show where to look for such no-repay money. You'll also see how to organize your real estate business so you're eligible for venture-capital funding.

And once you get your borrowed money, we show you exactly how to build your riches in income real estate. All on Other People's Money (OPM)!

Dealing with both Beginning and Experienced Wealth Builders (BWBs and EWBs), I've found that most of you have two interesting characteristics, namely:

1. *You can easily find* attractive income properties for investment purposes. And you can find these properties fairly quickly.
2. *Some of you have extreme difficulty* obtaining suitable financing for the excellent property you find. And you often search for months for that suitable financing with no success.

This book shows you how to solve—once and for all—your income real estate financing challenges. And it "takes you by the hand" to lead you to acquiring $1 million in real estate in one year, on borrowed money, in your free time.

While there are dozens of excellent books on investing in real estate, few focus on the Beginning or Experienced Real Estate Wealth Builder's main challenge—namely finding the money you need to buy, build, or renovate, the real estate of your choice. This book solves that problem for you.

And the book you're holding gives you hundreds of sources to finance every kind of income real estate. Starting with single-family homes, this book shows you—the Beginning or Experienced Real Estate Wealth Builder—how to find money for duplexes, triplexes, fourplexes, larger multiunit residential properties, industrial facilities, commercial stores, shopping malls, hotels, motels, nursing homes, mobile home parks, medical complexes, hospitals, mixed-use properties, storage facilities, new and used car lots, gas stations, golf courses, mega malls, senior housing, marinas, warehouses, and so on. Further, your friend, your author—me—is willing to try to help you get financing for any of these types of properties, if you're a reader of this book and any of my newsletters or self-study kits.

No matter what your credit score may be, this book shows you how to get the money you need to invest in income-producing real estate. And, if your supply of cash is limited, you're shown how you can get started financing your own income property, with little money. Using the methods I give you here, you will almost certainly find suitable financing for yourself for almost any kind of viable income real estate project. Why? Because you're shown dozens of different types of funding for your income and residential real estate deals. For each type of funding you're shown:

- **Who** can best use the type of funding described.
- **What** kinds of projects you can use the funding for.
- **Why** this type of funding can be beneficial to you.
- **Where** you can obtain the particular type of funding.
- **When** to use the type of funding in your deals.
- **How** to pay off your loan quickly from real estate earnings.

This book will shorten your struggle to find suitable financing to acquire your dream income property, quickly and easily. You'll work for just weeks—not months—to find the mortgage money you need. You get dozens of different creative ways to solve financing challenges you meet in building your fortune in income real estate.

A few of the different types of mortgage loans and venture capital covered in your book include:

- **Adjustable-rate mortgages.**
- **Assumable mortgages.**
- **Bad credit/No credit mortgages.**
- **Balloon mortgages.**
- **Biweekly mortgages.**
- **Blanket mortgages.**
- **Bridge-loan mortgages.**
- **Bullet mortgages.**
- **Conforming mortgages.**
- **Constant-payment mortgages.**
- **Construction loan with a takeout mortgage.**
- **Convertible mortgages (adjustable- or fixed-rate).**
- **Gifted down-payment mortgages.**
- **Graduated-payment mortgages.**
- **Growing-equity mortgages.**
- **Hard-money mortgages.**

- Hybrid mortgages.
- Home-keeper mortgages.
- Interest-only mortgages.
- Investor mortgages.
- Jumbo mortgages.
- LIBOR-based mortgages.
- No-doc/Lo-doc mortgages.
- Nonowner-occupied mortgages.
- Nonrecourse mortgages.
- Nonseasoned property equity mortgages.
- No-ratio mortgages.
- No-appraisal mortgages.
- No-seasoning mortgages.
- 100 percent first mortgages.
- 103 percent to 115 percent loan-to-value mortgages.
- 125 percent purchase mortgages.
- 125 percent second mortgages.
- Open-end mortgages.
- Pledged-account mortgages (PAM).
- Purchase-money (PM) mortgages.
- Reverse mortgages.
- Sale-leaseback mortgages.
- Seller-financed reverse-flip mortgages.
- Shared-appreciation mortgages.
- Shared-equity mortgages.
- "Soft" hard-money mortgages.
- Start-up mortgages.
- Super jumbo mortgages over $1 million.
- Term mortgages.

- **Third-position mortgages.**
- **Venture-capital mortgages.**
- **Wraparound mortgages.**
- **Zero-percent-interest mortgages.**

Besides the information provided in this book, I, as your author, stand ready to assist you, the serious real estate wealth builder, in finding a suitable loan for your "deal." This service is offered on a no-fee basis to readers of this book and subscribers to my newsletters described at the back of this book. So both BWBs and EWBs can use, and benefit from, this help. Others who will find the content of this book useful, along with the personal advice offered, are real estate brokers and salespeople, financial consultants, stock and bond brokers, construction contractors, land developers, and every other potential wealth builder seeking to finance his or her income real estate.

Further, the techniques I give you in this book can also be used by yourself and others to finance your personal residential real estate. Or you can use these methods to earn income by finding financing for clients seeking residential or commercial real estate for themselves. I can give you lenders you can work with as a Loan Originator or Loan Broker.

So come along with me, good friend, and learn the ins and outs of successful real estate financing to acquire $1 million in income real estate holdings in one year, or less, using borrowed money, in your free time, to build your wealth. Having this information on hand could make you a real-estate millionaire sooner than you think!

If you want to contact me in person, you'll find at the end of this book, in Chapter 12, my postal mail address, e-mail address, web site, business telephone, and fax numbers. You can contact me directly to have your real estate business questions answered! When you do so, you'll find a friend ready to help you in the business of acquiring $1 million in real estate in one year on borrowed money in your free time, to build your wealth!

Let's get started making you rich in real estate!

TYLER G. HICKS

How to Acquire $1 Million
in Income Real Estate
in One Year Using Borrowed
Money in Your Free Time

CHAPTER 1

Get Into, and Profit From, the World's Best Borrowed-Money Business

REAL ESTATE IS THE WORLD'S BEST BORROWED-MONEY BUSINESS. EARNING money from income real estate can make you richer sooner than you think. This book shows you how to acquire $1 million worth of income real estate in one year, or less, starting with little or no cash.

And while doing this your entire financial life will improve, as you'll soon see in this chapter. As proof of the results you can achieve, I include many real-life experiences from the thousands of readers who write, fax, e-mail, or phone me every year. Many of these happy readers tell me of their success in buying, and earning money from, income real estate.

Beginning Wealth Builders Do Amass Big Money

Some of these happy readers amass $1 million, or more, in income real estate in one year, or less. Most start on their own with a zero-cash investment. Since $1 million in assets represents a goal many Beginning Wealth Builders (BWBs) aspire to, I decided to use letters from these readers to show you how they reached their goal so quickly. This book gives you a number of these letters and the methods used to achieve the million-dollar goal in one year, or less. And you, too, can use the methods these Successful Wealth Builders (SWBs) use to achieve your income

1

real estate asset goal. At the same time, your financial life will become better than ever.

(The actual letters from these readers are available for your inspection in my New York City office. If you wish to inspect these letters, all I ask is that you give me a few days' notice so we can get the letters out of the safe deposit box where we keep them, and arrange comfortable seating for you in my office while you inspect the actual letters.)

Smart Thinking Builds Real Estate Wealth

The real estate holdings of these readers—which I call the *numbers*—prove that BWBs can acquire $1 million in income real estate holdings in one year, or less, while improving their financial lives immensely. For example, here's a letter a reader voluntarily wrote me telling what he did to acquire $1 million in income real estate assets:

> "In 10 months I bought 15 properties worth just over $1,000,000 with little, or no, money out of pocket. I, and my wife (couldn't have done it without her), are living proof that it can be done!
>
> "The first seven houses we bought with the owner holding a 10 percent second mortgage. Of these, three were bought with literally no money down (except the $8 Cashier's Check fee) where the owner rolled the closing costs into the note. The other four houses I used either a cash advance from a credit card or money from a 401(k) loan for the closing cost. All of the first seven I bought were with the owner holding paper.
>
> "The next eight were a sweet deal. This was a package deal with all eight from one seller. The total cost of the eight houses was $641,000. We split the sale up for financing. I, by the way, am a realtor. The owner was not willing to hold paper. So I had to come up with 10 percent down and the closing cost of roughly $19,000. Where there is a will, there is a way. I had the owner agree to

list his properties with me with a 10 percent commission. My broker had to agree to this, as well. I rolled my commission into the 10 percent down, so no money really changed hands. But, what about closing costs? I didn't have $19,000 lying around to plunk down. Or did I? After some searching for the right lender with the right terms, I took out a Home Equity Line of Credit (HELOC) on my primary residence. I don't mind that because the cash flow covers the note."   —Florida

Now you see you *can* acquire $1 million in income real estate assets in a year or less. Doing so will change your entire life and improve your standard of living enormously.

But before we show you what this great acquisition program can do for you, let me define exactly what we're talking about so we all have a clear view of the goal.

DEFINITION

The "$1 million in one year, or less, program" shows you how to acquire $1 million in *market value* of income real estate in the stated time span. One way this is done is to buy properties at below-market prices, fix them up, and either hold them for rental income, or flip them for a quick profit. The $1 million is the final *market value* of the properties you acquire—not what you pay for them. Your fix-up work is usually done by outside contractors working for you. Another way to succeed in this program is as shown in the previous letter—namely to acquire properties worth $1 million, or more, using borrowed money.

Now, here's what this million-dollar income real estate wealth building program can do for you.

You Build Your Real Estate Assets

When you acquire income real estate you become the owner of an *asset* that has value. Typical assets in real estate are buildings, land, a right of way, and so on. Each has a value that will generally increase your wealth when you own it. Acquiring assets is important for your financial health because:

- **Assets are an important part** of your Financial Statement (called your Balance Sheet). The more assets you have, the stronger—in general—is your Financial Statement.

- **Real estate assets are respected** everywhere, by everyone, as important elements in your financial picture.

- **Most real estate assets** rise in value as time passes. Your wealth increases as you sleep!

- **With more real estate assets** you can borrow against them to buy more income real estate that pays for itself and pays you a profit.

- **As your assets rise in value** your credit rating also increases because the greater the value of your assets, the stronger, in general, is your credit score since larger assets generally mean you are financially stronger and have more income to pay your bills on time, and in full.

You Acquire Large Assets in Your Free Time

When you start to build your income real estate wealth you will usually have a job or another business. So you'll have to look for real estate in your free time—on weekends, holidays, and vacations. This can be fun and profitable for you. Further:

- **Just a few hours a week** are needed by you to look for income real estate that can give you $1 million in assets in one year, or less.

- **You can arrange financing** in your off-hours by phone, Internet, postal mail, or e-mail.

- **Your employer never need know** about your spare-time income real estate work because it will not interfere with your normal weekday duties.

- **And if you don't have a job or a business** of your own, you can still get started in your free time.
- **No real estate license** of any kind is needed to buy, hold, or flip income real estate for your personal profit.

Use the Liberal Financing Available to You

Income real estate is a ***borrowed-money business.*** Few real estate investors ever pay cash for their property. Why?

- *Because it's easier, and more financially rewarding, to use Other People's Money (OPM).*
- *OPM gives you control of a valuable asset without having to use any of your own money.*
- *Control of a valuable asset using borrowed money is called Leverage—the secret to getting rich in real estate.*

You might pay cash for your home—called your *personal residence* in formal real estate language. Why? Because you may want to get rid of monthly mortgage payments. And owning your home "free and clear" gives you a feeling of safety and comfort. Sure, you'll have to pay real estate taxes. But if you're like me, your author, you'll look at these taxes as "tax-deductible rent."

Using the idea that real estate is a borrowed-money business you can start your wealth building with these thoughts:

- **Almost everybody borrows** to invest in income real estate.
- **OPM** is "the way to go" in income real estate today.
- **Hundreds of different loan programs** are available to you today to finance your start-up in income real estate. This book gives you almost all these programs.
- **You can start** with poor, or no, credit and get your needed financing.
- **And you can go from poor credit** to strong credit while your assets increase.
- **No other business offers to lend you money** to earn money.

- **You can "mortgage out"**—that is get cash money for taking over an income property using OPM—the only business in which this frequently happens.
- **Your author** can be a source of loan data for your income real estate wealth building. I assure you that you'll be treated cordially and sympathetically as your project is reviewed.

Obtain Large Assets Quickly in Your Free Time

Yes, you *can* obtain large income real estate assets quickly, starting with little, or no, cash. To do so you must:

- **Prepare a plan** detailing what kind of income real estate assets you want to own.
- **Include, in your plan,** specific dollar financial goals you want to reach.
- **List the steps you'll take** to locate the types of income real estate assets you want to own.
- **Estimate the time you'll take** to find, and take over, suitable real estate to allow you to reach your financial goal.
- **Focus on your goal every day** of the week. Take action on your goal every day so you make progress toward your final financial dollar number.

Now I know that preparing a plan might turn you off. "I want to get started fast," you say. "I don't have time to fool around with a complicated plan."

To which I say: "Your plan will be the most valuable step you take at the start of your million-dollar real estate wealth building. Why? It will guide you every day of the week while you look for, and negotiate, deals that can make you rich. So you *must* have a plan. And, in truth, it will be your Business Plan."

Write Your Real Estate Business Plan

To help you overcome the reluctance many BWBs have with preparing a Business Plan for their wealth building, our next reader letter includes data you can easily adapt to your locale and financial situation, if you want to run a similar real estate business. Or, if your future business is different, you can use the many elements he includes in his plan as a guide for your own Business Plan. To use this Business Plan as a guide, all you need do is:

- *Accept the type of properties* (single-family residential) covered in the Plan, or change the listing to the type of properties you want to buy.
- *Look at the dollar pricing numbers* in the Plan and see if they're within the typical price ranges in your area. If the numbers do not apply to your area, change them to numbers that are accurate for your locale.
- *Check the schedule for purchases.* If the timing seems too quick for you, extend the dates. And if you run over the 12 months suggested by this Plan by a month or two, don't panic! If it takes you 13 months to acquire $1 million of income real estate instead of 12 months, I'm sure you won't be angry with me! Why? Because you'll be following your own schedule, not mine.

Now we'll give you an Income Real Estate Business Plan summarized in an actual letter. You can use this Plan as a guide for your own Plan that can put you into the million-dollar class in one year, or less. Let's get started!

Planning Produces High Profits

"We buy 'distressed properties' at 70 percent, or less, of the fair market values in 'as-is' condition for cash. Most of the time there is no real estate agent or broker involved because the property may not be on the market when we buy it. 'Distressed properties' in our definition are: **Properties in disrepair, properties with tenant problems, or other emotional dissatisfaction with the property on the part of the owner.**

(continued)

"We look for sellers forced to liquidate their real estate to solve a cash need. And we look for sellers who are anxious to unload their properties that are 'in crisis.' This can result from many factors, such as tenant problems, tax issues, natural disasters—fire, flood, and so on, management or cash-flow problems, or vacancies. We've found this demographic group prefers 'peace of mind' instead of ownership problems.

"We have made ourselves proficient in three specific skills:

1. **Finding deals**—how to find real estate bargains.
2. **Funding deals**—acquiring money to fund transactions.
3. **Flipping deals**—reselling property quickly, profitably.

"One of the most difficult and critical components of our purchase strategy is the elimination of, or minimizing of, the down payment required to obtain the property. Quite often, the down payment represents a significant portion of the transaction. That is, the less money invested to turn the property, the higher the rate of return on the purchase. Here's our strategy to take advantage of a below-market purchase price:

"When a home owner signs a real estate contract to sell their property to us for 70 percent of the fair market value 'as-is' for cash, one of the ways we finance the deal is with a hard money lender that lends up to 75 percent of the fair future market value—that is, after fix-up. Most of the time we don't have to put any money out to buy the property (zero cash). Even money for the renovation is lent as long as the total loaned is not over 75 percent of the future fair market value.

"We are presently working with other entities anxious to join us as 'silent' investors. This will allow for massive growth while at the same time we will grow incrementally to protect all our investors.

"The terms of our financing are: _____ Lenders (the hard-money funder) provides a one-year loan. The cost of the money is 4 points (4 percent of $100,000, or $4,000) and 10 percent, interest only for the first six months. After that the rate goes to 14 percent and it is due in one year. We are currently working on raising capital without the need to make monthly payments.

"The reason we use _____ Lenders for financing is: Proactive closing of cash financing and escrow closure, which is so valuable to all the parties involved. We've found that sellers want to sell fast and we deliver. The average time for us to close a deal is six business days, or less. To accomplish this, our staff works zealously with the title company on a daily basis by pushing them to close in a rapid manner.

"_____ Lenders does not use credit or income for their approval. This allows us to buy an unlimited number of properties. All _____ Lenders requires is the collateral—that is, the property we want to buy. How does this work?

- There is no appraisal of the property required.
- We work with the fastest closing firm to get a title report.

"Banks and mortgage companies will typically be considered as a last resort. This is because of the long delays in processing mortgages. There is an estimated closing time of 30 to 45 days for these lenders. This precludes our ability to be proactive to all and that is why we try not to choose this avenue.

"Our investment strategy includes renovation of every property purchased. Homes that can be bought well below

(continued)

market value with very little repair are our best investments. But such houses are difficult to find. So we antici-
pate that every home will require at least cosmetic
improvements to bring the home up to maximum value
and allow it to be sold quickly.

"Over the last three years we've been in business our
purchases and holdings show these results:

Year 1: 4 properties bought; Cost = $376,000; Value = $1
million

Year 2: 11 properties bought; Cost = $1,887,000; Value =
$3,594,000

**Total cost for two years = $2,263,000; Total value =
$4,594,000**

**Gross Profit in two years = $4,594,000 – $2,263,000 =
$2,331,000**

"Now that you have the numbers of our organization,
here is information on our location and market: It is, and
has been, our goal to provide a unique service to our
growing and diverse community in northern California.
Our company's mission is sound. It is fostered with the
highest standard of excellence, dedication to quality, service oriented, detail attentive, with the goal to rebuild
our neighborhoods.

"We have surrounded ourselves with the 'best and
brightest' of professionals in diverse areas to address any
contingency that may occur. What we provide is unique.
We buy properties from others who wish to sell but do not
have the capital or liquidity necessary to fix up their
home and then sell it. This service is provided to sellers of
homes, investment properties, and apartment complexes in
'as-is' condition. We use in-house project management and
the best of contractors to restore the property to one that
transcends anyone's dreams.

"The area we chose to invest in is one in which we can
buy properties for 70 percent, or less, of the future fair

market value and resell within one month while on the market. This area has had a 40+ percent appreciation of housing prices. Further, there is recent demand for homes for first-time home buyers, our target market. Also, we know the area, as do most of our associates who work with us.

"We developed our strategy around the purchase of homes in the under-$150,000 range. This price represents homes on the lower end of the spectrum in the targeted neighborhoods. A price differential of at least 30 percent between our purchase price and the typical sales price is a requisite to each purchase. This allows us to absorb a renovation and acquisition expense of about $5,000 to $10,000 for each property and still net a minimum profit from each sale, with the potential of garnering six figures on the investment sales price. And our target neighborhood is well populated with significantly motivated sellers who will take cash in exchange for a substantial discount for a minimum of 70 percent, or below, of the fair market value, after fix-up."
—California

Focus on the Elements of Your Business Plan

Using this letter (which was sent to me in the form of a Business Plan) as a guide, let's extract the elements you'll use in your Business Plan—which I often call your Success Plan. These elements are:

1. **What you'll do** to acquire your million dollars in market-value real estate in one year. In this Plan it is: *Buy properties at 70 percent, or less, of future fair market value and fix them up for resale at a profit.*

2. **Select the area** in which you'll work. In this Plan it is: *A city in which owners of lower-priced homes need to get cash to take the next step in their lives. These, the letter writer calls his "targeted neighborhoods."*

3. **Choose the price range you'll focus on.** In this Plan it is: *Homes in the under-$150,000 price range. These are at the lower end of the spectrum of prices in the targeted neighborhoods.*

4. **Find suitable financing sources.** In this Plan it is: *A hard-money lender that charges points with an interest-only grace period and then a higher interest rate, with a one-year term limit on the loan.*

5. **Specify who will do the needed work.** In this Plan it is: *Experienced outside contractors, plus the company preparing the plan, are responsible for doing the rehab work.*

6. **State other important aspects of your business.** In this Plan they are:
    —*Estimated rehab cost for each property.*
    —*Acquisition price range for each property.*
    —*Market for sales—that is, first-time home buyers.*
    —*Condition of properties to buy—as is.*
    —*Rehab of each property as a business strategy.*
    —*Stated closing time for each purchase—six days.*
    —*Known interest-rate conditions for financing.*
    —*Specific type of seller targeted for purchase strategies.*

Now I know you may regard writing as a chore. And writing a Business Plan may be even more of a chore to you. But please hear me, as your friend and mentor, when I say:

> *Your Business Plan can be your most valuable tool in building $1 million in market-value real estate in one year, starting with little, or no, cash. Your Plan will outline what you intend to do. Then all you have to do is follow your Plan. Trust me, Business Plans do work for you. I have nothing to sell you but your success!*

Your Real Estate Road to Wealth Is Easy

Earning your fortune in real estate is easier today than ever before. And you can get started sooner than you think. Why? Because, in income real estate you:

- **Don't need a college education** to start. You can learn as you build your wealth. This book gets you started on little, or no, money.
- **Your race, gender, age, religion, and location** will not hinder you from starting, and succeeding in, owning income real estate of any type you like.
- **You have a friend in your author,** Ty Hicks. I'm ready to help you in every way I can. If you contact me, all I ask is that you submit your needs in writing because I take your request very seriously and I want to give you the best advice I can. A 60-second phone call is really not long enough to get the needed facts to give you a sensible answer!

 ## Your Key Ideas for Acquiring Large Real Estate Assets

❏ **Real estate** is the world's best borrowed-money business.
❏ **You can borrow money** to build $1 million in market-value real estate assets in one year.
❏ **While you build your real estate assets** you will improve your financial life and your credit score.
❏ **Smart thinking will help you** build your real estate wealth faster, and with less work on your part.
❏ **Real estate assets are respected** by all lenders. Hence, you can use your real estate assets to borrow money to buy more real estate.
❏ **You can build real estate wealth** working just a few hours per week in your free time.
❏ **Financing for your real estate business** can easily be arranged in your free off-hours time via telephone or Internet.
❏ **If you're employed,** your employer never need know about your off-hours real estate investing because it's your business, and yours alone!
❏ **No real estate license is required** of you as a property investor.
❏ **Hundreds of good, reliable loan programs** are available to you to finance building your real estate assets on borrowed money.
❏ **A comprehensive Business Plan** can guide you to acquiring $1 million in market-value real estate in one year on little, or zero, cash down.

CHAPTER 2

Pick the Type of Income Real Estate You Want to Acquire

You *CAN* BUILD YOUR FORTUNE IN INCOME REAL ESTATE IN YOUR FREE time, starting with no cash. The two letters in Chapter 1 should convince you that this great opportunity is there for you to grab. To convince you further, there's a third letter in this chapter that's a real winner! You'll meet it in a few pages.

To build your fortune you must first pick the type of income real estate you want to own, or flip (acquire and resell quickly). We'll overlook real estate development (going from raw land acquisition to full construction, and sale, of property) because this takes years of experience to acquire the needed skills.

Six Big Money Opportunities for You

There are six types of income real estate you can own to collect rents from, or to flip for a quick profit. These are:

1. **Multifamily residences—apartment houses.**
2. **Retail properties—stores, theaters, restaurants, and so on.**
3. **Commercial properties—small, and large, office buildings.**

14

4. **Industrial buildings**—factories, self-storage, and so on.

5. **Recreational properties**—tennis courts, marinas, bowling alleys, and so on.

6. **Single-family homes.**

Within each type of property there are subdivisions. To help you make a better choice, we'll give you the advantages and disadvantages of each type of property, and its subdivisions. By the end of this chapter you should be able to make a smart choice of your type of property.

If you're still puzzled, give your friend, your author, a call. I'll be happy to help in every way I can.

Multifamily Buildings Can Be *Your* Money Machine

Multifamily residential buildings—also called apartment houses—can build your real estate wealth faster than you might imagine. Starting with a two-family duplex, multifamily properties can contain as many as 10,000, or more, units. At the start, I suggest that you concentrate on 4 units and then go on to a 10-unit building as your next step.

Why? Because it does take experience and skill to deal with tenants and their many needs and wants. If all you plan to do is flip (sell quickly) multifamily units, then you must acquire negotiating skills. Both these talents take time to develop!

Multifamily residential properties have these characteristics:

Advantages

- **Multiunits reduce** the impact of apartment vacancies.
- **Rental income can be significant** when you have a large number of units.
- **Expenses can be spread** over numerous units, making the impact on you, the owner, less severe.
- **Financing is readily available** for well-kept multiunit properties because lenders know that the mortgage payments can be made from the cash flow from the building.

- **Section 8 tenants can provide you** with long-lasting and steady income from your rentals.
- **Many cities have waiting lists** of Section 8 tenants. So you, as a multiunit owner, have a steady supply of qualified tenants for your property.
- **Most multiunit properties rise in value** as time passes, making your investment more valuable. You earn money while you sleep.
- **You can have a management company** operate your multiunit property at a distance from you for a nominal fee.

An interesting letter from a Beginning Wealth Builder (BWB) shows the extent to which real estate riches can be built in your spare time with multifamily properties. This letter, I'm sure, will motivate you to get started soon. And it also shows you how you can acquire $1 million in real estate in one year in your free time, as this happy reader did.

Big Money in His Spare Time

"I have been investing in real estate in my spare time for 10 years. I have accumulated over $10 million worth of real estate with $6 million in equity. I must say that the ideas, resources and knowledge I gained from reading Ty Hicks' book are the big contributing factor in contributing to my success in real estate investing.

"Six years ago I was eagerly searching for lenders to finance my second income property. I had found a 16-unit apartment building in a nicer part of town listing for $600,000. The property was not in good shape (the appearance) because the out-of-town owner didn't take good care of it. Banks turned down my Loan Application. They said the rent was low (due to mismanagement) and I only had 5 percent down payment from credit cards and a personal loan. But I knew I could turn the property into a cash generator with some minor cosmetic improvements and careful selection of tenants. I read the IWS* Newsletter and found a Loan Broker who got me the loan to purchase the property. Thank you very much for your help."

—California.

*International Wealth Success—see Appendix for more information on this newsletter.

This reader submitted a list of his properties with his letter. This list is shown in Table 2.1, below. To protect the reader's privacy I deleted the addresses of his properties. Most of the properties are in contiguous cities in southern California, with one in northern California. Looking at this list you'll see that the total market value of his properties is more than $12 million. He owes $5,960,000 on these properties. Total monthly rents are $107,550. Expenses, including mortgage payments, total $71,990 per month. Profits—that is, his Positive Cash Flow (PCF)—is $35,560 per month, or $426,720 per year.

The listing shows this real estate BWB's properties. I'm sure you'll find the numbers both interesting and motivating!

Just think: Would another $400,000+ per year PCF into your bank account improve your life? Especially when the depreciation of your property shelters some, or perhaps all, of this income.

Looking at the PCF another way, this happy reader receives $35,560 per month/31 days per month = $1,147 per day in income from his real

Table 2.1
One BWB's Spare-Time Real Estate Holdings

Type	Market Value ($)	Monthly Rent ($)	Mortgage Payment ($)	Taxes* ($)	Net Income ($)
Motel	7,000,000	80,000	23,000	32,000	25,000
Apartment house	2,000,000	11,050	4,299	2,500	4,251
Apartment house	1,800,000	9,250	3,391	2,100	3,759
Apartment house	1,350,000	7,250	2,800	1,900	2,550
Totals	12,150,000	107,550	33,490	38,500	35,560

*Taxes, insurance, and maintenance.

estate. Would an extra $1,147 a day change your living habits? I'm almost certain that, for most people, it would.

Now let's look at the details of this excellent letter to see what gems of buying wisdom it contains. Here are the highlights:

- **The property being bought** is in a "nicer part of town," meaning that it has a good potential to rise in value.
- **An out-of-town owner** has neglected the exterior of the property and it needs cosmetic care to improve its appearance.
- **Rents are lower than others charge** in the area because the current owner mismanaged the property. This means there's a chance to raise rents soon after the property is acquired.
- **Though banks turned down his Loan Application,** he was able to get the loan he needed by working with a Loan Broker he found in the IWS newsletter.
- **Credit cards and a personal loan** were the source of his 5 percent down payment. This means he was able to obtain the property on zero cash.
- **Cosmetic improvements,** which are usually inexpensive, were all that were needed to make the building more attractive to prospective tenants.
- **Careful selection of tenants** could make the property more attractive to renters.

But multifamily properties may not be a complete "joy ride." As with other income properties, multifamily units have disadvantages. Here they are:

Disadvantages

- **Can present management challenges** if you are not an experienced multiunit operator.
- **May require expensive repairs** if the previous owner was lax about maintenance.
- **Rent collection can be a challenge** if you do not introduce mail and credit-card usage.
- **The down payment required** can be larger than for single-family homes, presenting an obstacle for some BWBs.

Retail Properties—Stores, Theaters, Restaurants, and Others

Advantages

- **Rental income** is often higher than for the same space rented to residential or industrial tenants.
- **Tenants are more dependable** than residential occupants because the space is needed to produce daily income; hence, the rent is paid on time, and in full.
- **Long leases**—multiyears—are common, with provision for annual increases of the rent as time passes.
- **A percent revenue-sharing clause** wherein you're paid a portion of the annual gross can be included in the lease for trophy locations.

Disadvantages

- **Your income** is somewhat dependent on the success of each of your retail tenants. If a tenant fails, your rent may be delayed, or not paid at all.
- **Vacancies may be longer** than with residential leases because retail tenants are not as numerous and are harder to find.
- **Intense competition** in an area might drive retail rents down, reducing your income.

Commercial Properties—Small, and Large, Office Buildings

Advantages

- **You deal with** business and professional tenants who respect you and pay their rent on time, and in full.
- **Tenants can be given** a Net, Net, Net lease in which they pay Taxes, Insurance and Maintenance, and square foot rental charges on their rented space.
- **Office buildings** tend to increase in value as time passes, giving you appreciation potential when you sell the property.

- **You can keep regular business hours** when you own an office building because your tenants generally observe weekends and holidays.
- **Sometimes you can use a long-term lease** from a highly credit-worthy tenant as collateral for a down payment loan to buy the office building.

Disadvantages

- **Large office buildings** require years of experience before you can do well financially with them.
- **Small office buildings** may be priced higher than a residential property giving you the same annual income.
- **Fewer office buildings** are sold by motivated sellers because owners are usually more sophisticated business people.

Industrial Buildings—Factories, Self-Storage, and Others

Advantages

- **Can be low-maintenance,** simple structures that your tenant assumes all responsibility for, freeing you of costly repairs.
- **When rented** to major tenants your income is assured, year after year, as the property rises in value.
- **Tax advantages** are available for such buildings in areas seeking to attract industry and the jobs it creates.
- **Long-term leases** from trophy tenants can be used as collateral for loans to buy more income property.

Disadvantages

- **Suitable tenants** can be difficult to find when business conditions are slow in a down economy.
- **When a vacancy occurs** it may take a long time—sometimes years—to find a suitable new tenant.
- **A building type may** go out of style for certain types of manufacturing operations and a vacancy can result.

Recreational Properties—Tennis Courts, Marinas, Bowling Alleys, and Others

Advantages

- **Can be popular with tenants** because few such properties are available in a given area.
- **You can charge** a profitable rental rate because there is little competition from other property owners.
- **Scarcity of needed recreational facilities** allows you to charge a percent of the gross sales in the property, in addition to rent.
- **Success with a facility** in one section of a highly populated area can lead to ownership of another—or several—facility in other parts of the area.

Disadvantages

- **Falloff of interest in a sport** can lead to a long vacancy in your facility; you have no control over sporting interest.
- **Mismanagement by your tenant** can result in late, or no, payment of rent to you.
- **Close supervision of your tenant** is necessary if illegal activities (gambling, drug dealing, etc.) are part of the sport housed in your facility.

Single-Family Homes Can Build Your Wealth

The single-family home has many advantages. And—good news for you—there are a number of types of single-family homes you can use to build your riches. These types allow you to combine other interests with your wealth building. Thus, under single-family homes you have:

- The detached, stand-alone traditional single-family home.
- Townhouse single-family home.
- Apartment in a multifamily building.
- Condo single-family home.
- Single-family detached vacation home.
- Mobile home in a mobile-home park.

Let's take a look at the advantages and disadvantages of each. Then you can make your choice of how you'll build your wealth in income real estate, after comparison with the five other types of properties discussed in this chapter.

Detached Stand-Alone Single-Family Home

Advantages

- **Easy to buy** in large numbers using many loan programs.
- **Can be financed** with down payment grants for zero-down deals.
- **Section 8 rentals** can give you a good, steady, dependable income.
- **You can have your tenant pay** for heat, air conditioning, yard maintenance, and so on.
- **Tenants can do simple maintenance**—painting, carpet cleaning, spackling, and so on—when you supply the materials.
- **Careful choice of tenants** can reduce management problems.

Disadvantages

- **Vacancy** can be a financial burden if you have only a few properties.
- **Tenants** can cause vandalism problems if they're not carefully selected.
- **Neighborhoods** may change, reducing the value of the home.

Single Apartment in a Multifamily Building (Apartment House)

Advantages

- **Can often be taken over** for NO CASH and NO CLOSING COSTS when first offered on the market.
- **Usually require less maintenance** than detached single-family homes because they're better built and have less exposure to the elements—snow, rain, hail, sun, hurricanes, tornados, and so on.

- **Are simpler to manage** and easier to rent because there's usually a larger need for apartments than for detached single-family homes.
- **Can be put on the market,** and rented, by a Rental Agent, for a small fee. This gives you more time for other real estate deals.

Disadvantages

- **Your rental income** may be lower than for a detached single-family home in the same area.
- **May be hard for you to find** in heavily populated areas because of the great demand for rental apartments.
- **Can take you longer** to assemble a "string" of these units than a group of detached single-family homes.

Condo Single-Family Home Units

Advantages

- **Simple, easy management for you** that can be done at a distance by yourself or by others.
- **No land or garden care by you or by your tenants**—the condo association does it all as part of your monthly fee.
- **You can finance these units easily**—often on zero cash, meaning you have a no-money-down deal!
- **Are usually easy to sell,** if you want to take a profit on your investment and buy other, more attractive, income property.
- **You can often buy older units** at low prices if there is new condo construction in the area of your property.

Disadvantages

- **You may find it hard to locate** a suitable condo in the area in which you want to run your single-family home rental business.
- **Newer units can be more expensive** than a detached single-family home in the same area in which you want to invest.

Single-Family Detached Vacation Home

Advantages

- **Can provide you with a high rental income** during the vacation season—often more than a year-round rental pays you in a less desirable area.

- **May provide you with tax-deductible trips** to desirable vacation areas when you travel to inspect your property, check on tenants, or do other work related to your income-producing real estate.

- **Is a "fun" type of business** because your tenants are in a happy mood—they're on vacation!

Disadvantages

- **May be hard for you to rent** during times of economic downturns or other conditions—war, shortages, stock-market debacle, and so on.

- **Can "go in and out of style"** as the types of vacations or the "in" vacation areas change in popularity.

Mobile Home in a Mobile-Home Park

Advantages

- **Sometimes you can buy them for almost nothing**—just $40 or $50 in some cases our readers have told us about in the warmer areas of the United States.

- **Are often low-maintenance structures** because they are made of long-lasting metals that resist corrosion or decay over the years.

- **Can be rented to the same family** for years, saving you time and money and allowing you to spend more time on other money-making deals you like.

Disadvantages

- **Tenants may be a less desirable** type because they are restless and don't stay in one location for very long. Such tenants may not treat your property too well.

- **Your mobile home** may have to be moved if the park closes or is sold to a new owner.

Townhouse Single-Family Home

Advantages

- **Seldom need major repairs** or maintenance because they usually are of recent construction.
- **Command higher rents** than detached single-family homes because they need less tenant work.
- **Rise in value quickly** when kept in good condition by the owner and his or her tenants.

Disadvantages

- **May cost more to buy or rent** than a stand-alone single-family home in the area you're investing in.
- **Can be difficult to find** because there often are few in an area in which you want to own rental property.

How to Choose Your Ideal Income Real Estate

Now that you know the advantages and disadvantages of each type of real estate you might own, or flip, you can choose your perfect fit. Here's how to make your choice.

1. Review the Characteristics of Each Income Method

You can earn your real estate income either from *rental income,* or by *flipping properties* soon after acquiring them. Or you can combine these two approaches.

Rental income earnings are characterized by:

- **A steady monthly income** that builds as time passes and you acquire more units to rent to tenants. You do not, in general, receive big blocks of cash from the units you rent to tenants.
- **Attention to tenant needs** on a daily basis, unless you use a management company that will save you time but reduce your net earnings from the property.

- **Ownership considerations** including regular payment of your mortgage, finding and supervising repair crews, collecting rents, paying insurance bills, and so on.
- **Finding suitable new tenants** when vacancies occur. You will often have to interview tenants yourself when you're first starting to build your wealth because you won't have the staff or a management company to do it for you.

To summarize rental activities, successful renters are *people persons*— that is, they enjoy dealing with people on a daily basis.

Flipping income activities are characterized by:

- **Big blocks of cash can flow into your bank account** each time you flip a property. But your income can vary wildly because you never know when you'll find a suitable property, or when you'll sell it. Compared to renting units, flipping can be like the weather—unpredictable on many days.
- **The need for an ability to negotiate** with buyers who want your property. You will seldom sell at your asking price. Instead, you'll price at a higher level than you want for the property and then negotiate down to your desired price.
- **A lack of love for any property.** Instead of "falling in love" with a building, you see its potential for resale. Your only interest in a property is how fast, and how profitably, you can resell it.
- **An ability to see the potential** others might see in a property you hope to buy low and sell high. This ability can be learned if you pay attention to values and trends in your area.

To summarize, if you're not a *people person,* you may find that flipping is a better business for you. Why? Because when you flip properties you deal with fewer people. And you're dealing with other business people who—in general—are easier to handle and more sensible than irate tenants in residential properties.

2. Select Your Income Method Based on Your Knowledge of Yourself

Only you know yourself well enough to make your income choice. But I can help you by saying:

- **If you enjoy working with people** such as tenants, then renting will probably be better for you.
- **If you are satisfied with the steady monthly income** from rentals that grows as time passes, then renting will probably be better for you.
- **If you are a calm, organized person** who enjoys a regulated lifestyle with predictable events each week, and month, then renting will probably be better for you.
- **If you enjoy** the ebb and flow of negotiations over price and terms, then flipping will probably be better for you.
- **If you like to rehab properties,** or direct crews that do this work, then flipping will probably be better for you.
- **If you get a thrill out of working** out a smart deal and earning a big chunk of money from it, then flipping is probably better for you.
- **If you find regular monthly collection** of rents is boring and unexciting, then flipping is probably better for you.

Put Your Real Estate Wealth Building Choice into Action

Rental Income Wealth Building

First, we'll assume, for this step-by-step procedure, that you've chosen *rental income properties* as your way to build real estate wealth. To ensure your success, we'll take you through each step of the rental process.

Once you've learned what you need to know about the rental process, we'll assume that you choose *flipping of real estate properties* as your way to wealth. Then, later in this chapter, you'll be shown exactly what to do to earn your real estate wealth flipping properties.

Now, here's what to do next for the rental income choice you made as your route to $1 million in market value real estate in one year:

1. **Pick the type of property** you want to own for your wealth building. Most BWBs choose single- or multifamily properties for their starter properties.
2. **Choose the area** in which you want to own your property. For most BWBs, its best to start with local properties, if the type you want to own is available in your area.

3. **Decide what type of people you want to rent to.** In rental real estate your prospective tenants are your market. If you define this market in advance—such as Section 8 (government-paid rents) in advance, it will help you rent your units sooner for a higher monthly amount. Thus, you might target newly married couples, blue-collar workers in nearby manufacturing plants, and so on.

4. **Look for suitable properties meeting your written goals.** Do this by searching the real estate section of your local papers on Sunday. Next, look in your telephone *Yellow Pages* under Real Estate Brokers for firms advertising your type of property. Contact them by phone, fax, e-mail, or postal mail. Tell them what you're looking for.

5. **Negotiate a suitable price** once you've found the type of property you want. For best results, try to pay no more than six times your Gross Annual Rental Income from the property. Thus, if your Gross Annual Rental Income from a property is $50,000, do not pay more than $6 \times \$50,000 = \$300,000$ for the property. Why? Because at a higher ratio, say seven or eight times, you may not have a PCF from the property. Positive Cash Flow means you have money left over EVERY month after paying ALL expenses, including your first and second mortgages. *YOU MUST HAVE A PCF FROM EVERY PROPERTY, EVERY MONTH!*

6. **Take over your selected property.** Allow three months to "get comfortable" with your new income property. Upgrade your property if it needs improvements. Raise the rents to reflect the better building your tenants are enjoying. Then start looking for your next income property. Keep your goal of $1 million in market value in view and you'll soon achieve what you set out to do.

Flipping Property Wealth Building

Now we assume that you want to build your real estate fortune *flipping properties.* When you flip properties you buy them at a low price and sell at a higher price. Your profit is the difference between your purchase price and your selling price, less the cost of improvements and legal consultation. Thus, if you buy a distressed property for $40,000, spend

$10,000 on rehab and legal work, and sell it for $75,000, your profit = $75,000 − $40,000 − $10,000 = $25,000. Now that you understand this, let's get you started flipping:

1. **Choose the type of property you'll flip.** Most BWBs start with single-family homes (SFHs) because these are usually available in abundant quantities and are the easiest to sell after being rehabbed. So we'll assume you're starting with SFHs.

2. **Find suitable properties to flip.** To earn money flipping, you want to obtain properties at less than their market price. Such properties are usually called "Distressed Properties." You'll find them:

   —**At local Sheriff Sales** advertised in the real estate section of your newspaper.

   —**At your local County Clerk's office** where "Lis Pendens," which is Latin for "suit pending," are published. Such lists are published when a suit has been filed because a property owner is behind in his or her mortgage or real estate tax payments.

   Using the Lis Pendens you can bid on a property before it goes to auction. Such an "early bird" action can get you desirable properties long before others discover them. Knowing what you want can get you results quickly.

3. **Take any needed rehab steps** to prepare your property for flipping. It's best to have a crew of experienced workers do this for you, unless rehabbing is your trade. Assuming it isn't, talk to mechanics in your area to find qualified people to do a quick fix up before flipping.

4. **Continue finding new properties and flipping them.** Keep your financial goal in view and you'll soon reach the $1 million in market value by finding, and flipping, desirable properties.

Recognize What It Takes to Succeed

Amassing $1 million in market-value income real estate is a great goal for anyone to achieve. And, as your friend and mentor, I want *you* to reach that goal. To do so you must recognize what it takes to succeed in achieving your goal. It takes:

- **Knowing exactly what you want to achieve**—in this case a stated sum ($1 million in a given time period of one year).
- **Knowing how you want to achieve your goal**—in this case by owning, or flipping, real estate.
- **Knowing how you will achieve your goal in rental income**—the types of property, the amount you're willing to pay, the typical closing time you'll endure, the type of tenant you're aiming to rent to, the type of lender who will finance your property, and what kind of work you'll do on each property to bring it up to the highest sale price you can get.
- **Knowing how you'll achieve your goal in flipping real estate**—the sources of your flip properties, the price you're willing to pay versus the expected sales price, the amount of fix up you'll do, the type of workers you'll hire to do needed rehab work, and the source of financing you'll use for the flipping you plan to do.

The best way for you to achieve you goal is to write a Business Plan covering what you'll do in either your rental or flipping business. While I know that writing may turn you off, nothing can beat a Business Plan you write to help you achieve your goal. Your Business Plan will:

- **Show you which** steps to take to get started.
- **Project the income** you can expect from your work.
- **Give you an insight** to your own thinking you may never have had before.
- **Put you on the path** to your $1 million goal in one year.

Again, I know writing may be painful for you. But as your friend and mentor, I'll tell you this:

I'll be happy to review your Business Plan free of any charge if you're a subscriber to one of my newsletters described at the back of this book. You'll be given pointers on how your Business Plan might be improved, if such work is needed. While you may not like to do the Business Plan, I'll help you with it!

Your Key Ideas for Real Estate Wealth Building

❏ **There are six big money making opportunities** for you in real estate today—single-family and multifamily homes, retail, commercial, industrial, and recreational properties.

❏ **You must evaluate** the advantages and disadvantages of each type before you decide which one you'll choose to build your real estate wealth.

❏ **You can earn money** in two ways with your real estate—rental income or flipping.

❏ **Before choosing** how you want to earn money in your real estate wealth building, analyze your likes and dislikes, needs and wants.

❏ **One of the best ways to create wealth** in real estate is to write your own Business Plan detailing what you intend to do, when you will accomplish your goals, and what your future earnings will be.

❏ **Your author** will be happy to review your Business Plan and help you with it, if you ask him to do so.

CHAPTER 3

49 Mortgages That Can Give You the Real Estate Funding You Need

To acquire $1 million in real estate in one year in your free time you'll need loans. And in real estate the loans you get that use the property as collateral are called **mortgages.** In this chapter, we give you numerous mortgages you can use to build your wealth in real estate.

A knowledge of mortgages can be a powerful tool for you in negotiating for, and buying, income real estate using borrowed money. Why? Because:

Knowing what mortgages are available allows you to suggest many different ways to fund a deal. And these suggestions can often lead you to a zero-down payment deal in which you acquire valuable property in just a few days.

So let's put you on the road to becoming an expert on mortgages. You'll find your road to borrowed-money real estate wealth is both fun and profitable.

For many of the mortgages listed in this chapter you are given:

- **Advantages** of the mortgage for you.
- **Disadvantages** of the mortgage for you.

- **How you can use** the mortgage.
- **Actual example** of use of the mortgage for a property.

When reading the data for each type of mortgage, please remember:

- **That you may have such a unique** real estate situation for your income property that the listed advantages and disadvantages may not apply to you and your property.
- **That the example given** for one type of mortgage may have dozens of other types of mortgages that can be used for the property. So do NOT assume that only one type of mortgage can be used for the property in the example.

And, as an aside, please do not call me, write me, fax me, or e-mail me saying you can finance an example property with 20 other types of mortgages. I know that! The examples are given to jump start your creativity into thinking of new ways for you to acquire $1 million in real estate in one year in your spare time!

Adjustable-Rate Mortgages

An *adjustable-rate mortgage* (called an ARM for short) is a real estate loan made to you generally at a low rate with the possibility that the rate will rise as time passes. The higher rate, if any, is tied to a well-known index, such as the U.S. Treasury Bill interest rate. One variation of the ARM is known as the *option ARM.* With an option ARM you have the right, during the term of your mortgage, to pay, in any one month, only the interest, interest and principal, or to reduce your payment to what you can afford that month. This gives you greater freedom in making payments on your mortgage. But the overall effect could be that the amount you owe increases as time passes. So I suggest that you think carefully before taking on an option ARM. And if you do take such a mortgage, be certain to make your scheduled payments every month to avoid going deeper into debt!

A *flexible payment mortgage* is like an ARM but when interest rates rise, your monthly payment stays the same, within certain stated limits. With an increase in interest rates, more of your monthly payment goes to pay interest and less to reduce your principal. Some Beginning Wealth Builders (BWBs) like the flexible payment mortgage because it ensures that their monthly payment remains constant. "I'll worry about principal reduction when I sell!" they say.

Now what are the pros and cons of ARMs for you, as a real estate wealth builder? We'll discuss them next.

Advantages for You

Your initial interest rate can be low—in some cases just 1 percent. This means your monthly mortgage payments of principal and interest (called P&I) can be lower than with a fixed-rate mortgage. And when you buy an income property you usually need—at the start—all the financial advantages you can get. A low P&I payment is a great starting advantage. Other advantages include the fact that lenders love to make ARMs. Why? Because the lender is protected against rising interest rates, should rates increase. Result? Some lenders may be less demanding about your qualifications for a mortgage. Thus, a lender may accept a lower credit score (your FICO rating, named for the developers of this credit rating system, Fair Isaac Corporation) when making an ARM loan to you. Some lenders will accept a FICO score as low as 500 when making an ARM. In my lending company we love to make ARMs because the Federal examiners are pleased with such loans when they're reviewing our books during our annual exam.

Disadvantages for You

Adjustable-rate mortgages can hurt you if interest rates rise. Why? Because you cannot control the national economy. So if T-bill rates (called the index rate) start to rise, your P&I will also increase. If you have a tight income and expense situation with a property having an ARM, you may be driven into a negative cash flow. This means you may have to "feed" the property, paying its expenses from other income. Take my word for it—you will not be happy putting money into a losing property every month. As your good friend, I have to warn you of this possibility. So while an ARM can look attractive, "do the numbers" on a "what if" basis BEFORE buying any income property with an ARM. That is, assume various higher interest rates and figure your P&I cost. If you're likely to get into a negative cash flow situation, don't buy the property!

How You Can Use This Mortgage

Use an ARM for income real estate for which you're trying to keep your monthly P&I payments as low as possible in an economic environment where you do not expect large increases in the index interest rate. Where there are large swings in the index interest rate, a fixed-rate mortgage is safer for you.

Example of Mortgage Use

You find a beautiful red-brick 10-unit apartment building on the tree shaded edge of town that's for sale by a bickering couple in the throes of divorce. Checking the building in the company of an engineer you find that: (1) The roof is in excellent condition, having recently been replaced; (2) The electrical system exceeds Code requirements; (3) The plumbing is modern, with all bathrooms having been updated five years ago; (4) Your Positive Cash Flow (PCF) before mortgage payments will allow you to pay no more than 3 percent interest on your long-term mortgage at the start. Since the property rents are under the going rate in town, you decide to risk taking an ARM with the hope of raising rents soon after you acquire the building. And since the building is 100 percent rented now, you feel that its good location, neat appearance, and modern apartments will allow you to keep it fully rented. With all these facts in mind, you select an ARM and buy this attractive income property. **Result?** You get an ideal building, follow your rental-increase plan over a two-year period, and wind up with a beautiful property giving you a strong monthly PCF while steadily rising in value. You're on your way to independence through rental real estate bought at a good price!

Assumable Mortgages

An *assumable mortgage* (often shortened to an *assumable*) is an existing loan on an income property that you can take over (assume) and make monthly payments on as soon as you get title (ownership) to a property. The usual assumable mortgage does not have a due-on-sale clause. Such a clause requires that the seller pay off the entire existing mortgage when the property is sold. When you assume a mortgage you do not have your credit checked by the lender. Thus, many BWB real estate investors like an assumable mortgage because their credit background does not come into consideration when they're buying the income real estate.

Advantages for You

An assumable mortgage saves you lots of time and bother. Why? Because with an assumable, you just start making payments without having to go through a credit check and a background investigation by a potential lender. Such reviews can take four to six weeks if there's anything in your background that worries your lender. With an assumable you can own a property in just four to six hours! You will also save any application fee a lender may charge because property sellers seldom levy such fees. To sum up: Speed, No Credit Check, Simplified Paperwork, the Assumable is Not Recorded in Your Name—it remains in the seller's name. Further, the seller is ultimately responsible for paying off the mortgage in the event you are unable to do so.

Disadvantages for You

With an assumable mortgage, you must accept the interest rate at which the mortgage loan was made. This rate may be higher than the current rate in the mortgage market. Thus, your P&I payment may be higher than you'd make on a new mortgage loan. And you cannot go to the lender to get the rate reduced because the lender will probably demand that a new loan be made at the same rate as the assumable loan. In most cases you will never inform a lender that you're assuming an existing mortgage. Why? Because if the lender knows, you will probably be subjected to a credit and background check. People with a history of bankruptcy, slow pays, and other credit infractions avoid a credit check like they avoid a plague!

How You Can Use This Mortgage

An assumable mortgage is ideal for people with past, or current, or both, credit problems. You can start your real estate career with the worst of credit, if you can buy property using an assumable mortgage. So if your credit score prevents you from getting a conventional (standard) mortgage, look around for properties having assumable mortgages. It could be your first step in building your million-dollar real estate portfolio!

Example of Mortgage Use

A good friend of yours wants to own condo apartments on the Florida Gold Coast that she will rent to vacationers during both the "high" (winter) season and the "off" season (summer). She has applied for several mortgages to buy condo apartments having an ocean view but each time she was turned down because her credit is weak. "Find a condo having an assumable mortgage," you suggest to her. Taking your advice she finds a beautiful 10th floor two-bedroom condo with ocean views to the north, east, and south. You can see cruise ships entering the Fort Lauderdale inlet when you look south from this superb apartment having an updated kitchen and bathrooms. And the seller says the long-term mortgage is assumable. Your friend, with the help of a competent real estate attorney signs a contract to buy the condo apartment using the assumable mortgage. Then, her only challenge is to come up with the down payment. You help her with this by taking out an equity loan on one of your properties and lending her the down payment. She collateralizes your loan with a 10 percent ownership in the condo. The assumable mortgage allows this BWB to buy an attractive beachfront condo that will have a waiting list of renters every year!

Bad Credit/No Credit Mortgages

Bad credit/no credit mortgages are usually made without a credit check of you, the borrower. This means that your credit score is not a factor in your acceptance by the lender. But the lender usually protects itself by charging a higher interest rate on your mortgage. Why? Because the lender has less information about you. Hence, the lender feels that it is at greater risk for a default. To compensate for this higher risk (whether it exists or not) the lender charges you a higher rate of interest on the mortgage. This could be 1.0 or 1.5 percent more than you'd pay if you had a credit check before the mortgage loan is made.

Advantages for You

Bad credit/no credit mortgages can help you get started in income real estate when you can't find a suitable property with an assumable mortgage and your credit isn't the strongest. True, you'll pay a higher rate of interest for your mortgage loan. However, the interest you pay on your income real estate is provable and tax-deductible. And, if you make your mortgage payments on time you have a good chance of refinancing your mortgage after 12 months. In a favorable interest rate climate, you may then be able to get a lower interest rate. You must "work the numbers" to see if the lower interest rate will produce savings greater than the cost of refinancing. Further, a bad credit/no credit mortgage can be a big help to you if you have never established a credit history. While this may sound unusual, there are plenty of people wanting to get started in income real estate who have no credit history of any kind. This is where the bad credit/no credit mortgage can be the key that gets you started.

Disadvantages for You

The major disadvantage of a bad credit/no credit mortgage is the higher interest rate you'll have to pay. In a tightly controlled income property situation the higher interest rate could cause you to have a negative cash flow. This might make you turn away from an otherwise attractive property. So it could take you longer to find a PCF property when you're using a bad credit/no credit mortgage.

How You Can Use This Mortgage

Use the bad credit/no credit mortgage when you have either situation in your credit history. Actually, this type of mortgage can make the difference between your becoming a wealthy real estate investor instead of nothing more than a salary hack locked into a dead-end job with a snarling boss who threatens to lay you off every day of the week. To rid yourself of the possibility of such misery, make use of bad credit/no credit mortgages!

Example of Mortgage Use

You're a young college student who wants to get into income real estate as soon as you can. But you don't have a credit history because you paid cash for everything up to now. You just found a beautiful 80-year-old Victorian mansion with 12 bedrooms that would be ideal for student housing. It has sweeping wraparound porches front and back with white hand-carved columns that were recently painted. What's more, there's an extreme shortage of student housing in your college town. The Student Housing Group will gladly recommend your mansion as a safe and secure dormitory for incoming freshman students. But you can't get a mortgage from a conventional lender, such as a bank, because you don't have a credit history. What to do? Look in your local newspaper for lender ads saying "Bad Credit/No credit loans Available." Or, as a subscriber to one of my newsletters, call me—Ty Hicks—and ask me to supply three or four suitable lenders in your area. It will take me a day, or so, to come up with lenders handling Bad Credit/no credit loans. Result? You have a good chance of getting your Victorian mansion you can easily convert to dorm rooms giving you a PCF of $2,000, or more, per month!

Balloon Mortgages

Balloon mortgages are loans backed by real estate that require either an interest-only payment or another token payment for a stated period of years, at the end of which the entire borrowed amount becomes due and payable. Thus, you might borrow $100,000 for five years at 6 percent interest with a monthly payment of interest-only of $500. On the 60th month of your loan the entire $100,000 would be repayable in full. Paying this mortgage off on a monthly P&I basis would cost you $1,933 per month. But at the 60th month your payment would be just $1,933, not $100,000. You would pay back a total of $115,980, for a total cost of $115,980 − $100,000 = $15,980. With interest only, your cost would be $500 per month × 60 months = $30,000 for the same $100,000 loan. However, your payments would be $1,933 − $500 = $1,493 per month less. If you could put the $1,493 saving in payments to work earning other income, your total excess loan cost could be less than the $30,000 − $15,980 = $14,020.

Advantages for You

The biggest advantage of a balloon mortgage for you is the reduction in your monthly payments on your mortgage loan. This advantage is especially important when you have a tight cash-flow property and you must reduce your expenses to the minimum. As long as you have a PCF from the property and you expect the property to rise significantly in value during the term of your balloon mortgage, this type of loan can be very good for your wealth building. Also, using balloon mortgages can help you build a large portfolio of properties in a short time—if that's your wealth-building goal. Using balloon mortgages, you can easily acquire $1 million in income properties in one year, or less!

Disadvantages for You

With a balloon mortgage you're not "cutting into" the loan principal if you pay only interest each month. This means you have a "big nut," as real estate professionals say, at the end of the balloon term. And unless the property rises high enough in value to repay the balloon you may have to dig into reserves to repay what you owe. Or you may have to take equity loans on other properties to repay the balloon.

How to Use This Mortgage

A balloon mortgage can be a powerful loan for you when you're dealing with properties that appreciate (rise) in value quickly. With some properties rising in value as much as 15 percent a year, you can easily repay the balloon at the end of its term by selling the property. And you'll show a nice profit on the sale because your "cost of money" for the balloon will usually be less than the appreciation rate of the property. So:

> *Use a balloon mortgage when you know that the property appreciation rate exceeds your cost of money and you can sell at a profit before the balloon term expires. You can project all of this in advance with a little pencil work.*

Example of Mortgage Use

You live in a large city having a former manufacturing area that is now deserted. Why? The manufacturers fled to areas having lower rent and labor costs. But the buildings that served the manufacturers have large floor areas with high (12-foot) ceilings. They're called "loft" buildings because of their large floor area and high ceilings. Recently, these buildings have been "discovered" by artists, sculptors, painters, and others needing lots of space for their work. Checking on recent sales, you see that a typical loft building can rise $100,000 in price in less than six months. You rapidly search for a suitable loft building to buy, and flip, quickly. Since you don't intend to hold the building for more than a few months, you look for a smaller property. You find a four-story (many are six-story) building that still has a rope-operated passenger and freight elevator in it! But its hard-wood floors are in good condition. And its tin ceiling will really appeal to the artistic crowd. To buy the building you negotiate a balloon mortgage because your payments will be lower and you are almost certain you can sell the building long before the balloon comes due. You buy the loft building for $400,000, putting just $4,000 down with a $396,000 30-year balloon mortgage. Within three months you sell the loft for $520,000 because the buyer just loves the rope-operated passenger/freight elevator! Your profit? About $80,000 after paying sales commission, interest, and other closing costs. Not bad for an ancient loft building that has suddenly come back into favor that you bought using a balloon mortgage. (Note: Some loft owners in New York City have made millions selling loft buildings, or condos in them, that they financed with a balloon mortgage.)

Biweekly Mortgages

With a *biweekly mortgage* you pay P&I every two weeks, instead of once a month. Each payment is one-half what your monthly payment would be. Result: In 12 months you've made 13 monthly mortgage payments by paying every two weeks. So a 30-year mortgage loan you've taken to buy an income property will be paid in full after just 19 years.

Advantages for You

By paying off your mortgage on a biweekly basis you shorten the term of your mortgage considerably. Further, the total interest cost of your mortgage is much lower. And your equity (ownership portion) in the property rises much faster than when you're making only monthly payments on your mortgage. It's a win-win arrangement for you if the income property has a large enough cash flow to handle that extra payment each year.

Disadvantages for You

You will be making one extra mortgage payment each year. In a tight cash flow property this extra payment might put you into a negative cash-flow condition. Also, you must arrange with your mortgage lender to have your biweekly payments properly credited to your loan account. If you don't do this in advance, an unknowing clerk in your lender's office may improperly enter your payment, leading to confusion and loss of term reduction to you.

How to Use This Mortgage

Use a biweekly mortgage when you want to pay off a property more rapidly than with a conventional mortgage. You may want the early payoff to collect more cash for yourself when you sell the property. Or you may want to reduce your total cost of a property by making 13, instead of 12, mortgage payments per year. There's a nice feeling when you pay off a property and some BWBs feel this is worth the extra payment each year. And—of course—your equity in the property builds faster than with a conventional mortgage. You can use this equity to get an equity loan on the property to buy other properties. And, as you know, the money you get from a loan is nontaxable when you receive it! That's why many BWBs use a biweekly loan to build equity faster for future loans.

Example of Mortgage Use

You're a mountain enthusiast, loving climbing and exploring in both the woods and on rocky trails. And you see that other mountaineer types love to spend their spare time in the woods and hills at the base of nearby mountains. So you decide to buy a mountain cabin for your own use and as an investment that will rise in value as time passes. But you don't want to be saddled with long-term payments on your mortgage. Looking around your favorite mountain-climbing area you find a neat little two-bedroom rustic cabin that's well built and in good condition. Contacting your bank, you arrange for a biweekly mortgage. This will cut the term of your mortgage while reducing your interest costs. Buying the mountain cabin, you enjoy it for a few years and then sell it for almost twice what you paid for it. Your biweekly mortgage saved you money while you enjoyed your mountain cabin and gave you a higher profit when you sold!

Blanket Mortgages

A *blanket mortgage* is a loan covering a property that can either be sub-divided and sold in smaller parts, or a group of buildings that can be sold individually without affecting the basic mortgage. Suppose you buy an acre of land using a mortgage loan to finance your purchase. You then subdivide the land into four quarter-acre lots because there is a strong market for such size properties in the area. A buyer approaches you and wants to buy one lot. You sell it to him and your blanket mortgage continues to cover your other three properties.

Advantages for You

A blanket mortgage allows you to finance multiple properties with just one mortgage. This saves your time, your money, and your gasoline for trips to lenders. You have much greater freedom to wheel and deal with buyers when your property is covered by a blanket mortgage. And lenders like blanket mortgages because less paperwork is needed to cover multiple properties.

Disadvantages for You

You may have more difficulty obtaining a blanket mortgage because your lender may not understand what you're trying to do with your property. And your lender may ask you to prepare a Business Plan in which you show how you intend to dispose of the property in pieces as time passes. While preparing such a Plan is good for you and your business, it does take time and may delay obtaining the mortgage for your property.

How You Can Use This Mortgage

You can use a blanket mortgage wherever you plan to acquire multiple properties for later development, resale, rehab, or demolition and re-placement. Your key is multiple properties or a situation in which you might take a single property and turn it into multiple properties by any of the methods listed above. The blanket mortgage protects you for future creative uses for the real estate you're buying.

Example of Mortgage Use

You've been a boater all your life and you want to blend your interest in boats with a business—namely a marina. You find a beautiful location on a picturesque tree-shaded nearby island ideal for a marina. After some negotiating you get an excellent price on two acres of prime waterfront land on this scenic island that has thousands of colorful blossoming flowers every summer. You will develop the land and put in boat slips that you intend to sell as "dockominiums." The buyer buys a slip and owns it. You receive cash for the sale that helps you pay off your mortgage. Preparing a comprehensive Business Plan, you approach a lender. Your Plan shows that you'll have 60 slips that you'll sell as "condos" for $40,000 each. This will give you 60 slips × $40,000 each = $2,400,000. Such a cash flow will allow you to "retire" (pay off) your mortgage and have cash left over for slip construction. So your Business Plan asks for a blanket mortgage to cover purchase of the island marina property, construction of the slips and service buildings, and a profit for yourself. Your blanket mortgage loan is made to you and you happily combine real estate and boating! Your blanket mortgage makes it all possible.

Bridge- or Swing-Loan Mortgages

You use a *bridge-* or *swing-loan mortgage* when you want to buy another property using your existing for-sale property as collateral for the loan to buy your next property. The loan "bridges" or "swings" between the two properties—the one you're selling and the one you plan to buy.

A *gap loan* is similar to a bridge loan but it is dependent upon certain conditions being met by an income property. Thus, when you are constructing a multifamily apartment house, a gap loan is used to meet expenses until a certain number of apartments—say 80 percent of those available—have been rented to suitable tenants. Then the final amount of the construction loan is released to the borrower.

Now let's look at the pros and cons of bridge loans and how you might use them in building your real estate wealth to $1 million in one year on borrowed money.

Advantages for You

There are several advantages for you offered by bridge loans. These advantages are:

- **You can get a bridge-loan mortgage** faster because your existing property collateralizes it.
- **Your interest rate on a bridge loan** is usually lower because the collateral (the property you plan to sell) is in place.
- **You have fewer credit requirements** to meet for a bridge loan because the collateral is easily checked and verified.

Disadvantages for You

Some lenders place tight time restrictions on bridge loans—such as 60 or 90 days. This may pressure you into paying more for your second property than you would if you had more time. Other lenders will give you a year to close the second deal. This is usually enough time for you to plan, and complete, an advantageous transaction in which you do not overpay!

How You Can Use This Mortgage

If you're trying to use a lower cost property to leverage yourself into a higher cost, higher income property, a bridge (or swing) loan mortgage can give you superior results. And you'll get your loan faster, with less red tape. Just be sure to get the longest term possible—at least one year!

Budget Mortgages

A *budget mortgage* is an amortizing real estate loan in which the lender requires the borrower to include one-twelfth of the estimated real estate taxes and insurance costs with each monthly P&I payment. The money for taxes and insurance is put into an escrow account, ready for payment when these charges become due. Having the tax and insurance costs paid monthly is an advantage for you, as a BWB in real estate, because it eliminates the worry over missing a payment and incurring a penalty. Hence, you'd be wise to have every income property mortgage set up as a budget mortgage. Doing so will give you more time to concentrate on the business aspects of your real estate.

Bullet Mortgages

A *bullet mortgage* is a short-term loan—usually of 5 or 10 years duration—with you paying interest only on your loan. Thus, it is an interest-only mortgage loan for 5 or 10 years, at the end of which the full amount you borrowed is due. The "bullet" name comes from the nature of the lump-sum amount for repayment. It hits you like a bullet! See "Interest-Only Mortgages" in this chapter for the advantages and disadvantages of such mortgages. In general, bullet mortgages have a shorter term than interest-only mortgages.

When an interest-only mortgage has a longer maturity than a bullet mortgage, it is called a *term loan* or term mortgage. Note that with any interest-only mortgage your total interest cost is much higher than with an *amortizing mortgage* in which you pay P&I monthly. With an interest-only mortgage you're paying interest on the full amount you borrow. With an amortizing mortgage, the principal is reduced with each payment you make, thereby reducing the total interest you pay. In some areas an interest-only mortgage is called a *standing loan* because the amount you borrow—the principal—is standing steady and is not being reduced by a monthly amortizing payment.

Conforming Mortgages

A *conforming mortgage* is a real estate loan whose paperwork conforms with the documents required by Freddie Mac (Federal Home Loan Mortgage Corporation) and Fannie Mae (Federal National Mortgage Association). Your loan, when prepared on these standardized documents, is termed a *conforming mortgage loan.* Your mortgage loan is also called a *conventional loan* (see following) because it complies with the standard documentation used by lenders. The reason why standardized documents are used is to permit the lender to sell the loan to Fannie Mae. When this happens the lender gets its money back to lend on other real estate mortgages.

Since these terms apply to mortgages described for you in later sections of this chapter, the advantages and disadvantages are detailed under their respective names.

Constant-Payment Mortgages

With a *constant-payment mortgage* you make the same payment every month, every quarter, or every six months, depending on the terms of your mortgage. Most constant-payment mortgages require a monthly payment. Thus, if you have a 25-year mortgage loan with a monthly P&I payment of $1,500, you will, when you make the last payment, have repaid the mortgage in full. With a constant-payment mortgage you know your P&I payment will remain the same for the life of your mortgage loan. This can be reassuring when the price of almost every other item in your life seems to be constantly rising. Constant-payment mortgages are good for you when you believe that interest rates will rise during the time you own an income property. If you had an ARM on a property, your P&I payment might rise as time passes, causing a negative cash flow to occur. REMEMBER: Negative Cash Flow is BAD; Positive Cash Flow is GOOD!

Construction Loan with a Takeout Mortgage

Construction loans pay for the building of a real estate income project— such as an apartment house, office building, commercial stores, motel, hotel, and so on. When you get a construction loan you generally own the land on which the project is built, control the land under a long-term lease (up to 99 years for some land), or have an option to buy the land. It is much easier for you to get a construction loan if you own, or control, the land on which the project will be built.

When you get a construction loan with a takeout mortgage, you either:

- **Have a construction lender** that requires you to place a long-term mortgage with it on satisfactory completion of construction and suitable "rent-up"—such as 70 percent of the units in an apartment house rented to credit checked tenants, or
- **Must obtain** a suitable long-term mortgage from an accredited lender *before* you will be granted the construction loan. The long-term mortgage is termed your *takeout*.

As a general guide for acquiring $1 million in real estate in one year on zero cash in your spare time, you should NOT take on a construction project unless you:

- **Are an experienced builder** of the type of property you plan to develop.
- **Have worked in construction** for at least two years before you start your project.
- **Understand the economics** of construction, or have an accountant who is experienced in real estate projects.

So, my advice to you is:

Work with built, existing real estate at the start of your career. Continue with this type of real estate until you have acquired $1 million in real estate in one year. Once you've achieved that goal you can consider starting a real estate construction project.

Conventional Mortgages

A *conventional mortgage* is a real estate loan from a bank, credit union, or other mortgage lender that is not guaranteed by a government agency, such as the Veterans Administration (VA) or the Federal Housing Administration (FHA). Further, a conventional mortgage normally requires a 20 percent down payment on the income property. This means the mortgage covers 80 percent of the cost of the property, or $80,000 on a property you pay $100,000 for, with a $20,000 down payment. You make a monthly constant P&I payment on your conventional mortgage. If your down payment is less than 20 percent of the price of the property—say $10,000 on a $100,000 property—then you must take out Private Mortgage Insurance (PMI) to cover a portion of the loan. Your lender will provide data on how, and where, you can obtain the PMI for your loan.

Advantages for You

There are thousands of conventional mortgage lenders. Thus, with some 15,000 banks and about 11,000 credit unions in the United States, you have some 26,000 conventional mortgage lenders. Add to this the number of mortgage companies and the total zooms. So the major advantage of conventional mortgage lenders to you is AVAILABILITY OF MONEY FOR MORTGAGES! The same logic applies to Canada and Europe where the number of mortgage lenders is large.

Disadvantages for You

The 20 percent down pay requirement can be a disadvantage for the BWB. But if you own other property in which you have equity (ownership) you can often take an equity loan for the down payment on your next income property. Note that the conventional mortgage does not prohibit you from using borrowed money for your down payment. And when you are required to get PMI, the cost can be an annoyance. Again, this cost is provable and tax deductible. So it is not too burdensome.

How You Can Use This Mortgage

Use conventional mortgages when you have a source of borrowed down-payment money and you're buying new, or relatively new, income property. Often, for new property, the seller will have a conventional mortgage in place for you. So all you have to do is sign a few papers, write a check for the borrowed down payment, and Presto—the property is yours! You get speed and convenience in a neat package.

Example of Mortgage Use

You want to buy a new townhouse you plan to rent for a monthly PCF. The townhouse is in a beautiful wooded community development with neat, curving streets that give a scenic view when you drive or walk. In the development, a large lake provides swimming and boating for residents. Your research shows that there's a shortage of desirable rental units in the area. Inspecting the townhouse, you find that it's a two-story, three-bedroom, 2.5-bath unit with spacious rooms, oak floors, and large windows with spectacular views of a golf course in one direction and colorful woods in the other direction. You can easily rent this townhouse to give you a $300-per-month PCF. And better yet, your tenant will pay all utilities—heat, light, lawn maintenance, and so on. You quickly accept the conventional mortgage the builder offers you and rent the income property the same day you put it on the market! Your new tenant gives you a three-month security deposit so you're off to a good start.

Convertible Adjustable-Rate Mortgages

A *convertible ARM* allows you to change from an adjustable interest rate to a fixed interest rate on your mortgage. You can usually convert any time after you have the mortgage for one year, or longer. Some ARMs allow you to convert up to the 60th month of your loan. After that you cannot convert from an adjustable to a fixed rate. While there may be a small charge for converting from the variable rate to the fixed rate (0.5 percent to 1.0 percent of the mortgage amount), the cost is much less than if you were to refinance the loan.

Advantages for You

A convertible ARM loan can give you a lower interest rate when you buy an income property. And a lower rate at the start of your real estate career is usually welcomed by most BWBs. Why? Because when you first buy an income property you may have unexpected expenses. So any savings you can obtain are welcome. Since most ARMs are offered at a lower interest rate than fixed-rate loans, you can save money during your first year or so of owning an income property. Just be sure you have a convertible clause in your ARM!

Disadvantages for You

If you don't have a convertible clause in your ARM, you may be saddled with a sharp rise in your interest cost, if rates rise. This may put you into a Negative Cash Flow situation.

How to Use This Mortgage

Use a convertible ARM when you want minimum cost during your first years of income property ownership. But to ensure that you have an opportunity to convert your mortgage to a fixed rate, you must be certain your ARM has a convertible clause in it! Your real estate attorney will check this for you. But to be doubly sure, check for yourself. And try to get the longest convertible time possible—at least 60 months, or longer.

Example of Mortgage Use

You're, we'll say, a tennis fanatic. You'd rather play tennis than eat or sleep! But you're also a real estate enthusiast. So you'd like to combine your love of tennis with your real estate wealth-building goals.

Looking around in your area you find an indoor tennis center with six clay courts for sale by an estate. Inspecting the building you find that it's a neat, sparkling white cinder block structure with neatly painted red doors and windows. Inside, the hard-clay courts are scrupulously clean and well marked. The nets are new, with shiny aluminum posts. The men's and women's locker rooms are clean, well maintained, and have new lockers, showers, and changing areas.

Going outside, you find four more attractive up-to-date new-surface tennis courts that will give you additional revenue during good weather.

These four courts are included in your purchase price. You're delighted with the entire project.

Checking with a mortgage broker you find that your interest rate on a fixed-rate mortgage will be 8.5 percent since this is a commercial mortgage project. But on an ARM your rate will be 5.5 percent. Since you don't trust the business records of the tennis facility because the estate never operated it (the owner is deceased), you opt for the ARM because your initial costs will be lower.

You tell your real estate attorney: "Be sure there's a convertible clause in the ARM. And get as long a convertible period as possible!" When you receive a copy of the ARM document from your attorney, you carefully read it—from start to finish—to be certain it does contain the desirable, and needed, convertible clause.

You take over the indoor/outdoor tennis facility and have an enjoyable time running your real estate business because it's part of your hobby. (But you really don't get much time on the courts because they're always busy with paying customers!) The method you use to take over this $500,000 facility is:

- **Long-term convertible ARM (25 years)** at 5.5 percent for 80 percent ($400,000) of the $500,000 purchase price.

- **Short-term purchase money (PM) mortgage (5 years)** from the seller for $120,000 which includes the closing costs. (The estate seller gives you the PM because he or she has not been able to find a buyer who understands tennis and wants to build a fortune in real estate.)

At the end of your first year in the tennis business you start to worry about an interest-rate rise. So you convert your convertible ARM to a fixed-rate mortgage. While your interest rate rises somewhat, you now know that your business is so profitable that you can afford the slightly higher cost. Further, you plan to raise your tennis court rental rates to give you the extra income to pay the higher interest rate!

"That's one of the advantages of having your own business," I tell you. "You can raise your prices to offset higher costs."

"You're right," you answer. "In fact, we'll also increase our profits when the income from the higher court rental rates starts to roll in. The higher interest rate pushed us to a price increase that we'd been considering for a long time. So the convertible ARM really was good for my real estate and tennis business!" you tell me.

Now what pointers should you gain from this example? They are:

- **An ARM can position you** for future protective and proactive business choices.

- **A convertible clause** is an absolute necessity in your ARM. Double-check every ARM document to see that you do get this important clause.

- **Keep careful expense records** so you can make a sensible decision about converting your ARM.

- **Get the longest convertible period you can.** Do not settle for less than 60 months. And get a longer term, if you can!

First Mortgages

The *first mortgage* is the most common loan secured by real estate. If the Loan-to-Value (LTV) ratio for an income property is 80 percent on a $100,000 total price, then the first mortgage is 0.80 × $100,000 = $80,000. Most first mortgages:

- **Are easy to obtain** because the value of the property exceeds the loan amount. For the aforementioned property, the value is 20 percent greater than the loan amount of $80,000.

- **Are readily available** from a variety of lenders—banks, credit unions, insurance companies, mortgage issuers, and so on.

- **Are usually made** at a lower rate of interest than any other mortgage loans (junior mortgages) on a property.

- **Are available** in a number of different forms—fixed rate, variable rate, adjustable rate, balloon, and so on.

With first mortgages relatively easy to obtain, it is much simpler for you to get started in income real estate. First mortgages are the "life blood" of income real estate. You will almost always have a first mortgage for income property unless you pay all cash for it. It is our suggestion throughout this book that you *not* pay all cash for the usual income property.

"Why not pay all cash for an income property?" you ask. "Because," we answer, "it's better to use Other People's Money (OPM) to finance your wealth building. Doing so gives you maximum leverage. And it helps you get started on little, or no, cash!"

Gifted Down-Payment Mortgages

As many of my newsletter and book readers know, I've been in the real estate and business lending fields for a number of years. And I can tell you this, good friend of mine, we lenders earn more money from our loans than from any other business activity. So, as lenders, we want to make as many loans as possible to reasonably well-qualified borrowers. Why? To earn more to send our kids to Ivy League Schools, have the car of our liking, and so on.

Result? We happily accept borrowers who have a "Gift Letter" from a relative stating that:

> *The relative will give the borrower a stated amount (usually the amount needed for the down payment on an income property) without any need of repayment of the money by the borrower. Such a letter allows us, as lenders, to make a long-term mortgage (15 to 30 years) to the borrower, even though we know the borrower is not putting up his or her own money.*

Advantages for You

You are allowed to purchase an income property with 100 percent financing—the *gifted down-payment loan* plus your long-term mortgage. And the lender will not be reprimanded by any regulatory agency for making this 100 percent loan because the Gift Letter will be in the lender's loan file.

Disadvantages for You

You may have difficulty finding a relative having sufficient funds to give you the money you need without having you eventually repay them.

How You Can Use This Mortgage

Use the gifted down-payment mortgage when you can't borrow your needed down payment for an investment real estate project from another source or by using equity loans on other properties you own.

Graduated-Payment Mortgages

A *graduated-payment mortgage* allows you to start your income real estate career with lower payments (and in some mortgages with no payments) for a stated period of time—typically five years. Then your payments increase for another stated period. For example you might obtain a graduated-payment mortgage thus:

> 8 percent interest for 5 years on a 35-year term mortgage.
> 8 percent interest for 5 years on a 30-year term mortgage.
> 8 percent interest for 5 years on a 25-year term mortgage.

Other graduated-payment mortgages may allow a *standing loan* during the first period where you pay interest only, no principal. This, of course, reduces your monthly payments on your loan. Graduated-payment mortgages have a number of variations you should know about. These are:

- **Variable-amortization mortgage** (**VAM**) in which your principal payments are lower at the start and then increase after a stated period of time.
- **Variable-payment mortgage** (**VPM**) in which the payments vary during the life of your mortgage.
- **Variable-rate mortgage** (**VRM**) in which your interest rate may change, based on some exterior standard, such as the Treasury Bill rate.

Advantages for You

The main advantage of any of these mortgages is to reduce your monthly payment during the early years of your ownership of an income property. This is when you need such help and a graduated-payment mortgage can provide that help.

Disadvantages for You

You pay off your debt more slowly with a graduated-payment mortgage. But few real estate BWBs hold an income property for the full life of the mortgage. They usually sell the property—at a nice profit—long before the mortgage is paid off. So the reduction of principal is a secondary consideration for them.

How You Can Use This Mortgage

Use the graduated-payment mortgage, or its variations, when you're first starting your real estate career. Having lower monthly payments can give you a strong PCF that will put you in the million-dollar class sooner!

Grants for Real Estate Down Payment

Probably the most frequent question asked of me when people call on the phone is: "Can I get a down-payment grant to buy an income property— either a Single-Family Home (SFH) or a Multifamily Home (MFH)?" The answer, good friend of mine, is "Yes, you may be able to get a down-payment grant for an income property of your choice!" Such a grant may give you 100 percent financing of an income property. There are organizations around the United States that do make **grants for real estate down payment.** To get such a grant you must:

- **Find a suitable income property** you want to buy.
- **Get the needed data** on the property—the Price, Income, Expenses, and Down Payment.
- **Contact a local organization** making down-payment grants.

- **Supply the needed paperwork** to get your down-payment grant.
- **Obtain your down-payment grant** and buy the property.

As you know, I'm sure,

You never have to repay a grant if you take the action for which the grant was made—that is, you buy the income property. The money is yours—with no repayment—ever.

Advantages for You

You get 100 percent financing of a desirable income property and never have to repay the down payment on the property. Your PCF will be higher because you're paying on only one mortgage—the long-term loan.

Disadvantages for You

You may have to spend a month, or longer, looking for an organization that makes down-payment grants. My company, IWS, Inc., specializes in finding down-payment grants for our readers. This service is available free to subscribers to our *Money Watch Bulletin* newsletter described at the back of this book. We cannot give you the sources of such down-payment grants here because they vary from one locality to another.

How You Can Use This Mortgage

Get a down-payment grant whenever you can to purchase an income real estate property that will show a PCF. A grant never affects your credit rating (FICO) score. Further, it does not appear on your debt-to-income ratio. Hence, getting a down-payment grant will not impede your getting other real estate loans, such as the many you are learning about in this chapter.

Growing-Equity Mortgages

When you have a *growing-equity mortgage,* your monthly mortgage payment is increased by an agreed-on amount—such as 5 percent or 10 percent each year. The increased amount is used to reduce directly the principal amount you owe. Result? You pay off your mortgage in full in about half the number of years for the same mortgage amount having a fixed payment each month. Thus, if you have a 30-year growing-equity mortgage, it will be paid off in about 15 years, compared to 30 years for a fixed-monthly payment mortgage.

Advantages for You

Your mortgage payments are smaller during the early years of your loan. But as time passes and your earnings increase from your income property, your payments rise. And your rising payments significantly shorten your payoff time for the mortgage.

Disadvantages for You

If your income falls during the later years of the life of your mortgage, the increased payments might be a burden. But this rarely happens and we hope it does not happen to you!

How You Can Use This Mortgage

Use the growing-equity mortgage when you plan to hold onto a property for a long time. Since you'll pay off the mortgage sooner, you'll be free and clear of any mortgage debt at an early age!

Hard-Money Mortgages

A *hard-money mortgage* is a loan based on the equity in a real estate property. In most hard-money mortgages the credit rating and the income of the borrower are unimportant. The equity in the property (the "hard" asset) is what collateralizes the loan.

Hard-money mortgage loans are characterized by high interest rates and high points. (A point is 1 percent of the loan amount, or $1,000 on a $100,000 loan.) Thus, you'll see hard-money loans at 16 percent interest and 10 points, or $10,000 on a $100,000 loan. But you can get a hard-money loan in just days, compared to weeks for a conventional loan.

Advantages for You

Speed in getting your money is the major advantage for you. And if your credit score is not the highest, a hard-money mortgage may be ideal for you.

Disadvantages for You

The high interest rate and high points can put you into a negative cash flow situation.

How You Can Use This Mortgage

When your credit is weak but you have, or can get, equity in a real estate property, a hard-money mortgage may be the best answer for you. Just be sure you get the amount of cash you need, after you pay the required points. And be certain you can make loan payments from the property cash flow.

Home-Equity Mortgages

When you own real estate having a market value greater than what you owe on the property, you are said to have *equity* or ownership in the property. And lenders—anxious to make more loans on the solid collateral that real estate is—will loan money to you using your equity in the property as collateral. This is termed a ***home-equity loan*** but it is really similar to a second mortgage on the property. You can take the proceeds from a home-equity loan in one lump sum or you can tap into the money on an as-needed basis. And since the loan is collateralized by real estate, the interest—in general—is tax deductible. You should, of course, see your tax advisor for the final word on the deductibility of the interest you pay on a home-equity loan. Home-equity loans are an excellent source of down-payment money to buy income real estate. With the rapid rise in real estate values in many areas, BWBs are using home-equity loans to leverage their income real estate holdings. Note: May be named HELOC = Home Equity Line of Credit.

Interest-Only Mortgages

Also called *zero-percent interest mortgages,* these loans can be both helpful and dangerous for beginners. Full details are given later in this chapter under the heading "zero-percent interest mortgages." See the information there for the advantages and disadvantages for you.

Investor Mortgages

When you buy your first few pieces of income real estate you're generally regarded as a part-time amateur. But once your total mortgages reach the limit set by many banks, namely $1 million, you'll have to apply for an *investor mortgage* for future real estate loans. By applying for an investor mortgage you're immediately informing the lender that you are requesting a loan to earn money from it. You're no longer an amateur! You're a professional investor who owns real estate from which you earn your livelihood.

Advantages for You

Investor mortgages enable you to borrow more than the typical bank limit of $1 million. Hence, investor mortgages can help you acquire large real estate holdings. Further, lenders will:

- **Treat you** with greater courtesy.
- **Be more willing** to negotiate the terms of your loan.
- **Give you a decision** faster than they do for the "amateur" applicant.

Being an investor makes you stand out from the rest of the crowd of mortgage loan applicants!

Disadvantages for You

Some banks, especially smaller ones, refuse to deal with investors. Why? Because they're afraid of risk takers, which is what investors are. Further, some lenders will charge a higher rate of interest for investor loans. "How much higher?" you ask. Typical rates will be 2 to 3 percent higher than conventional home mortgage loans. But as an investor you expect to have the property you buy pay all its expenses, including debt service. And in your debt service is the higher interest rate charged on investor loans.

How You Can Use This Mortgage

Use an investor mortgage as soon as you start approaching the $1 million in real estate loans. To get the fastest results from your investor loans:

- **Set up** a real estate holding company.
- **Have your attorney** advise you as to the best form of holding company—a full "C" corporation, or a limited liability corporation—"LLC."
- **Choose an appropriate name** for your company—such as Brookshire Real Estate; Coastal Holdings; Mountain Residential Real Estate; and so on.
- **Get a printer** to provide attractive letterheads, business cards, and mailing envelopes for you.
- **Tell every lender** you approach that you're an investor seeking investment funds for an attractive project.
- **Provide a comprehensive Business Plan** with every Loan Application you submit.

Jumbo Mortgages

Fannie Mae (Federal National Mortgage Association) has certain maximum first-mortgage loan amounts for the mainland United States and Puerto Rico and other maximum first-mortgage loan amounts for Alaska, Hawaii, and the Virgin Islands. These maximum amounts cover properties from one unit to four units. When a first-mortgage loan exceeds the maximum Fannie Mae amount for the number of units in the property, it is termed a ***nonconforming jumbo loan.***

Fannie Mae also sets maximum loan amounts for second mortgages. As for first mortgages, when a second mortgage exceeds the Fannie Mae amount it is termed a nonconforming jumbo second-mortgage loan.

You'll run into the jumbo loan term when your loan exceeds the Fannie Mae loan amount. Don't worry about it! It's a term lenders use when the loan exceeds the guidelines. If your property promises to be profitable and you qualify in other respects, you'll get the loan—jumbo, or not!

Junior Mortgages

A *junior mortgage* is any loan that does not have a first claim on the property for which the loan is made. Thus, a PM mortgage is usually a junior mortgage because it generally has a secondary position, after the first mortgage. Sellers are willing to accept a junior mortgage when doing so enables them to make a sale that otherwise might not go through. Further, if a buyer defaults on a junior mortgage the property reverts to the seller and any payments made by the buyer can be kept by the seller. From a buyer's viewpoint, a junior mortgage provides a way to purchase a property with no, or very little, cash down. Hence, a junior mortgage can be a powerful tool in getting started in income real estate on little cash of your own.

LIBOR-Based Mortgages

A *LIBOR-based mortgage* is an ARM loan whose interest rate is governed by the London InterBank Offer Rate. This rate is used in the international money market and is the rate one bank charges another for borrowed money. Your LIBOR-based mortgage rate will usually be a few percentage points above the current LIBOR rate. And, as the LIBOR rate rises or falls, so, too, will your mortgage interest rate, depending on the terms of your mortgage. LIBOR-based ARM loans are becoming more popular. But for a beginner, we suggest that you try to have your ARM based on the U.S. Treasury Bill rate. This rate is easier to find, and track, than the LIBOR rate.

No-Appraisal Mortgages

Almost every real estate transaction requires an appraisal of the property being bought, or sold, before financing is approved by a lender. A *no-appraisal mortgage* is a loan backed by real estate for which no appraisal is required for approval of the financing. Skipping the appraisal saves you money for those loans where the lender charges you the cost of the appraisal.

Advantages for You

A no-appraisal mortgage will give you your loan sooner because the time needed for the appraisal is cut to zero. And without an appraisal you can reduce the time needed to fix flaws found by an appraisal because needed repairs may not be included in the buying negotiations.

Disadvantages for You

An appraisal may discover serious flaws in a building and its structure. Such an appraisal can save you from making a serious error in buying a defective property that may cost big money and takes months, or longer, to repair. Unless you're a construction expert, be extremely careful before buying any property without an appraisal.

How You Can Use This Mortgage

Use a no-appraisal mortgage when it's to your advantage to be able to get a loan without having to bear the cost of an appraisal or spend the time waiting for an appraiser to become available. You must be sure, however, that the property is worth the amount you're paying for it. The only way to determine this is to make the appraisal yourself, or have an expert you trust do an appraisal for you. Take my advice—here and now—***Never buy an income property without an appraisal unless you're sure it's worth at least 50 percent more than you're paying for it!***

No-Doc/Low-Doc Mortgages

Lenders, as I've mentioned, are anxious to make as many loans as they can. Why? Because we lenders (I'm director of a large lending organization) earn more money from loans than from any other investment source. So we lenders spend hours and hours trying to figure out how we can make more reasonably safe loans.

One answer lenders developed is the *no-doc, low-doc mortgage.*

As the name implies, such mortgages are made with no documentation from the borrower regarding his or her income. Or, only a small amount of income documentation (low-doc) is required of the borrower.

No-doc, low-doc mortgages usually have a higher interest rate than the usual conforming mortgage. Why is this? Because the lender has less information on the borrower. So it's a riskier loan. To protect itself the lender charges a higher rate of interest.

Advantages for You

When you're first starting your income real estate career and don't have much of an earnings history, the no-doc, low-doc mortgage loan might be ideal for you. Just be sure that the income from the property gives you a PCF, after paying all expenses, including your debt service.

Disadvantages for You

The higher rate of interest on your no-doc, low-doc mortgage might cause a loss on your monthly income. If this happens, look around for a property that shows a PCF!

How You Can Use This Mortgage

Use a no-doc, low-doc mortgage when you're just starting. Or consider using one if you've had credit problems in the past that lower your FICO score.

Nonowner-Occupied Mortgages

Nonowner-occupied mortgages are used for smaller one- to four-family properties in which the owner will not reside. This type of mortgage is the same as any conventional mortgage except for the notation that the owner will not occupy the premises. When you're using a property to produce income for yourself it's important from an insurance-coverage standpoint that the mortgage be classified as nonowner-occupied so you have proper coverage of the risks involved when you have tenants.

Nonrecourse Mortgages

With a *nonrecourse mortgage* a lender cannot take any of your personal assets (your home, other income properties you own, your bank account, auto, etc.) if you default on payments for the property. The only asset the mortgage lender can act against is the property for which you hold the nonrecourse mortgage. Smart real estate investors try to get a nonrecourse clause written into their mortgages because such a proviso insulates them from legal action in the event the property goes into default. Your real estate attorney will handle the details of this clause if you ask that it be included in the mortgages you use to buy income properties.

No-Ratio Mortgages

When you apply for an income real estate mortgage early in your career you'll often find your lender checks your *debt-to-income ratio.* If this ratio—which is your monthly debt payments divided by your monthly gross income—is greater than 0.33 (or debt payments of 33 percent of your gross income) your lender may reject your Loan Application. You'll be told, "your debt-to-income ratio is too high. We have to reject your Loan Application."

For example, say your total monthly debt payments are:

Auto loan = $309
Credit cards = $802
Boat loan = $114
Personal loan = $186

Total monthly debt payments = $1,411
Gross income before withholding = $4,922 per month

Your debt-to-income ratio = $1,411/$4,922 = 0.287, or 28.7 percent. This is a good ratio and your Loan Application would probably be accepted.

But if your income were $3,922 per month, your debt-to-income ratio would be $1,411/$3,922 = 0.359, or 35.9 percent. Your Loan Application would probably be rejected by the usual lender.

To encourage more borrowing, some of today's lenders are making *no-ratio mortgage loans.* This means your debt-to-income ratio is not checked as part of your loan approval process. Or if it is checked, the ratio is ignored when your loan is approved. So you can have a high ratio, 45 or 50 percent, and your lender does not care. You must, of course, be able to repay *all* your loans every month without a struggle.

Advantages for You

A no-ratio mortgage allows you to get into income real estate despite earlier debts you may have taken on.

Disadvantages for You

A no-ratio mortgage may lead you to take on an excessive amount of debt. This can lead to monthly payment problems.

How You Can Use This Mortgage

Use a no-ratio mortgage when your debt-to-income ratio is so high you cannot obtain any other type of mortgage. But be careful not to take on more than one no-ratio mortgage unless you're sure you have a strong enough PCF to pay all mortgages while having a hefty cash reserve.

No-Seasoning Mortgages

Lenders often want "seasoning" of a mortgage before they will give you a HELOC, or any other type of loan, on a property. *Seasoning* is a record of on-time payments on your mortgage for 3 months, 6 months, or 12 months, depending on the requirements of your lender. A *no-seasoning mortgage* is one in which a lender does not require a record of on-time payments of a loan before the lender will make another loan to you for any purpose. (Some lenders call these loans *non-seasoned mortgages.*)

Advantages for You

When you're able to get a no-seasoning mortgage or HELOC you lever from one property to another quickly. Thus, if you buy an income apartment house at a price below its going market value, you can immediately use the property as collateral for another loan to buy your next property. This is termed *leverage*—using a smaller amount of money to control a larger amount. And if you buy your first income property—the apartment house previously mentioned—with borrowed money, your leverage is enormous. Why? *Because you're using borrowed money as the collateral for more borrowing!*

Disadvantages for You

If you don't pick your properties carefully you may become over leveraged. That is, you may have borrowed more money than the income from the properties allows you to repay. To avoid over leveraging you must always have a PCF from every property after paying all loans you have on each property. And you must make strong efforts at all times to keep your properties fully rented so you have enough PCF to repay all your mortgages with a comfortable amount left over.

How You Can Use This Mortgage

Use a no-seasoning mortgage whenever you need fast cash for another profitable real estate investment.

Example of Mortgage Use

You want to buy an attractive upscale 60-pad mobile-home park with a steady, and predictable, income. You plan to use borrowed money for the down payment on this tree-shaded park with a bubbling brook running along its back edge. A melodious waterfall is at the end of the brook at the southern edge of your neatly manicured grass lawns surrounding the owner's pad and neat powder-blue double-wide mobile home.

You don't plan to live in the mobile-home park. Instead, you intend to hire a park manager and have him or her live in the owner's home as part of his or her pay.

You borrow $50,000 from your credit-card line of credit, taking over the profitable mobile-home park for just 5 percent down on the $1 million total price. While the interest rate on your loan is high, you have a large enough PCF to repay both the down-payment loan and your long-term mortgage of $950,000.

Within three weeks of buying your first mobile-home park a 40-pad park just at the southern outskirts of your new park becomes available. Joe, the very active 98-year-old owner of the 40-pad park passed away in his sleep. Your immediate thought on hearing the news about Joe, and the availability of his park, is: "I've got to have Joe's park. It will give me a total of 100 pads. That's a real mobile-home park empire!"

You call your Loan Officer at the lender who gave you the $950,000 conventional mortgage on your first park. "Do you do no-seasoning mortgages?" you ask your Loan Officer, after giving details of the second mobile-home park you want to buy.

"Sure," he replies. "Get me an appraisal of your present mobile-home park and I'll tell you how much we can lend you."

Your appraisal for your first mobile-home park comes in at $1.2 million, giving you $250,000 in equity. "We'll lend you 100 percent of your equity, or $250,000," your Loan Officer happily tells you.

Working the numbers, you quickly see you can easily afford the second mobile-home park and its down-payment loan and long-term mortgage loan. So, using a no-seasoning mortgage you quickly acquire two attractive and profitable mobile-home parks!

100 Percent First Mortgages

With a *100 percent first mortgage* you receive the full price you pay for a property in your first mortgage. Thus, if you buy an income property having a full price of $500,000, your first, and only, mortgage will be for $500,000.

This gives you 100 percent financing of your income property. Your only other expenses in obtaining your mortgage will usually be for your closing costs and legal fees. In some purchases the closing costs can be "rolled into" your 100 percent loan, giving you a true zero-cash purchase. With closing costs of about 5 percent of the amount of the mortgage (a typical percentage) your total mortgage will be $500,000 + 0.05 ($500,000) = $525,000.

"So where," you ask, "can I get a 100 percent first mortgage?" Such mortgages are usually available for newly constructed properties that the builder wants to sell quickly. So look for new properties. "And where will I find them?" you ask.

Most such properties are in coastal cities—such as along the Atlantic, Pacific, and Gulf coasts. You will seldom find such properties in inland cities in the United States.

Advantages for You

A 100 percent first mortgage gives you a true zero-cash investment. If you want to acquire income property with zero down payment, a 100 percent mortgage will give you what you want.

Disadvantages for You

It is difficult to get a PCF from a higher priced 100 percent-first-mortgage Single-Family Home investment property. Why? Because with a higher priced SFH property it is difficult to charge a large enough rent to pay your mortgage, real estate taxes, insurance, and maintenance. The one exception to this statement is in places like the Hamptons, in Long Island, New York, where four-month summer rentals can go as high as $250,000 for a prime property. Hence, you must always "work the numbers" *before* you buy any income property. Don't let the attraction of a 100 percent first mortgage sway your financial decisions!

How You Can Use This Mortgage

You can use a 100 percent first mortgage for situations in which you'll get a minimal PCF from a property that will appreciate quickly. Then you sell it for a quick capital gain—called *flipping.* Some people earn large profits of 25, 35, or 40 percent on 100 percent first mortgages after holding the property just six months, or less. On the above $500,000 property you "bought" your profit would be $125,000, $175,000, or $200,000. "Sounds impossible!" you say. Not so, good friend. Any number of my readers report such percentage profits—especially on Florida's east coast, in the condo area. It can be done!

103 Percent to 115 Percent Loan-to-Value Mortgages

With a *103 percent to 115 percent loan-to-value mortgage* you receive either 103 percent of the price of the property, or 115 percent of it. Thus, with a $300,000 property your mortgage amount would be $300,000 × 1.03 = $309,000, or $300,000 × 1.15 = $345,000. Such a mortgage will give you 100 plus percent financing.

Why would lenders make such loans? There is a simple answer. As we said before, lenders generally earn more money from loans than from any other investment they have. Presto, lenders want to make more loans to earn more money! And since real estate usually rises in value as time passes, the extra money they lend on a 103 percent to 115 percent mortgage is quickly covered by the increased property value.

Mortgages of this type are most often used for new properties. So be sure to look for your 103 percent to 115 percent mortgage when you're thinking of buying new income property. You'll get yourself the 100+ percent financing that many BWBs dream of!

125 Percent Purchase Mortgages

The *125 percent purchase mortgage* resembles the 103 percent to 115 percent loan-to-value mortgage except that it provides you with more cash over the purchase price. Again, the 125 percent purchase mortgage is generally used for new properties. So be sure to look for it when you're considering buying a new income property.

125 Percent Second Mortgages

The *125 percent second mortgage* gives you additional money when you borrow on the equity in an income property. Thus:

- **You own** a $500,000 residential building that has a strong PCF.
- **Your equity** in this building is $300,000—that is, your present mortgage on it is down to $200,000. (Your equity = $500,000 − $200,000 = $300,000.)
- **You want to borrow** against this income property to buy another income building.
- **You see an offer** for a 125 percent second mortgage. So you borrow against your equity using it as a second mortgage.
- **You come away with** $300,000 equity × 1.25 = $375,000 using a 125 percent second mortgage.
- **You don't pay any income tax** on the $375,000 because a loan, in general, is nontaxable.

The 125 percent second mortgage can be important in your acquiring $1 million in real estate in one year in your free time on borrowed money. So keep an eye open for such offers. There are more of them around than you might think!

Open-End Mortgages

With an *open-end mortgage* you can borrow more money from your lender than the amount you use to buy the property. There's usually a cap on the amount you can borrow. For example:

- **You're approved for** a $500,000 mortgage on a property.
- **You use** $400,000 of this to buy a property.
- **You have the difference,** or $500,000 − $400,000 = $100,000 as an open-end mortgage.
- **You can request** the mortgage lender to advance to you any amount up to $100,000 of this open-end mortgage.
- **You may find** the mortgage lender restricts the amount that will be advanced to you to 80 percent of the appraised value of the property you purchased using the mortgage.

An open-end mortgage can be helpful to you when you need additional cash to rehab a property or to buy an additional property. To get this feature in your mortgage ask your lender for it BEFORE you agree to terms of the mortgage.

Package Mortgages

A *package mortgage* includes "personal" items, along with the real estate itself. Thus, a package mortgage can include furnishings, drapes, refrigerators, stoves, air-conditioning units, and so on. By including such items in the overall mortgage, the buyer is relieved of having to pay for these separately, thereby saving money. And a package mortgage can get you closer to a zero-down purchase because the money for the personal items increases the amount you can borrow! Keep that in mind when you're trying to buy an income property for zero cash down.

Pledged Account Mortgages

With a *pledged account mortgage (PAM)* the buyer puts cash into a bank account pledged to the lender. The lender draws on this account every month, taking money from it. This money is used to reduce the monthly mortgage payment the buyer makes to the lender. The overall effect is to reduce the buyer's monthly P&I mortgage payment during the first few years of the life of the mortgage. You can use such a mortgage when you have excess cash you want to use to reduce your P&I payment on an income property you buy.

Purchase-Money Mortgages

A *purchase-money (PM) mortgage* is a loan given by a property seller to the buyer to replace either all, or part, of the down payment required on the property. For example:

Property purchase price = $600,000.

Long-term first mortgage = 90 percent, or $540,000 at 6 percent interest.

Down payment required = 10 percent, or $60,000.

Seller accepts a $60,000 mortgage from the buyer, with P&I payable monthly over five years at 10 percent interest.

Buyer takes over the property with no cash outlay, except for the closing costs. And these might be included in either the long-term mortgage or the PM mortgage.

Purchase-money mortgages are popular for properties that have been on the market for a long time without selling. The seller reaches a point where he or she "just wants out" and is willing to help the buyer meet the financial requirements of the sale.

Advantages for You

A purchase-money mortgage is a powerful way for you to get income property with zero cash down. So look for such mortgages when you're seeking to start in income real estate with little, or no, cash of your own.

Disadvantages for You

It may take "a lot of looking" to find a PM mortgage for the property you're trying to buy. But the time spent looking will be well rewarded because you get ownership of an income property with little, or no, cash!

How You Can Use This Mortgage

Use a PM mortgage to acquire income property without having to take loans on other property you own, and without having to take cash out of your bank.

Example of Mortgage Use

You, we'll say, love golf. You "eat, drink, sleep and dream golf" day and night. You, I'm sure, know this type of person. And one of your dreams is to own your own golf course. Looking at one of the many golf magazines you read, you spot a nine-hole golf course for sale. True, it's not the 18-

hole golf course you dream about. But, the ad says, "there is room for another nine holes on nearby land that's part of the sale."

You contact the seller and find that he "wants out in the worst way," as people say. Talking price, he tells you he wants $1.5 million for the course, its rustic clubhouse, and locker rooms. He thinks his mortgage lender will finance 90 percent of the price, or $1.35 million. This means you'll have to come up with $150,000. "Let's take a look at the course," you tell the seller.

The two of you get into a golf cart and tour the nine-hole course. "It's beautiful," you say to yourself. Well planned on rolling countryside, its greens are neatly trimmed with no brown spots. And the hilly terrain will challenge any golfer. Sand traps are well maintained with neat white sand in the bunkers.

"I'll take it," you tell the seller. "But I'll need help with the down payment."

"How much help," the seller asks.

"I'll need the full down payment," you respond.

"Let me think about it and I'll call you in a few days," the seller says.

A week later the seller calls and says "I'll take a five-year 12 percent interest purchase-money mortgage for the down payment if you'll pay my asking price."

"You've got a deal," you quickly respond because you've "done the numbers" and know you can easily pay both mortgages and still have a PCF from the golf course. Besides, you can either develop the nearby, attached land into nine more holes, or you can sell off the land for a nice profit.

Bringing your attorney in you "do the deal" and become the proud owner of your own golf course, using a PM mortgage. The only negative is that you'll have to spend time on the business aspects of your golf course, giving you less time to golf!

Reverse Mortgages

When a home owner no longer owes any money on his or her mortgage, the property is said to be "free and clear." And if the owner wishes to take money out of the property, either in a lump sum or fixed or variable monthly payments, the owner can do so using a *reverse mortgage.* Such mortgages are generally used by people 62 years of age, or older, who want to supplement other income from a pension, Social Security, an annuity, and so on.

Advantages for You

If a relative or partner is eligible for a reverse mortgage you can use it as a source of a lump-sum down payment for income real estate. Just be certain to protect your reverse-mortgage source by buying a property that will retain its value for a long time. This will ensure that your lender or partner will not lose his or her income from the reverse mortgage.

Disadvantages for You

Your deal must be "solid gold" so it protects your reverse-mortgage relative or partner. So it may take lots of wheeling and dealing on your part to work out a satisfactory, and safe, arrangement to guarantee that the reverse-mortgage supplier gets his or her money back over a suitable period of time.

How You Can Use This Mortgage

Work with a relative or partner to get a lump sum from a reverse mortgage to be used for the down payment on an income property.

Shared-Appreciation Mortgages

With a *shared-appreciation mortgage* you get a loan from a lender at less than the going interest rate. Thus,

- **Suppose that current interest rate** on income residential property is 8 percent.
- **You tell a lender** that you will share one-third of the appreciation with the lender at the end of 10 years of ownership.

- **The lender agrees** and lowers your interest rate on the mortgage to 6.5 percent (1.5 percent less).
- **Your lower interest rate** is based on the lender's calculation of the appreciation that will be received at the end of 10 years. (If you sell the property before 10 years have elapsed, the lender will receive one-third of the rise in value to the date of sale.)

Advantages for You

Your monthly payment on the income property is lower because your interest cost is less. Hence, your PCF from the property is higher.

Disadvantages for You

While your interest cost is lower, you lose out on some of the appreciation of the property. In a rapidly rising market your loss of appreciation might exceed your interest-cost savings.

How You Can Use This Mortgage

Use the shared-appreciation mortgage where you're trying to reduce your interest cost and increase your PCF. Try to keep the shared-appreciation number as low as possible so you don't lose out on the rise in the value of the property.

Second Mortgages

A *second mortgage* is a loan secured by real estate that already has a first mortgage on it. The usual second mortgage is based on the equity (ownership) the owner has in the property. Thus:

- **Property** market value = $400,000
- **Mortgage** on the property = $300,000

- **Ownership equity** in the property = $400,000 − $300,000 = $100,000
- **Conventional second mortgage** available = 75 percent of equity, or $0.75 \times \$100,000 = \$75,000$

Thus, the owner could obtain $75,000 cash from a conventional second mortgage on this property. This money, which is nontaxable when received, could be used as a down payment on another income property, for repairs to the existing property, and so on.

In the frenzied market to make more real estate loans backed by good property, lenders are extending second-mortgage loans of 100 percent and 125 percent of the owner's equity. Not everyone believes such loans make sense. But the loans ARE being made and real estate BWBs are using the proceeds to buy more income property. You should consider using second mortgages to build your real estate wealth, provided you carefully analyze the numbers of each deal. Your author will be happy to help you do this, as a subscriber of one of his newsletters.

Seller-Financed Reverse-Flip Mortgages

A *seller-financed reverse-flip mortgage* is a loan used to finance hard-to-sell real estate. The seller, typically, has had the property on the market for a year, or longer, and it has not sold. Finally, the seller is approached by a hardworking, sincere beginner who has lots of ambition but little cash and less credit. The prospective buyer proposes the following: Since the seller has good credit and can easily borrow the down payment.

- **The seller borrows** the 25 percent down payment needed to take over the property.
- **Then the buyer will assume responsibility** for the down payment loan and will make monthly payments on it.
- **A long-term mortgage is obtained** for the balance of the selling price, giving the seller the cash he or she wants, comprised of the down-payment loan and the long-term mortgage.
- **The attorneys handling the sale prepare a "reverse flip"** document that says that if the buyer fails to repay the down payment loan the

property will revert to the seller (reverse flip) and all payments made by the buyer will be credited to the seller.

The reverse flip accomplishes several objectives for both the buyer and seller, namely:

- **The sale is made**—which is what the seller wanted.
- **The buyer gets** the income property—which is what he or she wanted.
- **The seller is protected;** in the event the buyer does not repay the down-payment loan, the seller recovers the property.
- **The seller no longer has responsibility** for the day-to-day operation on the property; it is in the hands of someone who wants it.
- **The seller has his or her cash** and can go on to other planned business activities, or retirement and no business!

Based on these facts, you may want to consider the reverse flip for your next income property. It works well, even when one has cash for the down payment and good credit!

Shared-Equity Mortgages

With a *shared-equity mortgage* you, as borrower, and the lender, share the equity (ownership) of a property. When you obtain a shared-equity loan the lender pays a portion of the down payment on the property. If you have a 50/50 shared-equity mortgage, the lender will supply one-half the down payment on the property.

When the property is sold, any remaining mortgage is paid off. Then the remaining profit on the sale of the property is split equally with a 50/50 shared-equity mortgage. Note that any other split may be used, such as 34 percent and 66 percent, and so on. The main reason for using a shared-equity loan is to reduce the required down payment on an income property.

Start-Up Mortgages

A *start-up mortgage* is a loan secured by real estate in which the first year is comprised of interest-only payments. In the second year the payments increase and become 2 percent higher than in the first year. And each year thereafter your payments rise by 2 percent until you reach a level where the payments are the normal principal and interest (P&I) for the mortgage at the interest rate and term under which it was granted. A start-up mortgage can have a term from 15 to 30 years, depending on the lender. Payments may be made monthly or biweekly. Start-up mortgages often have more liberal requirements than conventional mortgages.

Third-Position Mortgages

A *third-position mortgage* is a loan secured by real estate that is on a property having two other mortgages on it—a first mortgage and a second (junior) mortgage. This type of mortgage is also called a *third mortgage.* Should the property go into default, the lender for the third mortgage would be repaid only after the lenders on the first and second mortgages were paid in full. Some large properties may have as many as nine mortgages on them! The same payment procedure would be followed for each mortgage after the third. You can benefit from a third, or subsequent, mortgage by using it as a source of cash for property purchase, or improvement. Junior mortgages, seconds, and thereafter, usually have a shorter term (the payoff period) than a first mortgage. Thus, most junior mortgages have a five-year payoff term. This compares with 15 to 40 years for first mortgages.

Venture-Capital Mortgages

There are some venture-capital firms that invest in real estate that is rapidly rising in value. However, most venture capitalists are more interested in high-technology companies having products that will sell in large numbers, or at high prices in small numbers. If real estate is associated with such a company the typical venture capitalist will accept it as part of the technology deal.

As a general guide, you will obtain mortgage funding in the form of a loan much faster than via venture capital. Hence, unless you have real estate associated with a technology deal, you're generally better off using a traditional mortgage loan.

Wraparound Mortgages

A *wraparound mortgage* is a loan secured by real estate that includes an existing first mortgage on the property. (Experienced real estate people shorten the wraparound loan name to a "wrap" loan.) The lender for the wraparound mortgage receives a monthly payment from the borrower which includes principal and interest for both the wrap loan and the existing first mortgage on the property. For example:

- **A 10-unit residential income property** is for sale for $800,000. You want to buy it.

- **A first mortgage of** $500,000 at 7 percent interest exists on the residential property you want to buy.

- **A mortgage lender is willing to lend you** $200,000 at 10 percent on the property using a wraparound loan, with the total loan amount being $700,000 ($200,000 plus the $500,000 existing first mortgage).

- **You will need** $100,000 as a down payment on this property. This amount would come from equity loans you place on other real estate you own.

- **When the deal goes through** and you own this 10-unit residential property, you make monthly P&I payments on the $700,000 loan. Your lender uses part of your payment to retire the $200,000 loan and the remainder to repay the existing $500,000 first mortgage.

Advantages for You

A wraparound loan offers several advantages to you as a BWB seeking to start his or her real estate investing career. These advantages include:

- **You can acquire** a higher priced property using a wrap loan because approved financing (the first mortgage) is already in place.

- **You do not have to apply for,** nor be credit approved for, the existing first mortgage on the property. This saves you time and energy.

- **You make only one payment** per month on the loan for the property you buy using a wrap loan.

- **You do not have to pay points** on the existing first mortgage loan. Further, since the loan is already in place, you do not need an appraisal for that portion of the property.

- **You will often be able to get** a wrap loan much faster than a conventional mortgage. Hence, you can build your one-year real estate holdings with wrap loans faster.

- **You may be able to get a larger property** with a higher income with the same down payment amount with a wrap loan than you could with a traditional mortgage.

- **You have—in some cases—a better chance** of getting a wrap loan for a property than a full conventional loan, especially when your credit score is a trifle low.

Disadvantages for You

A wraparound loan may be difficult to understand at first. But if you think about it and follow the example given, you'll soon understand, and welcome, wrap loans!

Zero-Percent Interest Mortgages

With a *zero-percent interest mortgage* (also called a *no-interest mortgage*) you do not pay any interest on the mortgage for a stated interval—6 months, 12 months, 24 months. The objective of such a mortgage is to lower your monthly payments when you first buy the property. The idea is that as time passes your income will rise and you'll be better able to make P&I payments on the mortgage.

And, of late, new features have been added to this type of mortgage. There is an option feature in some of these mortgages. With this feature you can:

- **Pay the interest** due any month you choose to do so.
- **Avoid paying interest** at all during your zero-interest term.
- **Pay part of the interest** due in any given month.

While the zero-interest mortgage is attractive, you must read all the terms of your agreement. Why? Because the zero-interest feature can become expensive if you avoid paying any interest for a long period.

Advantages for You

You reduce your monthly payments at the start of your mortgage. This can help you get started in your income real estate career. Further, any interest you eventually pay is provable and tax-deductible against the income from your property.

Disadvantages for You

You can wind up paying large interest charges if you delay paying interest. And your equity in the property will increase less rapidly than if you pay P&I monthly. If prices of property fall in your area you could be in a *negative-equity position.* That is, you might owe more on the property that it's worth. So, for safety purposes, treat no-interest or zero-percent interest loans with great care. Better yet, give me a call BEFORE you accept a no-interest or zero-percent interest mortgage!

How You Can Use This Mortgage

Use this mortgage when you want to take over an income property with the lowest possible monthly payments. But be certain to analyze the numbers of your property *before* you buy it! And carefully read your mortgage so you're completely familiar with all its terms. You don't want to be socked with a huge interest charge when you're ready to sell the property!

Getting the Money You Need

You now have useful information on 40-plus mortgages you can use to acquire income properties worth $1 million, or more, in one year on borrowed money, in your free time. Your challenge in each real estate purchase you make is to choose the most suitable mortgage. To pick the best mortgage for yourself:

1. **Start with a mortgage** that allows you to make the smallest down payment possible. This will usually be a 5 percent down payment with a 95 percent long-term mortgage.

2. **Decide how, and where,** you'll borrow the 5 percent down payment. Earlier chapters give you many suggestions on this.

3. **If you can't find a lender** from which you can borrow the down payment, focus on another type of mortgage.

4. **Look at very low, or no,** down-payment government mortgages. See if any of these will allow you to acquire the income property without using any of your own money.

5. **Check your state housing finance agency.** The loan you need might be available quickly and easily at a lower cost through such a group. See Chapter 8 for zero/low-down state loans.

6. **If you run out of sources for your mortgage,** call your author, Ty Hicks at the number listed at the end of the last chapter in this book. You can fax, postal, or e-mail me data on your deal and I'll be happy to try to find a suitable mortgage for you, if you're a subscriber to one of my newsletters described at the back of this book.

 ## Your Key Ideas for Finding Mortgage Money Today

❏ **There are hundreds of different types of mortgages** available to you today. Your challenge is finding the best mortgage for each purchase you make.

❏ **Starting with the traditional,** and long-proven, conventional mortgage, you can go to dozens of other types of mortgages.

❏ **Be careful with any mortgage** that does not include principal reduction in your monthly payment. Interest-only mortgages can lower your payments but do not build your equity in an income property.

❏ **Know what might happen to interest rates** before you accept an ARM. You don't want your payments to "go through the roof!"

❑ **Look for assumable mortgages.** Such loans can put you into a property faster than you might ever think. And your credit does not come into question with such mortgages.

❑ **Use home-equity loans to leverage yourself** from one property to several. Your equity grows with the passage of time. Don't let equity go to waste—use it to build your wealth!

❑ **Never overlook the power of the Gift Letter.** Such a letter can get you mortgages for a variety of income real estate deals.

❑ **Put the "reverse flip" to work for yourself**—it can overcome all sorts of obstacles while providing big benefits for both the seller, and you, the buyer.

❑ **Never be afraid to use a junior mortgage—second, third, and so on**—to provide the funds you need to build your real estate wealth. Such loans are common and can be the difference between success and failure. And we want YOU to succeed in acquiring $1 million in income real estate in one year on borrowed money in your free time!

CHAPTER 4

Internet Financing of Income Real Estate Can Save You Time

The Internet permeates everyone's life today—including Beginning Wealth Builders (BWBs). And it has found its way into real estate financing of income property. So you must know what the Internet can do for you today to help you build your holdings of $1 million in real estate in one year on borrowed money.

To help you understand better what the Internet offers you as a real estate entrepreneur, we'll cover:

- **The types of loans** available on the Internet.
- **Advantages of getting loans** on the Internet.
- **Disadvantages of getting loans** on the Internet.
- **How, and where,** to get mentoring help.
- **Tips on working successfully** with Internet, and other, lenders.
- **Internet lenders** (some 700+) you can apply to.

Types of Loans Available on the Internet

Almost every type of real estate loan you might seek is available on the Internet. You just have to know where to look for the type of loan you need. Common types of loans available on the Internet include:

86

- **Residential** Single-Family Home (SFH) loans.
- **Multifamily Home** (MFH) residential loans.
- **Commercial property loans**—office buildings, hotels, motels, and so on.
- **Private loans** of various types and amounts.
- **Government loans** (federal, state, city) for many types of property.
- **International loans** for properties around the world.
- **Mixed-use real estate loans** (buildings with residences and stores or other commercial occupants).
- **Construction loans** for a variety of property types.
- **Rehab loans** to repair, improve, modernize, and fix up real estate of all kinds.
- **Miscellaneous loans** for many different real estate activities—acquisition, development, disposal, and so on.

Advantages of Getting Loans on the Internet

You enjoy several advantages when you obtain income real estate loans on the Internet. These advantages include:

- **Speedy decisions.** In general, you'll get a faster YES, or NO, answer on the Internet than when you apply in person.
- **Less time required** for filling out the Loan Application. You can generally fill in blanks on a computer screen faster than typing a paper application.
- **No face-to-face meetings.** On the Internet you rarely talk to a human being. So if you're shy, the Internet saves you the discomfort of facing someone.

Thus, the Internet is an ideal place for computer-literate real estate BWBs to find loans. But if you're still new to computers, the Internet can be a real challenge, compared to paper Loan Applications.

Disadvantages of Internet Loan Applications

Like anything else in life, the Internet has both advantages and disadvantages. Typical disadvantages include:

- **Little human contact.** On most Internet loan sites your "talking" is to a computer screen via fill-in boxes and e-mail.
- **Little chance to explain** your project, and its key features, to an understanding, human Loan Officer.
- **Little control over** avoiding having your credit score checked. With a human Loan Officer, to whom you can speak, you can say: "What are my chances of having this Loan Application approved?" If the Loan Officer says, "Oh, about 50 percent," you can say: "Please don't run a Credit Report on me until you tell me how can I improve this Loan Application, and I do what you advise." The Loan Officer will then help you improve the application to the point where it has a 95+ percent chance for approval. Then you can say: "Okay, run the credit check."
- **Little human involvement** with a Loan Officer who can give you advice based on his or her experience with similar loans. Such mentoring can often help you succeed much sooner, with less stress, than if you're just feeling your way along, unguided.

Now don't get me wrong, good friend of mine. Internet loans can be great for you. But when you're first starting out you may need some friendly, understanding human advice. You may get this from a lender with whom you meet and discuss your real estate project. With an Internet loan you may not have much chance to talk to a Loan Officer.

Cautions to Observe for Internet Borrowing

The Internet can be an important source of financing of income real estate for you. But you must be cautious when using the Internet as a financing source. Keep these important precautions in mind when seeking financing on the Internet:

- **Never pay Front Money or Advance Fees for loans** obtained through Internet lenders. No Advance Fee will ever be requested of you by a reputable lender. So refuse to pay any up-front fees for a loan that may never materialize. See a later section in this chapter for more details on Front Money and Advance-Fee schemes.

- **Always have a competent real estate attorney available** to advise you on loan terms and interest rates. Without an attorney you are on dangerous ground when it comes to real estate loans. Your attorney will review your loan agreements, promissory notes, contracts, and other documents associated with your funding.

- **Use a comprehensive source of Internet lenders** for your search for a suitable loan for your income real estate. The 700+ list of Internet loan sources in this chapter is a good starting point for your search.

- **Start with local lenders.** Why? Because they know real estate values in your area. Further they "speak" your language, having a similar accent and a local way of expressing ideas. And, if you want, you can probably visit local lenders and present your project to them in a persuasive and winning way. By working with local lenders via the Internet you overcome one of the major disadvantages of Internet borrowing—namely the lack of human contact as a way of presenting your project.

- **Check out whom you're dealing with on the Internet.** Try to deal with direct lenders, instead of Loan Brokers. Why? Because when you deal directly with a lender you save time. Further, reputable lenders will never ask you for a front or Advance Fee. And every reputable lender will provide its full name, address, telephone, and fax numbers on its Internet site.

- **Avoid providing personal information on the Internet** until after you've decided to work with a specific lender. Thus, data such as your Social Security number, corporate Employer Identification Number (EIN), bank account number, bank tracking number, and so on, are not generally needed until after you're ready to go ahead with a loan.

How, and Where, to Get Mentoring Help

As part of the service my firm offers to our newsletter subscribers and kit buyers, we mentor real estate beginners helping them:

- **Overcome the fear** that besets many beginners.
- **Analyze the numbers** of the projects one at a time, looking for Positive Cash Flow (PCF).
- **Find the money** they need for the down payment on the income property they want to buy.
- **Search for partners** that might be needed for their down payment on their chosen property.
- **Get successfully through** the first year of property ownership.
- **Use Private Lenders** to get the funding they need for both the down payment and long-term mortgage.
- **Occasionally borrow money** from their Private Lender author for the down payment on their income property. See the back of this book for more data on this service.

Such services, so far as we know, are not offered by Internet lenders. And when you're first starting to build your million-dollar real estate fortune, mentoring can make the difference between success and failure. So my advice to you, good friend of mine, is:

- **Find a mentor** you feel comfortable and safe with for your first few income real estate deals.
- **Work with your mentor,** listening to the advice and guidance you're given.
- **Follow your mentor's advice** after analyzing the probable outcome you can expect.
- **Check the actual results** of your real estate income against your mentor's estimate of what it might be.
- **Stick with a mentor** who projects good results for you, and delivers them!

Tips on Working Successfully with Internet, and Other, Lenders

When dealing with Internet and other lenders keep these facts clearly in mind at all times:

- *NEVER PAY FRONT MONEY OR ADVANCE FEES FOR ANY LOAN!* "What's an Advance Fee or Front Money?" you ask. An Advance Fee or Front Money is a payment you're asked to make BEFORE you receive your loan. And the amount you're asked to pay could range anywhere from $1,000 to $50,000, or more, depending on the amount of your loan. The stated purpose for the money could be any of several different scams, such as:
  —**Travel fees** to view the property or business.
  —**Credit checks** to ensure that your credit is acceptable.
  —**"Appraisal" fees** paid to consultants.
  Legal fees to prepare the Loan Application, and so on.

None of these are necessary with a legitimate lender. So don't let yourself be talked into Front Money or Advance Fees of any kind. You'll just lose your money and spend loads of time trying to recover it —usually unsuccessfully.

- **Give the lender enough time to evaluate your Loan Application.** This means you should start your loan search early. Don't wait until the last minute. Telling the lender "Time is of the essence," as some borrowers do, only gets you laughs! Time is always of the essence, especially the lender's!
- **Be businesslike at all times.** Just because a lender makes its services available on the Internet doesn't mean that it will cut corners for quick approval. Your income real estate project must "fly"— that is, it must make financial sense. You must have a PCF from the property. If you don't, getting an Internet loan could be extremely difficult.
- **Recognize that some Internet lenders have geographic restrictions** on where they lend money. If you find a lender that does not

lend in your area, simply move on to the next listed lender. There is not enough space in this book to list the geographic restrictions of each lender. Note that if a lender states that it lends nationally, this means that loans are made in all 50 states of the United States. International lending means the lender makes loans in most, or all, of the developed nations in the world.

Internet Lenders You Can Apply To

Since, as I've said before, all my readers are my good friends, I want *you*, as one of my good friends, to have as many real estate lenders as possible. So this chapter includes 700+ sources of Internet loans. These sources include:

- **Personal** and general loans.
- **Sub-Prime** loans.
- **Construction** loans.
- **No-Income verification** loans.
- **SBIC** (Small Business Investment Company)/private loans.
- **Commercial** real estate loans.
- **Hard-Money** loans.
- **Canadian** loans.
- **United Kingdom** loans.

Please recognize that some of the listed loan sources may be Loan Brokers while others may be direct lenders. You can quickly determine the type of organization you're dealing with as soon as you visit their web site. So far as we know, this is the largest published list of Internet real estate loan sources ever published in one book. This list will be valuable to you when you're on your third or fourth income real estate deal. For your first few deals, follow the mentoring plan shown earlier.

Internet Loan Sources

Personal/General Loans

quickenloans.quicken.com

www.1-personal-loans-online
.co.uk

www.auto-loan.com

www.banklady.com

www.bankofamerica.com

www.businesstart.org

www.cbaclenders.com

www.chase.com

www.citifinancial.com

www.eloan.com

www.entrepreneurfund.org

www.financial-services-online-fx
.com

www.icreditcentral.com

www.lbdc.com

www.lendingtree.com

www.loan-fast-cash-today-personal-
online-loan.com

www.loancrew.com

www.loansamerica.com

www.loansonline-now.com

www.loanweb.com

www.one-stop-online-loans.com

www.online-loans-center.com

www.online-personal-loans-office
.com

www.onlineloans.co.uk

www.peoplefirst.com

www.personal-loans.org

www.tbacloan.com

www.valoans.com

www.washingtoncash.org

Residential and Commercial Mortgage Loans

www.1cb.com

www.1stmortgage.com

www.1stnb.com/mortgage/fcm.htm

www.aami.net

www.accesslending.com

www.acs-inc.com

www.advisorsmortg.com

www.aegismtg.com

www.agtexas.com

www.ahomeloan.com

www.aimamerican.com

www.alaskapacificbank.com

www.alaskausatrust.com

www.alphamortgageusa.com

www.alservices.com

www.americahomekey.com

www.americanunsecured.com

www.ameriquestmortgage.com

www.amnetmortgage.com

www.amortgagecorp.com

www.anb.com

www.ApprovedHMC.Com

www.asbonline.com

www.austinmba.org

www.bank.guarantygroup.com

www.bankers.fprsi.com

www.bankersassistance.com

www.bankfranklin.com

www.bankheritage.com

www.bankofamerica.com

www.bankrcrb.com

www.banksourcemtg.com

www.barclayassociates.com

www.bbwcdf.com

www.beaconrealtycapital.com

www.bearstearns.com

www.benchmarkfin.com

www.berkshiremortgage.com

www.bmandg.com

www.bnmortgage.com

www.bokf.com

www.botw-ep.com

www.capitalmort.com

www.cbainfo.com

www.cfabalaska.com

www.ch-cpa.com

www.ch-mortgage.com

www.chase.com

www.choicelender.com

www.citicorp.com

www.citifinancial.com

www.cnmcs.com

www.coastalbanc.com

www.collateral.com

www.comfedbank.com

www.commercialfinancingusa.com

www.communityhomeloan.com

www.compassweb.com

www.continentalamerican.com

www.ContinentalTrust.com

www.continuityprograms.com

www.corsicanabank.com

www.countrywide.com

www.crockett-nb.com

www.croscom.com

www.ctxmort.com

www.cvcb.com

www.cypressmtginc.com

www.dallasmortgagebankers.com

www.dcccd.edu

www.directorsmortgage.com

www.e-mortgagedirect.com

www.emortgage.com

www.equibanc.com

www.equityexpress.com

www.esbmortgage.com

www.ewmortgage.com

www.executivemortgagegroup.com

www.extracomortgage.com

www.fabtexas.com

www.fanniemae.com

www.farristurner.com

www.fbandt.com

www.fbsmortgage.com

www.fcmchou.com

www.feiwellhannoy.com

www.ffbctx.com

www.FFunding.com

www.fgbjax.com

www.fhhlc.com

www.fhmtg.com

www.fieldstonemortgage.com

www.financialshop.com

www.first-franklin.com

www.first-mortgagefunding.com

www.firstam.com

www.firstamericanbankfab.com

www.firstcollateral.com

www.firstcommandbank.com

www.firstfedsf.com

www.firstfundingusa.com

www.firsthomemtg.com

www.firstmagnus.com

www.firstpennbank.com

www.firstpreference.com

www.fiserv.com

www.fla-mortgage.com

www.floridabankmortgage.com

www.floridamortgagecorp.com

www.fnbalaska.com

www.fnbchestercounty.com

www.fnbgranbury.com

www.fncinc.com

www.fnf.com

www.fnis.com

www.fortworthmba.org

www.franklinamerican.com

www.frostbank.com

www.fsb.com

www.gemortgageinsurance.com

www.gkbaum.com

www.glasermortgage.com

www.glo.state.tx.us/vlb

www.gmac.com

www.gmacrfc.com

www.greenmort.com

www.greenparkmortgage.com

www.gregg-valby.com

www.guarantygroup.com

www.guardianmortgageco.com

www.hankamer.com

www.HeritageMTG.com

www.hibernia.com

www.hiberniabank.com

www.hmgtexas.com

www.homecomings.com

www.homefundingfinders.com

www.homeloancorp.com

www.homeside.com

www.hometrust.com

www.householdfinance.com

www.houseloan.com

www.houston-mba.com

www.houstonsavings.com

www.hud.gov

www.hwallp.com

www.iboc.com

www.imaginesolutions.com

www.info1online.com

www.insurance.guarantygroup.com

www.irwinmortgage.com

www.iseva.com

www.jeffersonmortgage.net

www.jlmdirect.com

www.josmg.com

www.journeyhomeloans.com

www.jw.com

www.kdhco.com

www.kennedycpas.com

www.key.com

www.keymortgagelink.com

www.kpmg.com

www.krymick.com

www.legacytexas.com

www.litton.c-bass.com

www.ljmelody.com

www.loansyourway.com

www.lockeliddell.com

www.lonestarbank.com

www.lonestartitle.com

www.lottstatebank.com

www.lowestloan.com

www.malonemtg.com

www.martellmortgage.com

www.maverickmortgage.com

www.mcafeemort.com

www.mcc-cpa.com

www.mccalla.com

www.mdgibson.com

www.mgic.com

www.midcitiesmortgage.com

www.midrid.com

www.milestonemortgage.com

www.missionmortgage.com

www.mitchellmortgage.com

www.mortgage-advantage.com

www.mortgage-makers.com

www.mortgage.wellsfargo.com

www.mortgageresourcenet.com

www.mountainwest-bank.com

www.mpmortgageonline.com

www.mtmckinleybank.com

www.mvfcu.org

www.mwfinc.com

www.myprovident.com

www.nascopgh.com

www.national-city.com

www.nationalclosingsolutions.com

www.natlbank.com

www.nbclending.com

www.networkmtgserv.com

www.next-home.com

www.nfri.com

www.northmarq.com

www.northrim.com

www.omniamerican.org

www.onholdexchange.com

www.onlinedocuments.com

www.onstaff.com

www.optiononemortgage.com

www.pacfirst.com

www.PatriotBank.com

www.peirsonpatterson.com

www.plusonemtg.com

www.pmigroup.com

www.popularmortgage.com

www.primelending.com

www.pulaskimortgage.com

www.radianmi.com

www.randadocsaol.com

www.realtymortgage.com

www.recenter.tamu.edu

www.reliabank.com

www.republicstatemortgage.com

www.republictitle.com

www.residentiallending.com

www.rmcv.com

www.rmic.com

www.rmmc.com

www.rockportmortgage.com

www.sacu.com

www.samortgagebankers.com

www.sandwgroup.com

www.saxononline.com

www.sebringcapital.com

www.sierrafunding.com

www.sierraviewfinancial.com

www.smimortgage.com

www.smiservices.com

www.southside.com

www.southstarfunding.com

www.southtrustmortgage.com

www.southwestfunding.com

www.southwestguaranty.com

www.ssfcu.org

www.stanmor.com

www.statebanktx.com

www.sterlingcapital.com

www.stonehillgroup.com

www.summitmtg.com

www.swbc.com

www.synergymortgage.net

www.tdsf.com

www.texanscu.org

www.texasbank.com

www.texascapitalbank.com

www.texaslandtitle.com

www.texasmortgagespecialist.com

www.texasreversemortgage.com

www.tgic.com

www.the.loangoddess.com

www.ticatitle.com

www.tmslp.com

www.traviswolff.com

www.truenorthfcu.org

www.txcommunity.com

www.txstbk.com

www.ufcu.org

www.ugcorp.com

www.uhmconline.com

www.unitedbancmtg.com

www.us.kpmg.com

www.usam.net

www.venture-encoding.com

www.waterfieldgroup.com

www.wcmlending.com

www.wellsfargo.com

www.wrstarkey.com

Sub-Prime Loans

www.accredhome.com

www.aegismtg.com

www.agencymortgage.com

www.ameriquestmortgage.com

www.amerisave.com

www.citifinancial.com

www.d1online.com

www.myafsloan.com

www.ncen.com

www.wamu.com

www.wellsfargo.com

www.householdfinance.com

Construction Loans

www.203k.net

www.alliancefinancialcorp.com

www.amcore.com

www.americancm.com

www.americanmortgageco.com

www.amerisphere.net

www.amicapital.com

www.apfmultifamily.com

www.archonfinancial.com

www.arcscommercial.com

www.bankgranada.com

www.bankofhemet.com

www.boh.com

www.bondstreetcapital.com

www.builderonline.com

www.businesscash.com

www.c-loans.com/onlineapp

www.calcenterbank.com

www.calnetbank.com

www.cambridgecap.com

www.canada.ml.com

www.caplease.com

www.capricap.com

www.cfcurry.com

www.churchconstruction.com

www.cit.com

www.citizensbank.ca

www.clms.ca

www.cmcapitalcorp.com

www.co-operativetrust.ca

www.coastcapitalsavings.com

www.cobshomes.com

www.collateral.com

www.commercialending.com

www.constructionloans.com

www.cplloans.com

www.cwbank.com

www.davispenn.com

www.dcxcapital.com

www.ebsb.com

www.encinostatebank.net

www.ezprivatemoney.com

www.fgmf.com

www.flaloans.net

www.fremontnational.com

www.fundyourdeal.com

www.gab.com

www.galaresources.com

www.gcpcap.com

www.gecapitalrealestate.com

www.generalbank.com

www.genoasavings.com

www.glacierbank.com

www.glaser.com

www.gmaccm.com

www.greatnation.com

www.hardtoplaceloans.com

www.harlowcapital.com

www.hometrust.ca

www.hsbc.ca

www.ibank.com

www.intesabci.ca

www.jacksonclyburn.com

www.key.com

www.lincap.com

www.loansbyredrose.com

www.lospadresbank.com

www.mandtbank.com

www.mcap.com

www.metrosavings.com

www.ml.com
www.montrosemortgage.com
www.myconstructionloan.com
www.onecapitaladvisors.com
www.palender.com
www.pbtok.com
www.peoples.com
www.peoplestrust.com
www.pncrealestatefinance.com
www.pwbank.com
www.pwfunding.com
www.redcapitalgroup.com
www.rehabhome.com
www.riversidebanc.com

www.rivesleavell.com
www.sccb.com
www.scotiabank.com
www.scotmor.ca
www.stearns-bank.com
www.tdcanadatrust.com/fnbank
www.tomatobank.com
www.unionhomeloan.com
www.valleybankhelena.com
www.vitekinc.com
www.wachovia.com
www.wachoviasec.com
www.wamu.com
www.zieglerloan.com

Private-Money and Hard-Money Loans

www.1hardmoney.com
www.alcobc.com
www.allcityservices.com
www.altfunding.com
www.atlantahardmoneyloans.com
www.bayviewfinancial.com
www.BlueCrownFunding.com
www.coastallajollafunding.com
www.commercialending.com
www.cplloans.com
www.creativefinancialcorp.com
www.floridahardmoneylender.com
www.FundingEdge.com

www.galaresources.com
www.gecapitalrealestate.com
www.gracecapitalgroup.com
www.HamiltonCommercialLoans
  .com
www.hardmoney-loans.com
www.hardmoney.com
www.hardmoneycorp.com
www.hardmoneyfunding.com
www.harlowcapital.com
www.heartlandcapitalgroup.com
www.investwell.com
www.ironwoodcap.com

www.kennedyfunding.com

www.lafayettefinancial.com

www.libertyfinancialco.com

www.lljcapital.com

www.loan-solution.com

www.LoansByTrista.com

www.metmtge.com/contact.htm

www.metrofundingcorp.com

www.minneapolishardmoney.com

www.mlamortgage.com

www.mortgageholdings.com

www.myprivatelender.com

www.PaceLending.com

www.pacificmortgage.com

www.pioneerwest.com

www.portfoliolending.com

www.prestige.1st-web site.com

www.privateinvestorloans.com

www.privateloanfunding.com

www.quantumfunding.com

www.readymort.com

www.refinancecash.com

www.rehabfunding.com

www.rehabmoney.com

www.spectrum-mortgage.com

www.statewidellc.com

www.sunvestinc.com

www.thefundingsolutions.com

www.thenorrisgroup.com

www.tinvex.com

Venture Capital, Small Business Investment Companies, and Private Financing

www.1hardmoney.com

www.allcityservices.com

www.altfunding.com

www.anjgroup.com

www.atlantahardmoneyloans.com

www.bayviewfinancial.com

www.BlueCrownFunding.com

www.captec.com

www.coastallajollafunding.com

www.commercialending.com

www.creativefinancialcorp.com

www.eastoncapital.com

www.ecenturycapital.com

www.edfvc.com

www.edisonventure.com

www.eg-group.com

www.emigrantcapital.com

www.equinoxcapitalinc.com

www.esevc.com

www.exeterfunds.com

www.facilitatorfunds.com

www.fequity.com

www.firstnewenglandcapital.com

www.floridahardmoneylender.com

www.frontierfunds.com

www.FundingEdge.com

www.galaresources.com

www.gemini-investors.com

www.gmacapital.com

www.gmbltd.com

www.gracecapitalgroup.com

www.grosvenorfund.com

www.HamiltonCommercialLoans
   .com

www.hamiltonventures.com

www.harbert.net

www.heartlandcapitalgroup.com

www.housatonicpartners.com

www.hudsonventures.com

www.independentbankerscap.com

www.investam.com

www.investwell.com

www.ironwoodcap.com

www.Irwinventures.com

www.jeffcap.com

www.jpmorgan.com

www.kinderhookcapital.com

www.lafayettefinancial.com

www.lasallecapitalgroup.com

www.lcapital.com

www.libertyfinancialco.com

www.libertyview.com

www.lljcapital.com

www.longworth.com

www.madisonpartners.com

www.magnetcapital.com

www.mainstreet-resources.com

www.mainstreethouston.com

www.marquette.com

www.medallionfinancial.com

www.metmtge.com/contact.htm

www.metrofundingcorp.com

www.mezzcap.com

www.midmarkcapital.com

www.minneapolishardmoney
   .com

www.mlamortgage.com

www.montreuxequity.com

www.morgankeegan.com

www.mortgageholdings.com

www.mtncap.com

www.mvpartners.com

www.mwvcapital.com

www.myprivatelender.com

www.navigatorequity.com

www.nccapital.com

www.newspringventures.com

www.njtcvc.com

www.norven.com

www.ocpcapital.com

www.PaceLending.com

www.pacesettercapital.com

www.pacificmortgage.com

www.patriot-capital.com

www.petracapital.com

www.pinecreekcap.com

www.praesidiancapital.com

www.prairie-capital.com

www.prestige.1st-web site.com

www.prismfund.com

www.privateinvestorloans.com

www.privateloanfunding.com

www.prosperoventures.com

www.radiusventures.com

www.randcapital.com

www.readymort.com

www.rcdriverventures.com

www.refinancecash.com

www.rivervest.com

www.rockycapital.com

www.rusticcanyon.com

www.salemcapital.com

www.saugatuckcapital.com

www.scvp.com

www.seacoastcapital.com

www.selbyventures.com

www.selectcapitalcorp.com

www.shepherdventures.com

www.sightlinepartners.com

www.smartforest.com

www.smithwiley.com

www.springcap.com

www.stcloudcapital.com

www.stonehengecapital.com

www.summerstreetcapital.com

www.swbank-stl.com

www.tamarackcapital.com

www.telesoftvc.com

www.thenorrisgroup.com

www.thewalnutgroup.com

www.tinvex.com

www.tonkabayequity.com

www.tridentgrowth.com

www.Trilogycap.com

www.uven.com

www.vacapital.com

www.velocityep.com

www.wasatchvc.com

www.watersidecapital.com

www.westburypartners.com

www.whitepines.com

www.wmfg.com

www.zonpartners.com

www.northatlanticcapital.com

Commercial Loans

www.accessbusinessfinance.com

www.allbank.com

www.amsouth.com

www.baccorp.com

www.bfec.com

www.bofa.com/businesscapital

www.capitalsource.com

www.citizensbank.com

www.clearblueventures.com

www.commercefunding.com

www.crestmark.com

www.equifin.net

www.exim.gov

www.fbcapital.com

www.gecfo.com

www.gmacccf.com

www.hilcocapital.com

www.ibm.com/financing

www.mbfinancial.com

www.profininc.com

www.puritanfinance.com

www.quantumfunding.com

www.sterlingbancorp.com

www.tabbank.com

www.wffoothill.com

www.wittern.com

No-Income Verification Loans

apex.instantlender.com

www.agfmortgage.com

www.alpinemtggroup.com

www.americanfinancialcredit.com

www.ameristarmadison.com

www.atlantamortgagegroup.com

www.bankatcommerce.com

www.bluewatermtg.com

www.camelotmortgage
   corp3174625400
   .worldpages-ads.com

www.canadasbestmortgage.com

www.cnbanytime.com

www.coastalfinancialco.com

www.coloradomortgage.com

www.commitmentmortgage.com

www.countrywide.com

www.creativemortgagefunding.com

www.CrossroadsUSA.com

www.directorsmortgage.net

www.ewmortgage.com

www.fairviewcommerciallending
   .com

www.fairwaydfw.com

www.firsteastern.com

www.firstmerit.com

www.floridamortgage.net

www.fountaincityfinance.com

www.hamilton-mortgage.com

www.hamptonroads.com/clients
/hometown-mortgage

www.homesavings.com

www.houstonmortgage.com

www.loansmortgage.com

www.manhattanmortgage.com

www.marketplacehome.com

www.marylandlowrates.com

www.meritfinancial.net

www.metrofunding.com

www.midamericabank.com

www.myamerifi.com

www.pemconline.com

www.pfsimortgage.com

www.reliancemortgage.com

www.seloan.com

www.southernfidelity.com

www.suntrustmortgage.com

www.tricornet.com

www.veteransadvantage.com

International Internet Loan Sources

France

www.socgen.com

www.societegenerale.fr

Germany

www.bayernlb.de

www.commerzbank.com

www.db.com

www.dbrealestate.com

www.dghyp.de

www.lbs-bw.de

India

www.globaltrustbank.com

www.indian-bank.com

www.bank-of-china.com

Japan

btmna.com

www.btm.co.jp/english/index
.htm

www.smbc.co.jp

Switzerland

www.credit-suisse.com

www.csfb.com

www.ubs.com

Canada

www.21stcenturyent.com

www.cwbank.com

www.firstline.com

www.alterna.ca

www.hsbc.ca

www.royalbank.com

United Kingdom

www.onlineloans.co.uk

www.personal-loans.org

www.barclays.co.uk

www.bankofscotland.co.uk

www.natwest.com

Be a Proactive Internet Loan Seeker

You now have the tools you need to find income real estate loans on the Internet. Here are the proactive steps for you to take to get the real estate loan you seek:

1. **Contact selected lenders on the previous list.** Ask for data on their loans—amount, term, interest rate, geographic area, and so on. Use your own computer or one at your local public library, high school, Boy/Girl Scout troop, and so on. Download the Loan Applications you think might be suitable for your investment goals. Fill out the Loan Application and submit it to the lenders you've chosen. Wait for an answer. We hope it's YES!

2. **Use the IWS computer service** in which we'll download 12 Internet Loan Applications of your choice and send them to you via postal mail, fax, or e-mail—whichever you choose. You fill out the Loan Application and return it to us. We'll type the application for you and submit it to your chosen lender(s). The lender's answer will be faxed, e-mailed, or postal mailed to you. See the back of this book for more information on this computer service.

3. **Use the IWS Internet web site** www.iws-inc.com on your computer to click on selected lender sites. Submit your application and wait for an answer. With both these services I'll be happy to advise you on any questions you may have. See the back of this book for data on this service.

Remember, as your good friend, I'm here to help you acquire $1 million in real estate in one year on borrowed money. So if you want to go the Internet route to your funding, follow the ideas in this chapter. And—as one of my newsletter subscribers—you can always call me for personal, step-by-step mentoring help. I'm at the phone day and night to answer your questions and give any guidance you need.

Ten Steps to Start Using Internet Money Wisely

Using your Internet money wisely can put you into the big time faster than you might imagine. To use your Internet money wisely, take these proven steps when you're starting your million-dollar real estate career.

1. **Real estate is a borrowed-money business**—from start to finish. Try to put the minimum amount of your own cash into any income real estate property you plan to buy.

2. **Remember—at all times—that your income real estate is a *business.*** Every property you buy—except your personal home—is purchased for the income it can deliver to you. You buy income property for only one reason, namely the money you will earn from it in terms of rental income and any eventual appreciation.

3. **Never look at a residential income property** with the thought that you will personally live in it. You're buying the property because your analysis of the numbers shows that the real estate will give you a PCF. You're buying an income-producing asset—not "a pretty building on a hill."

4. **Real estate and time are interlocked.** The time can be long, or short. When the time is long you look for both monthly rental PCF and annual appreciation to deliver the profit you seek. Short-time real estate profits depend on quick turnover, called *flipping.* Your profit comes from the price difference between what you paid for the property and what you can sell it for.

5. **Your first step after buying income real estate** is to raise the rents to increase your PCF from your purchase. Raising the rents also increases the value of your property. Why? Because the higher

the income of a property, the larger the amount investors are willing to pay for it!

6. **Know, before you buy, the precise profit** you will earn from every income property you invest in. Analyze the Income and Expense Statement of every income property BEFORE you buy it. If the statement puzzles you, fax, e-mail, or postal mail it to me and I'll do a quick, and thorough, analysis of it free of charge if you're a subscriber to one of my newsletters.

7. **Get into the habit of saving your profits from each property.** Build a cash reserve you can use to buy other income properties. You need not spend your savings for a down payment. Instead, use your savings as collateral for a down-payment loan. Then you'll be getting into your next income property on zero cash—the Ty Hicks way!

8. **Be the ideal landlord.** How? Be available to your tenants 24 hours a day, seven days a week, called 24/7 for short. Accept credit-card rent payments—its faster and safer for you. Give the tenants a toll-free number to call you for help, or repairs. Offer to supply materials (paint, spackle, wallboard, etc.) so tenants can improve their spaces so they are more comfortable. They'll love you for the attention and consideration you give them. Result? You'll have many fewer, or no, vacancies in your income properties.

9. **Prepare a Business Plan for your real estate future.** True, a Business Plan may be a chore to prepare. But it WILL give you a view of your real estate business, and yourself, that you've never had before. And, as a subscriber to one of my newsletters, I'll be happy to review your finished Business Plan completely free of charge. Any improvements that might be made to your Plan will be suggested to you in a friendly and helpful way. You are, after all, my good friend!

10. **Dedicate yourself to acquiring $1 million in real estate in one year.** Use every one of the 365 days in the year to advance toward your goal. Don't take holidays off. Instead, work toward reaching your goal. You'll have plenty of free time AFTER you reach your

goal. Chapter 12 in this book gives step-by-step directions for filling each of those 365 days with positive advances toward your goal. And—of course—you always have your good friend—Ty Hicks—to advise and encourage you along the way!

Your Key Ideas for Getting Internet Financing

❏ **There are hundreds of Internet sources of financing** for your real estate investments. You can use some of these, if you have access to a computer or a computer service.

❏ **Many different types of loans are available** from Internet lenders. You, of course, must know the type of loan you need for your investment.

❏ **Internet loans have several advantages**—decision speed, no need for a face-to-face interview, quick filling out of your Loan Application. All these features save you time when applying for your real estate loan.

❏ **Disadvantages of Internet loans** include little human contact, less chance to explain your project to a Loan Officer, little or no control over whether your credit is checked.

❏ **Be certain to observe the cautions** listed in this chapter when seeking an Internet or any other loan. Being cautious can save you time and money.

❏ **Use a mentor for your first few real estate deals.** Why? Because using a mentor can prevent you from making big mistakes, can save you time, and put you in the winner's circle faster than you think.

❏ **Be proactive in seeking loans** from Internet lenders. Follow the suggestions in this chapter and your chances of getting the loans you seek are much better.

CHAPTER 5

Private Lenders Can Be Your Real Estate Money Supply

<small>An often-overlooked source for real estate financing of all types</small> is Private Lenders. A Private Lender is:

- **A nonbank source of loans** and money assistance for real estate purchase, construction, development, or rehab.
- **A nonbank money source** that is free of the usual federal and state regulations conventional lenders must follow.
- **A nonbank lender** that may operate without a Loan Committee or other groups making loan decisions.
- **A nonbank money source** that will read, and listen to, your real estate project presentation and make a decision based on your profit projections and the potential of your project.
- **A nonbank lender** that may also be in the real estate business and can be sympathetic to your plans and goals.

You can use Private Lenders to your advantage in building your million-dollar real estate empire in one year, or less. Here's how.

Why Private Lenders Can Be Good for Your Wealth Building

Private Lenders can be good for you and your wealth building for several reasons. Thus, when you deal with Private Lenders, most of whom are experienced real estate or business people, you'll find that they:

- **Usually seek less documentation** for your loan than other lenders because they rely on a written Project Description from you.

- **Seldom do a credit check** on you personally, relying instead on their personal "gut" appraisal of you as a real estate person.

- **Can deliver your money sooner**—often in just a few hours, if necessary—for your income real estate project.

- **Are easier to talk to** and deal with than most other lenders (banks, mortgage companies, insurance funds, etc.) because they admire the Beginning Real Estate Wealth Builder, and want to help you. Further, some Private Lenders are in their own business and they understand the mentality of the wealth builder.

- **Can be a regular, repeatable, source of money** for you—the Beginning Wealth Builder (BWB) or Experienced Wealth Builder (EWB)—if you repay your real estate loan regularly, and on time.

- **Will work with you** if you have a sudden and unexpected expense with your property that causes you to be late with your monthly payment on your mortgage.

- **May be willing to make a down payment loan** and a long-term mortgage to you, allowing you to get ownership of an income-producing property on zero cash from your pocket.

You can use Private Lenders for both single-family and multifamily residential properties. Likewise, if commercial, industrial, or retail properties are your way to real estate wealth, there are Private Lenders that will work with you to finance them.

With all the plusses that private lending offers, is there any downside? Yes, there is. Since private lending is essentially unregulated, you must be careful in choosing the lenders you deal with.

Why? Because some lenders may ask you for large—$1,000 to $100,000—up-front fees before you get your loan. Also known as *Front Money* or *Advance Fees,* such payments are completely unnecessary. Further, in some areas of the country, they are forbidden. Hence, as a general guide for your success in borrowing money from any type of lender for income real estate:

> *Never pay "Front Money" or Advance Fees for any loan! Such fees are NOT a necessary part of obtaining any mortgage loan. So if a lender asks for an Advance Fee for a loan before you obtain your funding, refuse to pay it!*

As you know, you can call me, day or night, as a subscriber to one of my newsletters and I'll be happy to answer any real estate business questions you may have. Since readers ask dozens of questions each week about Private Lenders, the next several subheadings in this chapter are in question form. And the questions in each subhead are those readers ask most frequently. So this chapter should answer your major questions about Private Lenders. If it doesn't, give me a call. Here's your first Private Lender question:

What Kind of Loans Can I Get from a Private Lender?

Private Lenders make almost every type of real estate loan needed by BWBs seeking to build riches in income property of many different types. Thus, some of the Private Lenders your author works with make these types of funds available to BWBs:

- **First mortgages** for income properties of almost all types.
- **Second mortgages** for income properties of two units, or more— residential, commercial, retail, and so on.
- **Down payment loans** for properties whose income can pay off both the first mortgage and the down payment loan.
- **Bridge loans** to help you buy another property using your present property as collateral for the loan. If you do not want to use your present property as collateral, you may be able to use actively traded

stocks or bonds, a vehicle (auto, truck, airplane), and so on, as collateral for your bridge loan. Some bridge loans do not require repayment until after you purchase the desired property.

- **Construction loans** for new, and existing, properties of almost all types you might want to build, develop, or rehab.
- **Equity loans** where you use the portion of what you own of a property as collateral for a loan. Also called a *Home Equity Loan* (HEL) or property equity loan.
- **Investor loans** for real estate wealth builders who might not be able to get a loan from traditional lenders (such as banks) who think investor loans are too risky for them.
- **Foreclosure-purchase loans** that help you to buy foreclosed, or pre-foreclosed, properties at less than the market price, that you later hold for rental income or flip (resell) for a quick profit.
- **Mortgage note purchase loans** that you use to buy purchase-money notes a seller receives in place of cash from a buyer.
- **Other types of real estate loans** for almost any need you might have. Thus, you can get loans for raw land, rehab loans to repair income property needing such work, conversion loans to change a building from a hotel or school to residential condos, developer loans to convert raw land into housing or industrial projects, and so on.

What Should I Do to Get Private Lender Loans?

Here are eight easy steps for you to take to get loans from Private Lenders. Be certain you understand, and take, each step to get the real estate money you need:

1. **Figure how much money** you need for your real estate purchase, or rehab. You MUST know the AMOUNT of money you'll need and the PURPOSE of your money request—that is the real estate activities you'll use the money for.
2. **Prepare a short Executive Summary** telling Private-Money Lenders and investors: **(a) What** type of real estate you'll invest in;

(b) **Why** your real estate will perform better than competing properties; (c) **Which** marketing methods you intend to use to rent, or flip, the property you obtain with the money you're seeking; (d) **When** your real estate project will break even and start earning money, if you're starting from a condition of zero income, such as when you build a new housing complex. Be sure to give your Private Lenders full information on your project. Never try to hide important data from them. You'll be refused a loan faster than you can imagine! Later in this chapter you'll find an example of a typical Loan Submission Letter.

3. **Get information on Private Lenders** you might work with. Your book gives you several later in this chapter. And IWS, Inc., my BWB help company, has hundreds. See the back of this book for the *Private Loan Money and Funding Kit.* Or you can go on the Internet to (www.iws-inc.com) and see what's in this kit. If you do not have access to the Internet, try a computer in your local Public Library.

4. **Contact Private Lenders** making the type of real estate loan you seek. Do this by writing a letter, or sending an e-mail, telling the lender about your project. Include your Executive Summary you prepared in Step 2, previously. Send out as many letters and e-mails as you have time for. Wait until you hear from one, or more, lenders. Good data gets loans!

5. **Read each loan offer carefully.** Why? Because you want the best deal possible. Never settle for 2nd class when you can go 1st class! And remember, ***NEVER PAY FRONT MONEY FOR ANY LOAN.***

6. **Pick the best offer you get.** Have an attorney review any agreements you must sign. No Private Lender is out to harm you. But you MUST be careful in all your dealings.

7. **Arrange for the loan money to be transferred** to your business bank account. Have your bank call you when it receives "good funds" from your loan. NEVER spend your loan money before you get it!

8. **Guard your loan money** so no one but you can use it! Remember: "Spending other people's money is the easiest thing in the world

to do." Never let others spend YOUR money! Keep tight control of it.

Getting private money is easy when you have a good real estate project that you describe well, and accurately, to prospective lenders. So take the time to understand, and write up, your project. Doing so can lead to success in getting the real estate funding you need for a profitable real estate deal. For best results when dealing with Private Lenders, remember:

Private Lenders have funds of their own or funds from investors who want to invest in profitable real estate as silent partners. The Private Lender is working alone and is not governed by strict laws, except the usury limits on the amount of interest they can charge on loans they make. Most Private Lenders rely on their personal opinion of a borrower and the borrower's real estate project when making a loan decision.

Where Can I Find Suitable Private Lenders?

Private Lenders are all over the landscape! You just have to look in the right places for them. Good places to look include:

- **Your large-city** Sunday newspaper under "Capital Available."
- **Local business** magazines in industrial and manufacturing areas.
- **Business newspapers** and newsletters such as the *Wall Street Journal* and *International Wealth Success.*
- **The "Private Loan Money and Funding Success Kit"** described at the back of this book.
- **Local attorneys** and accountants who have wealthy Private Lenders as clients.
- **Members of** nearby golf, tennis, and yacht clubs.
- **Business capital clubs** that meet monthly to hear presentations by BWBs seeking funding.
- **Angel groups** in various parts of the country.

- **Internet sites** under the heading "Private Lenders."
- **Your author,** me, Ty Hicks, who has access, through research, to data on hundreds of active Private Lenders.

What Services Can I Expect from Private Lenders?

Most Private Lenders will give you excellent service, compared to busy, crowded, and overworked Loan Officers in other money sources. You can expect Private Lenders to:

- *Give you full attention* at the time they're reviewing your Loan Application, and during any interviews you may have with them.
- *Show interest in your Loan Application* and the real estate you plan to put the loan money into when you receive the funds.
- *Cooperate with you* by getting your money to you when you need it to close a real estate deal you're working on.
- *Speed up your loan approval process* when you need a fast response to win a deal which others may be competing with you to close. Funding speed never kills any real estate deals!
- *Supply ongoing help to you* to ensure the success of your real estate project so you're able to repay your loan on time, and in full.

To help your Private Lender give you the better service you expect from him or her, take these Smart Borrower Steps to help both yourself and your lender:

1. **Prepare a detailed Loan Package** on the specific real estate property, or project (such as a development or rehab job) you need the funding for. **REMEMBER:** You can talk all you want about the great deal you need funding for. But a lender won't really have a clear picture of your proposal until he or she sees it in writing. A Loan Package can tell a winning story for you! Further, you must have a Loan Package available for a Private Lender to make a favorable decision on your Loan Application. To help you prepare your Loan Package, Figure 5.1 shows a typical Loan Package Submission Letter. Figure 5.2 shows the Income and Expense Statement for the

Date
President
Private Real Estate Lender
789 Main Street
Any Town 00000

Dear President _____:

Enclosed is a Loan Package for a desirable and profitable real estate income property located at 444 Main Street, Anytown, for which we are applying for a First Mortgage Loan of $340,000, or 65 percent of the purchase price. The balance of the purchase price will be paid in the form of cash and notes. This Loan Package includes:

- A filled-out Loan Application.
- A Profit and Loss Statement for the property.
- A recent Appraisal of the property.
- A Description of the property.
- Three photographs of the property.
- A description of the Business Experience of the Applicant(s).
- A listing of the Insurance Policies covering the property.
- Deed, Title, and Mortgage information for the property.
- The Annual Net Operating Income for the property is 40.7 percent, which is typical for properties in the area.
- Operating Expenses for this property are similar to those in the area in which the property is located.

If you have any questions concerning this property and the loan we are seeking we'll be happy to answer them.

Very truly yours,

Signature

Your Name

Figure 5.1   Typical Loan Package Submission Letter

```
Bayview Crossing Apartments
444 Main Street, Anytown
20 units at $675.00 per month rent

Gross Income:  Gross annual rental income            $162,000
               Vacancy reserve (Fully
                  rented now)                            8,100
               Adjusted rental income                  153,900
               Laundry income                              600
               Gross annual income                    154,500

Gross Expenses:  Annual, for
   year end 12/31
Real estate taxes, water, sewer       12,900
Heat and electricity                  33,500
Insurance                             11,000
Payroll                               14,800
Payroll taxes                          2,400
Trash removal                          2,300
Repairs and supplies                  11,800
Elevator maintenance                   1,400
Advertising                            1,100
Professional fees                        300
Telephone                                300
Total expenses                                          91,800
Net Operating Income before
   Debt Service                                         62,700
Price of building:  $520,000
Annual Debt Service:
First Mortgage:  $420,000 @ 8 percent
   for 30 years                       37,000
Purchase Money
Mortgage:  $100,000 @10 percent
   for 10 years                       15,900
Total Debt Service                                      52,900
Net Operating Profit                                     9,800
```

Figure 5.2   Typical Income and Expense Statement used
for submission to a Private Lender

income property covered by the Submission Letter. The other items mentioned in the letter—Filled-Out Loan Application, Appraisal, Description, Photographs, Business Experience Description, Insurance Policies, Deed, Title, and Mortgage Information, will be made available to you by your seller.

2. **Establish a friendship** with your Loan Office or other contact at the Private Lender. Most Private Lenders are working for themselves. So you're talking to the "top honcho." Being friendly with your direct Private Lender can put you into the big loan leagues quickly. REMEMBER: Borrowing money is not an adversarial relationship! Instead, it is a friendly relationship and a shared interest in real estate and its moneymaking future.

3. **Do not push your Private Lender** for an instantaneous answer. You will usually get your approval in just hours. So don't pressure your Private Lender. It only causes friction.

4. **Be familiar with ALL the numbers of your deal.** Don't be caught stuttering about unknown numbers. Know the **Price,** the **Annual Income,** the Annual **Expenses,** and the **Down Payment** better than you know your own name and you'll get your loan!

Are There Any Other Good Reasons for My Using Private Lenders?

Yes, there are many good reasons for a real estate BWB to work with a Private Lender. Here are a number of these reasons, as I see them. Perhaps you can see how you might use one, or more, of these benefits in your million-dollar real estate wealth building. Various Private Lenders may offer one, or more, of these benefits to you:

- **Loans** from $100,000 to $100 million.
- **Interest-only loans**—reducing your monthly payment when it can help you most of all.
- **International loans** for real estate of many types.
- **Payout times** from 6 months to 30 years.
- **Loan Broker fee** of up to 5 percent of the loan paid to you if you act as a broker to bring new loans to some Private Lenders.

- **Specialists in loans** called "Difficult to make"; "Hard to Approve"; "Less Than Perfect Credit"; "Loans to People in Bankruptcy"; "Loans to People after Bankruptcy."

- **100 percent loan on Sales Price** after rehabilitation of a real estate property needing upgrading.

- **Loan Brokers** can deal directly with Private Lenders to get loans for their clients.

Now not every Private Lender offers all these benefits to you. Some lenders may offer only one of these benefits. So you must check with each Private Lender to determine which benefits—if any—it offers. If the first Private Lender does not offer the benefit(s) you're seeking, go on to the next one. *When you seek, you may find. If you don't seek, you're sure not to find what you're looking for!*

Where Can I Find Private Lenders?

This often-asked question is easy to answer. Here, based on research that I did, is a list of Private Lenders you might wish to contact for your real estate loan. For best results with these lenders:

1. **Contact the lender** by phone, e-mail, or postal mail before sending any documents or a Loan Application to them.
2. **Ask what types of loans** the Private Lender makes.
3. **Present,** in brief form, the type of loan you seek.
4. **Question your contact** about their interest, or lack of it, in your loan.
5. **Obtain their Loan Application** and submit it in typed form to the Private Lender.
6. **Wait** for a decision.

List of Private Lenders

Now here's a listing of Private Lenders that might be interested in your real estate proposal. Follow the rules immediately above before submitting your real estate Loan Application.

Alford, Marsh & Associates, 127 Dreher Road, West Columbia, SC 29169. Tel: 803-939-098; Fax: 803-926-0610; E-mail: MONEYDE836@aol.com; hometown.aol.com/moneyde836/index.html.

Allcity Services, Allcity Finance, 643 Broadway, Suite 301, Saugus, MA 01906. Tel: 781-233-4850; E-mail: Allcity@shore.ne; www.allcity-services.com.

ARI Properties, Inc., Atlanta Hard Money Loans, 4780 Ashford Dunwoody Road, Suite 213, Atlanta, Georgia 30338. Tel: 404-421-5578; Fax: 404-806-6133; E-mail: wade@AtlantaHardMoneyLoans.com; www.atlantahardmoneyloans.com.

Bayview Financial Trading Group, 2665 South Bayshore Drive, 3rd Floor, Miami, FL 33133. Tel: 305-854-888; Fax: 305-854-2031; E-mail: BFTG@bftg.com; www.bayviewfinancial.com.

Blue Crown Funding, Inc., 3943 Irvine Boulevard, Suite 172, Irvine, CA 92602. Tel: 714-544-2738; Fax: 714-544-1460; E-mail: charlesw@bluecrownfunding.com; www.BlueCrownFunding.com.

Chandler & Associates, Inc., 18811 Pintail Lane, Gaithersburg, MD 20879. Tel: 301-527-0023; Fax: 775-640-1055; E-mail: brian1414@comcast.net.

Coastal La Jolla Funding, 7709 Eads Avenue, La Jolla, CA 92037. Tel: 858-456-2423; Fax: 858-225-3683; E-mail: craig@coastallajollafunding.com; www.coastallajollafunding.com.

Continental Mortgage Capital, 2141 N University Drive, #220, Coral Springs, FL 33071. Tel: 954-603-0420 or 954-575-077; Fax: 954-575-9421; E-mail: lenning@trillions.com; www.commercialending.com.

Creative Financial Corporation, 420 East 111th Street, Suite 1110, New York, NY 10029. Tel: 212-534-2795; Fax: 240-526-7165; E-mail: info@creativefinancialcorp.com; www.creativefinancialcorp.com.

Fairfield Financial Services, 3327 SE 50th Avenue, Portland, OR 97206. Tel: 503-775-6725; Fax: 503-241-4903; E-mail: info@altfunding.com; www.altfunding.com.

Funding Edge, 4211 Gardendale, Suite 200, San Antonio, TX 78229. Tel: 210-249-2111; Fax: 210-249-0211; E-mail: leon@FundingEdge.com; www.FundingEdge.com.

Gala Resources, LLC, 1212 Avenue of the Americas, 6th Floor, New York, NY 10036. Tel: 800-372-3393 or 212-302-884; Fax: 212-302-8832; E-mail: AlanH@galaresources.com; www.galaresources.com.

Grace Capital Group, Six Venture, Suite 270, Irvine, CA 92618. Tel: 949-788-0999; E-mail: jbk@gracecapitalgroup.com; http:/www.gracecapitalgroup.com.

Hamilton Commercial Loans, 840 N 5th Street, Hamilton, IL 62341. Tel: 217-847-6481; Fax: 510-743-0770; E-mail: info@hamiltoncommercialloans.com; www.HamiltonCommercialLoans.com.

Hardmoney.Com, Platinum Funding, Inc., 2882 Nostrand Avenue, Brooklyn, NY 11229. Tel: 800-HARD MONEY; E-mail: Ptoiv@hardmoney.com; www.hardmoney.com.

Hard Money Funding, Inc., 12627 San Jose Boulevard, Suite 203, Jacksonville, FL 32223. Tel: 904-425-3955; Fax: 904-425-3959; E-mail: info@hardmoneyfunding.com; www.hardmoneyfunding.com.

Hardmoney Loans, Moore & Levy, 6034 Hazeltine Avenue, Van Nuys, CA 91401. Tel: 818-712-9502; E-mail: info@HardMoney-Loans.com; www.hardmoney-loans.com.

Heartland Capital Group, LLC, 2535 E. Southlake Boulevard, Southlake, TX 76092. Tel: 817-748-2599; Fax: 817-748-5601; E-mail: drockaway@heartlandcapitalgroup.com; www.heartlandcapitalgroup.com.

Investment Exchange, 234-5149 Country Hills Boulevard, Suite 131, Calgary, Alberta, Canada T3A 5K8. Tel: 403-208-2964; Fax: 403-208-2965; E-mail: info@tinvex.com; www.tinvex.com.

Investors Mortgage Holdings, Inc., 6991 E. Camelback Road, Suite C-158, Scottsdale, AZ 85251. Tel: 602-889-341; Fax: 602-889-3412; E-mail: info@mortgageholdings.com; www.mortgageholdings.com.

Investwell, UMTH Lending Co., 5740 Prospect, Suite 1000, Dallas, TX 75206. Tel: 214-237-3300 ext-140; Fax: 214-237-3301; E-mail: welowe@umth.com; www.investwell.com.

Ironwood Capital, 200 Fisher Drive, Avon, CT 06001. Tel: 860-409-210; Fax: 860-409-2120; E-mail: info@ironwoodcap.com; www.ironwoodcap.com.

Lafayette Financial, 1427 Finley Lane, Alamo, CA 94507. Tel: 888-576-6534; E-mail: Wayne@lafayettefinancial.com; www.lafayettefinancial.com.

Liberty Financial, 14700 Firestone Boulevard, La Mirada, CA 90638. Tel: 714-523-540; Fax: 714-523-5444; E-mail: libertyfinancialco@msn .com; www.libertyfinancialco.com.

LLJ Capital, LLC, Glenpointe Center West, 500 Frank W. Burr Boulevard, Teaneck, NJ 07666-6883. Tel: 201-287-153; Fax: 201-287-1531; E-mail: admin@lljcapital.com; www.lljcapital.com.

Loan Solution, Inc., 21618 Golden Triangle Road, Santa Clarita, CA 91350-2615. Tel: 661-251-9075; E mail: info@loan-solution.com; loan-solution.com.

Met Mortgage Corp., 501 56th Street, West New York, NJ 07093. Tel: 201-866-480; Fax: 201-866-9477; E-mail: hardloans@metmtge.com; www.metmtge.com/contact.htm.

Metro Funding Corp., One Kalisa Way, Suite 310, Paramus, NJ 07652. Tel: 866-302-636; Fax: 201-262-6910; E-mail: info@metrofunding-corp.com; www.metrofundingcorp.com.

Minneapolis Hard Money, Onward Financial, 4780 Ashford Dunwoody Road, Suite A457, Minneapolis, MN 55346. Tel: 612-226-0351; E-mail: info@minneapolishardmoney.com; www.minneapolishard-money.com.

MLA, INC., 30521 Schoenherr Road, Warren, MI 48088. Tel: 586 751-1111 or 313-617-1198; Fax: 586-751-2553; E-mail: information@mlamortgage .com; www.mlamortgage.com.

Mortgage Bankers, Ltd., 4621 Horizon Circle, Suite 3, Baltimore, MD 21208. Tel: 800-854-9077 or 410-922-710; Fax: 410-922-4564; E-mail: Banker7000@aol.com; www.refinancecash.com.

Norris Group, 18710 Van Buren Boulevard, Riverside, CA 92508. Tel: 951-780-5856; Fax: 951-780-9827; E-mail: thenorrisgroup@pacbell .net; www.thenorrisgroup.com.

North American Capital, LLC, 31st Floor Bryan Tower, 2001 Bryan Street, Suite 3110, Dallas, TX 75215. Tel: 214-485-280; Fax: 214-999-0478; E-mail: mark@hardmoneycorp.com; www.hardmoneycorp .com.

Pace Lending, 133 E. Bay Street, Jacksonville, FL 32202. Tel: 904-396-0072; Fax: 407-210-0075; E-mail: paul@PaceLending.com; www.PaceLending.com.

Pacific Mortgage Funding, 11924 E. Firestone Boulevard, Norwalk, CA 90650. Tel: 562-864-4006; E-mail: info@pacificmortgage.com; www.pacificmortgage.com.

Prestige Mortgage Services, Subsidiary of 1st-Family Inc., 202 North 8th Street, Lakeside, OR 97449, Mail to: P.O. Box 656, Lakeside, OR 97449. Tel: 214-452-9938; Fax: 775-310-7739; E-mail: prestige95@hotmail.com; www.prestige.1st-website.com.

Private Investor Loans, Inc., 3405 Ridgemont Drive, Mountain View, CA 94040. Tel: 650-967-250; Fax: 650-964-8684; E-mail: info@pi-loans.com; www.privateinvestorloans.com.

Private Lender Inc., Zoltan Padar Mortgage Broker, 333, 1333-8 Street SW, Calgary, Alberta, Canada T2R 1M6. Tel: 403-616-9114; Fax: 403-256-5971; E-mail: zoli@myprivatelender.com; www.myprivatelender.com.

Private Loan Funding Corp., 26311 Junipero Serra Road, Suite 150, San Juan Capistrano, CA 92675. Tel: 949-248-3844; Irvine, CA 92612; E-mail: chad@privateloanfunding.com; www.privateloanfunding.com.

Quantum Corporate Funding, 1140 Avenue of the Americas, New York, NY 10036. Tel: 212-768-1200 or 800-352-2535; Fax: 212-944-8216; www.quantumfunding.com.

Ready Mortgage Corp., 833 E. Arapaho Road, Suite 112, Richardson, TX 75081. Tel: 972-889-7323; E-mail: c-pttit@readymort.com; www.readymort.com.

Real Estate Investors Group, P.O. Box 266735, Weston, FL 33332. Tel: 888-228-6324 or 954-608-6774; Fax: 954-252-2380; E-mail: andrabr9@bellsouth.net; www.floridahardmoneylender.com.

Regatta Capital, Ltd., 222 Milwaukee Street, Denver, CO 80206. Tel: 303-329-3479; Fax: 303-329-0303; E-mail: SReplin@aol.com; www.1hardmoney.com.

Private Lenders can be your source of real estate money. To be successful with such lenders you must be completely businesslike in all your dealings with them. Go the extra mile in preparing your real estate proposal for Private Lenders. If in doubt, furnish more information, instead of less. Why?

Because Private Lenders are often entrepreneurs in their own right and they enjoy evaluating another wealth builder's approach to earning a fortune. So you never go wrong when you provide detailed information to Private Lenders!

Some real estate wealth builders never deal with a bank, established mortgage lender, credit union, or other regulated lender. Instead, they start their real estate investment career with a Private Lender and stay with that lender for all their investments. Other real estate BWBs work with a group of five or six Private Lenders and get all their deals funded by them. So take your pick—deal with one Private Lender, or several. Your key objective is:

- **Get the real estate loan** you need.
- **At an acceptable** interest rate.
- **With the term** (number of years) you feel comfortable with.
- **In a reasonable** amount of time—one week, or less.
- **Without paying** Front Money or an Advance Fee of any kind.
- **While acquiring a property** that will give you a Positive Cash Flow from the first day you own it.

Build Your Wealth as a Private Lender Client or Finder

You can build your riches faster in real estate using Private Lenders in two ways, namely:

1. As a client of one, or more, Private Lenders getting loans for yourself.
2. As a finder for one, or more, Private Lenders, finding clients for your lenders.

A good way to act in both these capacities while getting funding for yourself and finding funding for others is to:

Form your own group of three, or more, Private Lenders from whom you hope to obtain your own funding, and loans for clients you bring to your Private Lenders. Bring deals to your Private Lenders as a group—either for yourself or for a client of yours seeking a loan.

To form your own group of Private Lenders to get real estate loans for both yourself and others take these easy, and fun, steps:

1. **Choose several Private Lenders** you think you might want to work with, based on the type, and size of, loans they make. Use the IWS Kit "Private Loan Money and Funding" to find suitable lenders. You'll find the Kit listed at the back of this book.

2. **Have a preliminary interview** with each target lender on the telephone. During your interview get data on the types of loans you might get for yourself.

3. **Ask about being a finder** for the Private Lender. Have the person you're talking to give you full details on the commission you'll be paid, when you'll receive your payment, and so on.

4. **Become friendly** with your contact person at each Private Lender. Establish a rapport with this person by finding items of interest to both of you. Work at establishing a first name relationship as quickly as you can.

5. **Ask for bare-bones details** of previous loan deals the Private Lender has made. Get data on:
   • **Loan** amount.
   • **Term** (payoff time).
   • **Purpose** of loan.
   • **Type of** property for which the loan was made.

6. **Slant your real estate loan deals** so they resemble the deals the Private Lender has already made. Similarity of deals makes for speedy approval.

7. **Send your Loan Application** to your friend at the Private Lender. Do the same for any client deals you may have. Be sure to call your friend before you send your application to alert him or her that it will be arriving on his or her desk soon.

8. **Be willing to alter your Loan Application** if your friend at the Private Lender advises you to do so.

9. **Follow these steps** and your chances of getting your real estate loan will zoom. And you may find your income from client commissions, which can run as high as $100,000 for large loans, may give you the down payment money you need for your real estate deals!

Your Key Ideas for Getting Financing from Private Lenders

❏ **Private Lenders** can provide real estate funding to you faster, with less paperwork, fewer credit checks, and greater friendliness than many highly regulated lenders can.

❏ **Private Lenders** can be a steady source of real estate loans for you and may even make down payment loans to you for your wealth building.

❏ **Private Lenders** make dozens of different types of real estate loans, including first and second mortgages, bridge loans, construction loans, down payment funding, and so on. And your credit rating is usually less important with Private Lenders than it is with more traditional lenders.

❏ **Private Lender** loans can by obtained sooner, and with less paperwork, if you follow the eight key steps given to you in this chapter.

❏ **Private Lenders** can be found in numerous sources, many of which are listed in this chapter.

❏ **Private Lenders** can be both your source of real estate funding and your source of loans for clients you find who need loan money. You will be paid a finder fee by your clients for finding them funding from Private Lenders.

CHAPTER 6

Self-Starter Real Estate Financing for Beginning Wealth Builders

As you learned in Chapter 3, there are *conventional* and *nonconventional* mortgages available to real estate wealth builders. Likewise, you'll find that there are conventional and nonconventional ways to find real estate loans for yourself. This chapter deals with nonconventional ways for you to obtain the real estate financing you need.

As I said earlier in this book, you have a friend in your author. So I want to give you every way I know of to get the money you need to acquire $1 million in real estate in one year using borrowed money. Let's get you started using completely approved and fully acceptable nonconventional ways to raise the money you need for your deals.

Two Ways for You to Find Money Today

Just as there are two broad categories of mortgages (conventional and nonconventional), there are two broad ways for you to raise the money you need:

1. **Acting on your own** to find funds for both yourself and others.
2. **Using others** to find for you the money you need.

We'll look at acting on your own first because such action can often bring you the result you seek—quickly. Meanwhile, you might even earn money while helping others find the real estate money they need.

1. Acting on Your Own

Become a Loan Originator for a Local Lender

A Loan Originator is a person who serves a local lender:

- **As an Independent Contractor**—that is, not on the lender's payroll. You're your own employer!
- **Finding people seeking mortgage loans** for a residence or for commercial property of some kind.
- **Earning a commission** (usually 40 percent of the lender's loan fee, though this can vary from one lender to another). Your commission is paid by the lender—not by the borrower.
- **Working under the lender's license** instead of a personal license; thus, you generally do not need a real estate license to be a Loan Originator for a licensed lender.
- **Keeping your own business hours** because you're paid for getting successful borrowers, not for how many hours you work. Sometimes you can find a successful borrower with just 10 minutes of talk—there's no need for long hours of work.
- **Concentrating your efforts,** in general, for just one lender, instead of working for several at the same time.

"So why," you ask, "is being a Loan Originator important for me?" It is important for you for several reasons, namely:

- **As a Loan Originator** you learn which lenders are loaning money for what types of properties.
- **As a Loan Originator** you quickly learn what qualifications your lender, and its competitors, are looking for in borrowers.

- **As a Loan Originator** you see what loan amounts are popular with your lender, and with its competitors.
- **As a Loan Originator** you can (in six months, or less) get a good "feel" for which types of properties get quick funding from local lenders.
- **As a Loan Originator** you see how your own Loan Application should be tailored to be approved by your lender, or by its competitors. You become a "street-smart" borrower.

"So how," you ask, "can I become a Loan Originator?" The answer is:

- **Check your local banks** and mortgage companies by calling, e-mailing, or writing them.
- **Tell the lender** you'd like to become a Loan Originator for him or her. Be willing to complete any needed paperwork.
- **Agree to whatever** simple requirements they have, including any training they may require.

If you can't find a local lender using Loan Originators, ask for the name and address of an associate of your author, Ty Hicks. This associate of mine offers Single-Family Home Loan Originator opportunities in 17 states at no cost of any kind to you. Another associate of mine offers nationwide multifamily Loan Originator spots to ambitious people. Full data on these opportunities are available free to two-year subscribers to my newsletter, *International Wealth Success*. See the back of this book for full information on it.

Pick the Type of Properties You'll Work With

Loan Originators usually specialize in one type of property. You should decide early on, which type of property you'd like to work with.

The easiest way to start as a Loan Originator is with residential properties—usually single-family homes (SFHs). With the SFH:

- **There are more** Loan Originator spots available.
- **Your training is shorter,** and easier, for beginners.
- **You can usually earn** your first commission sooner.

If you're an experienced real estate person you can specialize in multi-family (apartment house), industrial, or commercial properties. With such properties:

- **Your commission is larger** because—in general—prices are higher.
- **Sales usually take longer** because the paperwork is more complex.
- **Your training time will be longer** than for SFHs because there's more for you to learn.

Be a Finder for Loans for Others and Yourself

As a Loan Originator you work for just one lender in a restricted geographic area—one city or one state. But as a Finder, you:

- **Work for many different lenders** who seek your services.
- **Work nationally,** and if you want, internationally.
- **Work on a commission basis** for the firm, or person, seeking the loan.
- **Work as an Independent Contractor** and are not on anyone's payroll.
- **Work using your own money** for telephone calls, auto gas, and so on. Your commissions will far exceed these expenses.

"So, why," you ask, "should I be a Finder instead of a Loan Originator?" There are a number of good reasons. As a Finder:

- **You're working for yourself,** not some giant financial group.
- **Your commissions can be much larger,** dollar-wise, because you're not splitting them with the lender.
- **You can work worldwide.** You're not restricted to one small area. Your international commissions can be much higher than domestic ones because the deals are usually larger.

How to Set Yourself Up as a Finder

You can become a Finder in just one day. All you need do is take these simple steps:

1. **Register your business** with your County Clerk if you plan to operate under an assumed name, such as ABC Finding Services. (In general, you do not have to register your business if you operate under your own name. However, you must check this out with a local attorney to learn the rules in your area.)

2. **Have letterheads printed,** or print them yourself on your computer, giving your business name, address, telephone number, and e-mail address, if any.

3. **Advertise your services** using classified ads in national papers and magazines. As a newsletter subscriber you can advertise free of charge in my two newsletters, *International Wealth Success* and *Money Watch Bulletin,* described at the back of this book. Some readers report good results with such ads. A typical classified ad you might run is:

Need money for real estate or business? We can find it for you. Call 123-456-7890 day or night.

Your typical commission for finding real estate or business loan money will be 5 percent on the first $1 million, 4 percent on the second $1 million, and so on. Doing some arithmetic on this, that's $50,000 on the first $1 million, $40,000 on the second $1 million. So you can easily see that finding can be much more lucrative for you than being a Loan Originator.

Being a finder can give you a lifetime career, once you get a few clients and close some deals. People will seek you out, asking you to take on their finding assignments. And if you "deliver the goods"—that is, find money for your clients—new customers will plead with you to take on their business.

Establish Yourself as a Financial Broker

A Financial Broker finds loans for clients, just as a finder does. But the Financial Broker often performs other duties, such as:

- **Bringing two companies together** for a profitable merger.
- **Searching for, and finding,** key personnel—such as a Sales Manager, Chief Financial Officer, and so on.
- **Consulting with a firm's management** to prepare plans for future expansion, downsizing, and so on.
- **Helping a company to go public**—that is sell its stock to investors.

As you can see, acting in any of these capacities requires previous business experience. That's why becoming a Financial Broker takes both education and time. However, you can use your previous business experience to become a Financial Broker to find real estate loans for both yourself and your clients.

To establish yourself as a Financial Broker, follow the steps given earlier for finders. And be sure to get some education concerning fees, lenders, typical agreements to use, and so on. You should also have a working arrangement with a competent attorney who can advise you on legal matters you encounter in your work as a Financial Broker.

Get the Know-How You Need

Being a Financial Broker is lots easier, more profitable, and less challenging if (as in any other business) you know what you're doing—from day one. While you can study various business books and pick up snippets of information here and there, it's best to use a focused course that will give you the facts, and procedures, you need to succeed. For example, look at this letter:

> "Received **Financial Broker Kit** yesterday morning. Using info in it, closed deal for $463,750 yesterday afternoon. Thank you. Best regards."   —Tennessee

While the letter writer might have been working on his deal before he received the Kit (he didn't say in his letter), he did use info in it to close his deal. You'll find the *Financial Broker Kit* listed in the back of this book. It is one example of how know-how can get you the results you seek.

Other sources of Financial Broker education include college extension courses, correspondence "distance learning" instruction, and personal one-on-one meetings with your good friend, your author, in conjunction with your using the Kit mentioned before as your basic introduction to this exciting, and financially rewarding, business.

Another reader writes:

"Besides investing in income real estate, I'm also a Financial Consultant, thanks to your **Financial Broker Kit.** I make about $60,000 a year in that business alone. I could earn more than $100,000 a year if I didn't have the demands of five children and a wife who wants to spend my income on several family vacations every year."

—New York

Become a Loan Officer with an Active Lender

When you become a Loan Officer with an active lender you go on the lender's payroll as an employee. While this may seem like "giving up the ship" because you're agreeing to work for someone else, listen to me, your good friend. The lender will:

- **Train you** on the ins and outs of many types of real estate loans.
- **Show you** how to handle the papers associated with real estate loans.
- **Guide you** on how to best qualify a borrower so he or she can be granted a loan.
- **Help you understand** interest rates, mortgage calculations, and loan payoff procedures.
- **"Get you up to speed"** on real estate loans in about six months, allowing you another six months to find your income properties worth $1 million, or more.

To become a Loan Officer and reap the benefits listed above, you should take the following steps:

1. **Prepare a resume** of your previous experience emphasizing any real estate jobs you've held or education in the field.

2. **Specify that you want to be a Loan Officer** with a real estate lender and that you look forward to whatever training the lender offers.

3. **Be willing to undergo** any training the lender requires.

Training to be, and acting as, a Loan Officer for an active lender can give you a fast education in real estate borrowing and lending. While spending six months in such a job may seem like a diversion from your goal, it really isn't. You'll be learning the "nuts and bolts" of real estate finance. This will probably be the most important learning of your lifetime! So consider becoming a Loan Officer for a brief period. It can put big bucks into your bank account sooner than you think!

Form Your Own Mortgage Company and Make Loans

As a Loan Officer you're an employee on a payroll. The other extreme is to be in your own business and be self-employed. A good way to do this in real estate is to:

> **Form your own mortgage company with investors putting up the money you'll lend and have a licensed real estate professional on your Board of Directors to supervise the real estate aspects of your lending.**

While forming your own company may seem like a challenge (and it is), there are several advantages to this way of raising money for your income real estate projects. These advantages are:

- **You run your own "show,"** deciding which loans you'll make and which loans you'll reject. Your loan decisions are based on the creditworthiness of the borrower, the term (how long the borrower has to repay the loan), the amount of the loan, and the purpose for which the money will be used.

- **You earn profits for yourself** on loans funded with Other People's Money (OPM) while having little more than your time at risk. It's a win-win deal for you!

- **You will find business easily** because—according to your author, Ty Hicks—money, not water, is the universal solvent! When you have money to lend, people will be after you day and night, applying for the loan (or loans) they need. How do I know? I'm a Private Lender to my two-year, or longer, newsletter subscribers. The loans I make are for short-term real estate down-payment funds (three to five years) at 6 percent simple interest rate. Some kind of collateral is asked for on each loan.

- **You will quickly learn** what type of loan you're eligible for. Applying for such a loan will be easy for you because you already know what types, amounts, purposes, and so on, lenders welcome when they make loans. You have an insider's edge that can get you your loan faster than you might think.

2. Using Others to Find Loans for You

Using others to find loans for yourself can have several advantages for you, namely:

- **You save time** because someone else is doing the "grunt" work of contacting lenders, getting details on the loans they make, looking over the application, and so on.

- **You don't deal directly with Loan Officers** until you're ready to accept the loan. This saves you from the probing questions sometimes asked during a loan interview.

- **You can evaluate potential lenders from afar.** This allows you to choose a lender you believe will be best for your deal.

- **You pay a nominal fee** to the person or organization finding the loan for you. This fee can usually be "rolled into the loan" so no money comes out of your pocket or bank account.

- **You can spend more time** "doing your real estate business thing" to earn money, instead of chasing after potential lenders.
- **You avoid the embarrassment of rejection** because the word is given directly to your Loan Finder, instead of to yourself. This face saving is often worth whatever fee you pay when you eventually get your loan.

Which Types of Loan Finders Should I Use?

This question is often asked when I first talk to Beginning Wealth Builders (BWBs) about getting assistance in raising the money they need for the income real estate they wish to buy. The answer, really, is simple. And it is:

Use the type of Loan Finder you're comfortable with for the income real estate project you wish to finance.

Thus, if you're working with a real estate broker on the purchase of the property, the Mortgage Broker in his or her office might be an excellent choice. Why? Because a local Mortgage Broker:

- **Knows properties** in his or her area.
- **Knows lenders** in his or her area.
- **Knows what kinds of deals** "fly"—that is, get loans.
- **Knows how to "massage"** a Loan Application for faster funding.
- **Knows when to drop** one lender and go on to the next.

So if you're dealing with a real estate broker, ask to speak to his or her Mortgage Broker. Your funding may be as close as the next desk!

If a Mortgage Broker isn't available, try a Financial Broker who is familiar with real estate in the area in which your future property is located. Why use a Financial Broker? Because an experienced Financial Broker can:

1. **Contact lenders** specializing in the type of property you want to buy.
2. **Tailor your Loan Application** to the needs of chosen lenders.
3. **Advise you on the best amount** to request for your loan. While $128,672 may be the amount you need, $130,000 may be a better

number to use, based on the Financial Broker's earlier dealing with selected lenders.

4. **Negotiate the interest rate** to a level you are willing to accept, based on the expected Income and Expenses of the property.

5. **Advise you on the term** (loan duration) the lender prefers, so you can see if the proposed term allows you to have a Positive Cash Flow from the property you're planning to buy.

"So where," you ask, "can I find a suitable Financial Broker?" One of the best places is my newsletter, *International Wealth Success*. Each month it lists numerous Financial Brokers who might help you. And, as a subscriber, you can advertise free of charge every month in the newsletter to find a qualified and friendly Financial Broker for your deal.

You can also use a Finder to seek the loan you need. When considering using a Finder, keep these thoughts in mind:

- **Deal only with experienced Finders.** Amateurs will just waste your time. So be sure to ask for a resume from each prospective Finder so you get an idea of what he or she has done in the past.

- **Never pay a Finder a front or Advance Fee.** The fee you pay a Finder should be stated in a written agreement document signed, and dated, by yourself and the Finder. Your fee is paid after the loan the Finder negotiated is delivered to you in the form of "good funds" in your bank.

- **Limit the amount of personal information** you give a Finder. You will reveal such information to the lender once your Loan Application has been approved.

You can also work with Loan Originators in your area having them find the loan you seek. Most Loan Originators work with just one lender. So you must determine—in advance—if the lender a Loan Originator represents makes the type of loan you seek. Thus, you would not work with a single-family home Loan Originator for a multifamily home loan. Likewise, the reverse.

You'll find Loan Originators advertising in the newsletter mentioned before. You may also find them advertising in your local newspapers—both daily and weekly. Follow the same procedures listed earlier for Loan Finders.

This chapter gives you numerous ways to self-start your financing for acquiring $1 million in real estate in one year on borrowed money. Put these ways to use and you'll soon be on your way to your goal—in your spare time! Just remember, your good friend, Ty Hicks, is here to help you every step of the way.

Your Key Ideas for Self-Starter Financing of Your Real Estate Fortune

- ❏ **There are two ways to self-start** your real estate financing—(1) acting on your own, and (2) using others to find the loan money you need for income real estate investing.
- ❏ **When acting on your own** you can work as a Loan Originator, a Finder, a Financial Broker, a Loan Officer at a lender, or form your own mortgage company with investors to make mortgage loans. Each role has its advantages for you.
- ❏ **Before you become a Loan Originator,** pick the types of properties you want to work with—single-family, or multifamily. Your earnings per transaction will be smaller with single-family homes. But if you're just starting, single-family homes will usually produce earnings sooner.
- ❏ **Finders can set up easily.** But you must know mortgages and how they work before you can really help people. So be sure to read this entire book carefully before getting started as a Finder.
- ❏ **Financial brokers handle** both real estate and business loans. As with a Finder, you must get training and enough knowledge of loans and mortgages before you can really help people get the loans they seek.

❏ **Working as a Loan Officer** can give you valuable experience and training. You might even have one of your associate Loan Brokers approve your Loan Application! Why? Because once you know what your lender seeks in a loan you can prepare a Loan Application that is almost impossible to refuse!

❏ **Forming your own mortgage company** using investors to supply the needed funds is an advanced way of raising money for your deal. You should have experience with mortgages and lending before taking this step!*

❏ **Using others to raise money for you** can save you time and embarrassment, while you continue working at acquiring the real estate you want.

---

* See page 260 in the Appendix for "Offering Circular for a Real Estate Mortgage Company, M-8."

CHAPTER 7

Bad Credit/No Credit Financing Is Possible for You

THE MOST FREQUENTLY ASKED QUESTION (MFAQ) I GET FROM READERS OF my two newsletters and many books is: "I messed up my life a few years ago. So now I have bad credit. How can I get started buying income real estate?"

These people made a wrong turn in life because of:

- **Divorce**—where one spouse runs up big credit-card debt to get even.
- **Illness**—major medical bills can lead to late payments or bankruptcy.
- **Job loss**—with a resultant reduction in income and late, or no, payment of bills.
- **Student loans**—are a nuisance to repay so some people skip out on them, hoping they will go away but they never do.

I've Found My "Dream Property" but My Credit Is Bad

When these people come to me they've often found a "dream property." It's usually a multifamily building that will give them a strong Positive Cash Flow (PCF)—often as much as $10,000, or more, per month, after

141

paying ALL loans they've taken on to buy the property. The $10,000+ per month PCF has their brain spinning.

"What can I do," they moan. "I just have to have this property with that gorgeous cash flow!"

My answer will vary, depending on the reader's credit situation. To help you, or a relative or friend, cope with such a situation, here are valuable answers.

Use Lenders That Accept Bad Credit

Some lenders will work with bad-credit applicants if:

- **The property you want to buy is in good condition and has a strong PCF.**
- **You have a sensible Business Plan for the property showing how it will pay for itself when you're managing it.**

What kinds of lenders may overlook bad credit and look at the property instead?

- **Private Lenders**—see Chapter 5—may overlook bad credit if the property (called the *Subject Property*) has a strong cash flow.
- *Yellow Page* lenders may accept bad credit for loans backed by strong property. So look at your local large-city *Yellow Page* telephone book. Look under the "Mortgages, Loans," and "Real Estate" headings. In it you may find lenders that advertise: "Bad Credit Okay"; "Bankruptcy, No Problem"; "Judgments, No Problem"; and so on.
- **Read your local** large-city newspapers. In these listings you may find ads for real estate loans using many of the same terms you'll see in the *Yellow Pages*.

Check Out Sub-Prime Lenders

As you know, I am Director of a large lender that makes many different types of loans. But the largest category of loans we make are real estate loans. More than 75 percent of the loans we make every year are for real estate.

In making these loans we classify borrowers thus:

A credit = a person with excellent credit (FICO score = 700+); no history of late pays, slow pays, or no pays.

B credit = people with a few missed or late payments. But the payments were eventually ALL made. Some payments, though late, were caught up with later—with double, or triple, payments (FICO score = 600).

C credit = many missed payments, late pays, or other credit problems on loans (FICO score = 500, or less).

D credit = no, or very few, payments on loans made to the person. Such people may ignore any loans they receive and seldom repay the debts they have with lenders.

Any loan made to a borrower with less than "A credit" is called a ***subprime loan.***

To protect themselves, lenders charge a higher interest rate to borrowers having less than **A** credit. But lenders today are finding that:

Sub-prime borrowers are worth giving another chance at receiving, and repaying, a loan. If you have bad credit, you could be given that second chance.

Sub-prime borrowers are nearly a $1 trillion market for lenders; to ignore such a market is foolish for people like myself and the lender for which I am a Director.

Sub-prime borrowers are usually so happy to get a new loan they repay right on time, in an attempt to improve their credit rating while showing their appreciation.

Sub-prime borrowers today mostly seek loans for real estate—either for an income property to improve their cash flow, or for a first home.

Work with Interested Sub-Prime Lenders

Sub-prime lenders want to make loans as much as, or perhaps even more than, you want a loan. If you work with an interested sub-prime lender you increase your loan-getting chances enormously.

"So what is an 'interested sub-prime lender'" you ask. The answer is:

An interested sub-prime lender is one actively seeking to loan money on worthwhile real estate deals at—possibly—a higher rate of interest than that charged by conventional money sources, such as banks.

Interested sub-prime lenders indicate—in their informational material—that they make loans to:

- **People** with imperfect credit.
- **Investors** with good projects but with little cash.
- **Beginning Wealth Builders (BWBs)** with lots of drive and ambition.

Dealing with interested sub-prime lenders can get you the real estate money you need faster than from conventional lenders. And you'll find that some of these sub-prime lenders will welcome you, even if your credit is not the best—say a FICO score of 525, or so.

Where to Find Sub-Prime Lenders

Finding sub-prime lenders is a challenge. But don't get discouraged! There may be sub-prime lenders in your area. If there aren't any sub-prime lenders in your area, you can work with national sub-prime lenders. To find local sub-prime lenders, take these easy steps:

1. **Use the methods given before for lenders that accept bad credit.** That is, look in your local telephone *Yellow Pages* under "Mortgages," "Real Estate," and "Loans." Some sub-prime lenders advertise there. Contact each such lender. Ask for his or her Lending guidelines. See if you can qualify—you probably can. Also, look in your local large-city Sunday newspaper in the real estate section under "Mortgages." Some sub-prime lenders advertise there. They will identify themselves by lines such as "Good credit not needed." Or "Bankruptcy? No problem!" Follow the procedure mentioned here.

2. **Look in the directories** published by IWS, Inc., listed at the back of this book. You'll find many sub-prime lenders listed there. Follow the procedure in Step 1.

3. **Look at membership lists of associations of sub-prime lenders.** Choose a lender in a large city near you, or in the city in which you reside. Contact the lender by phone, fax, e-mail, or postal mail. Get full data on the lender's criteria for loans. Keep contacting lenders until you find one whose criteria you can meet. Then apply for your loan. Use the qualifying phrases given earlier to choose your lender.

4. **Look at the selected list that follows.** Contact one or more of these lenders to see if they're interested in your project. Data given here is based on the informational materials released by the listed lenders. Since business objectives may change, it is important that you contact the listed lenders to determine if they are interested in your project. The lenders listed here are based on research I did to find sub-prime lenders you might work with.

List of Sub-Prime Lenders

Accredited Home Loans, 15090 Avenue of Science, Suite 200, San Diego, CA 92128. Tel: 858-676-2100; Fax: 858-676-2170; www.accredhome .com.

Advanced Financial Services Inc., 25 Enterprise Center, Newport, RI 02842. Tel: 401-846-3100 or 800-644-3327; www.myafsloan.com.

Aegis Mortgage, 11111 Wilcrest Street, Suite 250, Houston, TX 77042. Tel: 713-878-0100; www.aegismtg.com.

Agency Mortgage Corp., 6000 Sagemore Drive, Suite 6302, Marlton, NJ 08053. Tel: 800-905-9970; www.agencymortgage.com.

Ameriquest Mortgage Corp., 1100 W. Town and Country Road, Orange, CA 92868-4600. Tel: 714-541-9960; Fax: 714-634-0674; www. ameriquestmortgate.com.

Amerisave, 3525 Piedmont Road, 6 Piedmont Center, Atlanta, GA 30326. Tel: 866-970-7283; www.amerisAvenue.com.

Citifinancial, 301 Saint Paul Street, Baltimore, MD 21202. Tel: 410-332-1574; www.citifinancial.com.

Decision One Mortgage, 6060 JA Jones Drive, #1000, Charlotte, NC 28287. Tel: 704-887-2700; www.d1online.com.

Household Financial Services (HFC), 2700 Sanders Road, Prospect Heights, IL 60070. Tel: 847-564-5000; www.householdfinance.com.

New Century Financial Corp., 18400 Von Karman, Suite 1000, Irvine, CA 92612. Tel: 949-440-7030; Fax: 949-440-7033; www.ncen.com.

Washington Mutual Inc., 1201 3rd Avenue, Seattle, WA 98101. Tel: 206-461-2000; Fax: 206-554-4807; www.wamu.com.

Wells Fargo Home Mortgage, 420 Montgomery Street, San Francisco, CA 94163. Tel: 800-411-4932; www.wellsfargo.com.

Find a Partner and Get the Property You Want

If your credit is not the best, you must take giant steps to overcome this disadvantage. While taking a partner may not appeal to you, look at the benefits you can reap:

1. **You can buy the income property you want** when you have a partner with strong credit. Thus, you achieve your first goal—income property ownership.

2. **As you make each payment on the loans** you get to buy the property your credit rating improves. So while you're earning an income from your property you're also improving your credit rating!

3. **With the passage of each day** your ownership portion of the property (called your *equity*) increases. Thus, your Net Worth (what you own) rises as you sleep!

4. **As your credit rating score rises** and as your equity ownership increases your whole financial life becomes better. You become a more attractive borrower to lenders. Soon they may be chasing you, begging you to accept their loans!

5. **So, even though taking a partner who has good credit** may "turn you off," it could be just what you need to start acquiring $1 million in real estate property in one year.

When I suggest taking on a partner who has good credit so you can get both the down-payment and long-term mortgage loans:

- **I am not suggesting** that you give your prospective partner half ownership of the property.

- **Instead, I suggest** that you negotiate with your prospective partner, pointing out that buying the income property is your idea, that you will look for and evaluate possible properties, and that you will operate the property on a daily basis.

- **Based on these facts** you will offer your partner a 3 percent or 5 percent ownership in the property, along with a 50 percent share in the rise in the property's value at the time of sale. Most partners will agree to such terms.

So you see, taking on a partner is really not an onerous task for you. Instead, it gives you an opportunity to overcome poor credit and get into property ownership quickly.

How and Where to Find a Partner

Your best chance of finding a suitable partner is often in your local area. Why is this? Because:

- **You and local people** "speak the same language." By that I mean that you understand each other.

- **You and local people** know property values in your area better than most outsiders.

- **You and local people** can form a greater bond of trust than you can with strangers.

To find partners locally, take these easy steps:

1. **Prepare a short Business Plan** detailing what type of property you want to own, the typical profits a partner might earn, and what a partner's ultimate profit might be on sale of the property.

2. **Contact members of local** golf, country, and yacht clubs, telling them about your plans to invest in local, or nearby, income real estate. Tell them you have a Business Plan you will show to prospective partners.

3. **Meet with people interested in becoming a partner** by "lending" you their credit. Show enthusiasm when telling these prospects about your proposed income property purchase. Be completely honest in all your projections of costs and profits. But at the same time know what you're talking about. Impress your prospects with your strong work ethic, your reliability, and burning ambition to make every income property profitable.

4. **Call, or write, local medical, dental, and other health professional groups.** Tell your contact that you'd like to present an investment opportunity to their members at their monthly business meeting. Ask for 10 minutes of their time, during which you'll describe the real estate business opportunity to their members. You will also distribute data (your Business Plan) on the project. Many such groups are looking for speakers who can give an interesting presentation of the real estate business opportunity they have.

Once you have a partner with good credit you can move ahead to buy your first income property. Be certain to have the advice of a competent real estate attorney. That person should: (a) advise you on your partnership agreement, with particular attention to the percentage of ownership (make it as small as possible) you give up, and (b) the legal aspects of your property purchase.

Now let's look at other ways you can overcome bad credit, or no credit, and still get started in owning income real estate.

Get Owner Financing for Your Income Property

Some property owners are so anxious to sell they will overlook your credit rating and credit history. You must, of course, convince the seller that you will do a good job of managing the property you're taking over. To get owner financing (also called *seller financing*), take these easy steps:

1. **Look for property ads saying** "Owner financing," "Financing available," or any other version of these thoughts. You may be able to find such offers in your local large-city Sunday newspaper ads.

2. **Contact the advertiser quickly.** Don't wait! The offer may be snatched from your hands in just moments. Call, or visit, the advertiser as soon as you can.

3. **Analyze the property immediately.** Do a quick figuring of your Gross Rent Multiplier (GRM) by dividing the Price of the property by the Annual income of the property. If your GRM is between three and seven, you're on to a possible fortune. (I, as your author, will do a full free analysis of the numbers of your property if you're a one-year, or longer, subscriber to either of my wealth newsletters described at the back of this book.)

4. **Make a verbal offer on the property,** subject to the owner financing both the long-term mortgage (15 years, or longer) and the down payment, if your attorney later approves of the purchase. Such an offer should hold the property long enough for you to contact your attorney and get a quick opinion as to the legal aspects of your purchase.

5. **Move ahead with buying the income property** if the numbers work out (you MUST have a PCF) and your attorney believes there are no legal risks for you.

6. **Improve the property where it needs work,** using outside contractors if you can't do the work yourself. Then rent the property for a monthly PCF, or flip it for a profit. Owner financing can usually help you reach your financial goals, no matter what your credit rating is!

Why Consider Owner, or Seller, Financing?

Now why do I recommend that you consider owner, or seller, financing? There are a number of good reasons why you can benefit from owner financing, including:

- **You negotiate with just one person,** the seller. This means you don't have to make a trip to the lender's office. You save time, energy, and money!

- **You don't have to be interviewed by a lender.** Why? Because your seller is your lender! You're being "interviewed" while you're negotiating the sales price.

- **Bad credit/no credit may be acceptable** to the seller because he or she sees how honest and reliable you are. And such a seller is often willing to overlook a few past problems because he or she has probably had the same challenges. Or perhaps someone in his or her family has had similar credit problems.

- **The loan terms offered by private sellers** are often much more flexible than those forced on you by banks and other mortgage lenders. So you have greater freedom in negotiating your loan payment schedule and amount.

- **You can arrange an installment sale** so the seller has a smaller tax burden and is more willing to sell to you. To be sure you get the property, you can offer the seller his or her asking price. Nothing makes a seller happier than being paid the asking price! Your seller will be more willing to agree to monthly payments (an installment sale) because he or she is getting the asking price and saving taxes. Win/win for you and the seller!

- **Most seller financing deals** go through without a credit check. So your credit score is not reviewed. This means you have one less inquiry on your Credit Report. Result? Your FICO score does not go down because of an inquiry.

- **To make your seller happier** you can name him or her as the beneficiary on the property insurance policies until such time as you have reached a certain repayment level. This means that in the event of a fire, tornado, hurricane, or other disaster, the seller's asset is protected by insurance. Any payments you have made will also be covered by the insurance.

- **Seller financing is an excellent way** to transfer property that is otherwise nonfinanciable because it does not meet lender requirements. Thus, if a property fails building code rules but you can bring it into compliance because you have access to competent mechanics, seller financing is the way to go.

- **Your seller will usually be delighted** that you have an attorney review the terms of the deal. Why? Because the attorney also (in a way) protects the seller because the deal meets the local legal requirements. And a competent attorney will demand that a title search be made, to protect you. Likewise, your attorney will demand a termite inspection of the property—again to protect you.

- **Some sellers will agree to an interest-only loan** to ensure that the deal goes through. While an interest-only loan has risks for you (see Chapter 3), this type of loan can get you the property you seek.

- **As a final step in getting seller financing** you can have your attorney prepare papers to assign the deed to the seller. Why? In the event that you fail to make the required payments the seller can recover his or her property without a complex foreclosure action. This saves time and money. But it also gives the seller one more good reason to offer you 100 percent financing regardless of your credit rating or history of a bankruptcy. Again, WIN/WIN!

Here's a letter from a reader showing what you can do in income real estate if you have drive and dedication:

> "I can't put your book down! It has been absolutely phenomenal. I started my real estate investment career about 18 months ago. Since then I've purchased 17 single-family homes with a value of over $1 million. I've mortgaged out (taken cash out of these properties) more than $150,000 and have a positive cash flow of about $4,000 per month from the rents." (As an aside, these properties have given this reader $8,333 per month for 18 months, plus about $4,000 in PCF rents, or $12,333 per month, which is $2,868 per week! Not bad for a beginner!)
>
> —North Carolina

Join Your Local Apartment Owners Association

By joining your local Apartment Owners Association you can meet people who own income property in your area. And, after a while, some of these owners might offer you one or more properties they want to sell. You, as an ambitious BWB might be able to:

- **Convince an older seller** that you're just the right person to buy his or her beloved property and continue to offer the same fine service to his or her tenants for years to come.

- **Show the seller** that your written plans for the future of the property will improve its worth, upgrade its facade, modernize its interior, and give its tenants a better quality of life. You're the best potential buyer they've ever met. You're such a desirable potential buyer that your credit rating need not even be checked.

- **Help the seller save on income taxes** by arranging a legal and legitimate *installment sale* of the property to you in which you do not put down any cash. To arrange such a sale you must have the advice of a competent accountant and real estate attorney. Older members of the Apartment Owners Association may be unfamiliar with the many tax advantages to them of an installment sale. If you introduce them to the possibilities it is likely that they may pick you as the ambitious buyer they've been looking for, regardless of your credit rating!

Form a Limited Partnership to Raise Money to Buy Your Properties

A Limited Partnership is a popular way to raise money for income real estate. In such a partnership the limited partners invest anywhere from $5,000 to $5 million each per participation to enable the partnership to buy, and operate, investment real estate.

You, as General Partner, run the partnership, receiving a salary and other employee benefits. And you are usually awarded one participation as your reward for developing the partnership's Business Plan and running it on a daily basis. For most Limited Partnerships you do not have to spend eight hours a day operating it. Thus, you can have other business activities you can conduct for additional income. To form your Limited Partnership, take these easy steps:

1. **Choose the type of real estate** you think can earn big money for your future limited partners. Keep in mind at all times that investors seek profits from their investment choices. So the higher the profits you can offer them, the more likely they are to invest.

2. **Prepare a Limited Partnership Offering.** This is a Business Plan that tells what types of properties the partnership will invest in, how much profit might be expected from each property, and what "Exit

Strategy" (eventual sale of the properties and return of investors' cash) will be followed. While this Offering is not a sales document, it does give your potential investors an idea of what their future income from the partnership could be. You will find a typical real estate Limited Partnership Offering Agreement in the "Real Estate Riches Success Kit" listed in the Appendix at the back of this book. Such an Agreement can serve as an example when you decide to prepare your own. Your Agreement must be reviewed by a qualified attorney before you seek any investors for your Limited Partnership.

3. **Contact potential limited partners** and describe your proposed investment. Be certain to follow any local, and national, rules governing Limited Partnerships. Your attorney will explain these to you. Follow the steps given under the "How, and Where, to Find a Partner" section in this chapter to search for your future limited partners.

4. **Keep in mind at all times** that "it's the deal that counts, not your credit rating!" Set up a profitable Limited Partnership and you can overcome poor credit, no credit, bad credit, and so on!

Establish a Real Estate Investment Trust to Raise Big Bucks

A Real Estate Investment Trust (called a REIT [rhymes with "feet"] for short) is used to raise big bucks for many types of real estate investments. Thus, if you plan to raise $5 million to $250 million for real estate, consider a REIT. Again, your credit rating has no bearing on the REIT. What does count is the uniqueness of your REIT. "What do you mean by that," you ask. Here's your answer.

REITs are used to raise big money for almost every type of real estate known. Thus, there are dozens of apartment house REITs. So if you propose another such REIT it may not attract much attention. But if you'd like to start a REIT for:

- Apartment houses for handicapped people.
- Apartment houses for the elderly.
- Apartment houses for low-income people.

your chances of getting funding are much better. That's what we mean by the uniqueness of your REIT.

Starting your own REIT can help you acquire much more than $1 million for real estate in one year, or less. To do so you must have highly competent legal and accounting advice. While such guidance is expensive, some REIT founders pay for the advice with funds from the REIT public or private offering.

For help in forming your REIT, we suggest you use the helpful kit, *"How to Build Your Real Estate Fortune Today in a Real Estate Investment Trust"* Kit described in the Appendix at the back of this book. Again, your credit does not come into play in a REIT. What counts is whether the REIT can make money for its investors. You, as the REIT founder, share in its profits and property ownership.

Fund Your Commercial Real Estate with Hard Money

You've heard, we're sure, the term *hard money* if you've been in real estate for a while. Briefly:

> **Hard money is a loan based on the hard asset in a real estate transaction, namely the land and the building, if any.**

And hard money is characterized by several features, namely:

- **Higher interest rate** than prevailing rates in the area.
- **Faster closings**—sometimes within one week.
- **Less paperwork** than with traditional real estate loans.
- **Focus on the hard asset,** not the borrower's credit rating.

You can accumulate real estate using hard-money loans without ever having your credit reviewed. What a lender seeks in hard-money loans is:

- **A suitable commercial property** with strong income.
- **Potential for** income increases in the future.
- **Dedicated potential owner** (such as you) who will work to increase the value of the property.

"So," you ask, "what kinds of commercial properties are suitable for hard-money loans?" Here are typical properties that Hard-Money Lenders consider lending on:

- Apartment complexes.
- Townhouse developments.
- Residential (single-family homes) subdivisions.
- Strip centers and shopping malls.
- Hotels and motels.
- Golf courses.
- Nursing homes.
- Office buildings.
- Mixed-use (residential and commercial) properties.
- Industrial buildings.
- Mobile home parks.
- Plus many other types.

I'm sure t hat you can find one, or more, suitable properties among this list. And—best of all—you can own these properties even when you start with bad credit!

One way to start getting hard-money commercial real estate loans is to act as a Loan Broker for clients seeking such loans. With one Hard-Money Lender you earn 40 percent of the lender's profit on every funded loan. And this lender says commissions of $20,000, $30,000, and $40,000 are not unusual. Again, your credit rating does not have any influence on your commissions or your work as a hard-money Loan Broker.

Once you "learn the ropes" of hard money, you can find, and get financed, a project of your own. This will put you on your road to acquiring $1 million in real estate in one year in your free time. To get started as a hard-money Loan Broker with the goal of getting such funding for your own projects, see the "Hard Money Commercial Real Estate Finance Video Training Course" in the Appendix at the back of this book.

Assume an Existing Mortgage to Get Started

Your whole key—when you have poor, or no, credit—is to acquire ownership of at least one property and build from there. An excellent way for you to get your first property without your credit (or lack of it) getting in the way is to:

1. **Take over a property** having an Assumable Mortgage in which you start making payments one month after you acquire the property.

2. **Gain ownership** with NO credit check, NO review of your credit history, NO questions about your FICO score.

3. **Look for Veterans Administration and FHA mortgages** that are assumable. With such properties you can get started owning income real estate sooner than you might imagine.

4. **Search for insurance-company-issued mortgages.** Some such mortgages allow assumption without paperwork or other processing of any kind. Keep in mind that when you assume a mortgage you also become responsible for paying all of the seller's other obligations related to the property, including real estate taxes, mortgage payments, trash collection, fuel costs, maintenance of the building, and so on. Hence, you MUST have a PCF from the property.

5. **Have your attorney** (and you MUST have one) advise you as to the best way to assume ownership of the property. When you take title *"subject to an existing mortgage"* you become personally responsible for the mortgage payments. But when your attorney has you take the property *"subject to the mortgage"* you are not personally responsible for making the mortgage payments. You must, however, make these payments if you wish to eventually own the property. As you know, I'm just a real estate investor and business advisor, not an attorney. Hence, you MUST have these cautions reviewed by your attorney and you should follow that person's advice—not mine!

As you can see, assuming a mortgage can be a great benefit to you. But you must have competent legal guidance so your transaction is trouble free. Having a competent real estate attorney's advice will ensure a smooth and trouble free assumption of property by you.

Your Key Ideas for Overcoming Bad Credit/No Credit

❏ **Bad credit/No credit** will not prevent you from building real estate riches if you follow the guidelines in this chapter.

❏ **You can still acquire** your "dream property," even though your credit may not be the best.

❏ **Use lenders that accept** bad credit and you have a good chance to acquire the income real estate you seek.

❏ **Check out sub-prime lenders.** These lenders are accustomed to working with people having less than perfect credit.

❏ **Work with interested sub-prime lenders.** They may provide you with the financing you seek, despite past credit problems.

❏ **You can find sub-prime lenders.** All you need do is follow the easy directions given in this chapter.

❏ **Find a partner with good credit** and you can probably get your income real estate quickly and easily. Then rebuild your credit so you can go out on your own.

❏ **Follow the guidelines in this chapter** to find a qualified partner who can help you acquire the income property needed to build your riches.

❏ **Get owner (or seller) financing** for your income property. You can get your money much faster, and with hardly any extra paperwork.

❏ **Join your local Apartment Owners Association**—you can learn a lot from other members and they might sell you an excellent property.

❏ **Form a Limited Partnership to finance** your income properties. Such a partnership can get you started quickly.

❏ **Establish a Real Estate Investment Trust** (REIT) to fund your big real estate deals.

❏ **Fund your commercial real estate** with hard money and you'll get more deals closed.

❏ **Assume an existing mortgage** to get started with poor, or no, credit; you can prosper with zero cash down.

❏ **Never do any real estate deal** without the help and advice of a competent real estate attorney.

CHAPTER 8

Little-Known Alternative Money Sources for Real Estate Loans

WHEN YOU'RE LOOKING FOR A REAL ESTATE LOAN OF ANY KIND THE USUAL steps include applying at:

- **Banks.**
- **Credit unions.**
- **Mortgage brokers.**

Yet there is a little-known source few people are aware of. And even those who do know really don't try very hard to learn of all the programs this source offers, such as:

- **First-time** home-buyer programs.
- **Affordable-housing** programs.
- **Construction loans** for a variety of projects.
- **Rehab loans** for many types of buildings.
- **Multifamily property loans** and other assistance.
- **Historic preservation** of selected structures.

Get to Know Where You Can Find Funding

"So what is the source?" you ask. The source is your *STATE HOUSING FINANCE AGENCY.* In Canada it's your *Province Housing Finance Agency.* While the name of such an agency varies somewhat from one state or province to the next, the general goal is the same, that is:

- **Finance** needed real estate within the state or province borders.
- **Help provide** better housing and industrial facilities.
- **Encourage** the rehabbing of worthwhile buildings and homes.
- **Preserve** historic structures for future instruction of, and enjoyment by, state residents, and others.

You can contact your state housing finance agency by mail, by phone, by fax, by e-mail, or on the Internet. And you can download forms, letters, and other documents from the Internet from most state and province sites. For best results you should:

- **Decide in advance** what type of financing you need.
- **Focus on** that type of financing when contacting the agency. Some agencies are very large and you can get "lost" if you're not focused on the type of funding you need.
- **Treat agency employees with respect.** These people are helpful and anxious to do a good job for you. Be polite and you'll get great results!
- **Type ALL the forms** you must submit. Be businesslike in everything you do and you have an excellent chance of getting the real estate financing, or loan guarantees, you need from your state or province finance agency!

Important Money Availability Data for You

Here, for your use, are 53 housing finance agencies you can contact for data on their programs. For each agency you're given the name, address, telephone and fax numbers, toll-free phone number, if available, Internet address, and major types of programs offered.

Note that, in many states, you do not have to be a state resident to benefit from some of the programs offered. The real estate must—of course—be located in the state or province offering the benefits. In most states, if you are a resident, the benefits will be available to you in a shorter period of time.

"What happens," you ask, "if I'm not on the Internet and I want to download Loan Applications and other loan data for my state?" Your author will gladly have his staff do this for you free of charge for your state if you're a two-year subscriber to one of his newsletters described at the back of this book. Just ask him after you subscribe.

Now here is your list of state housing finance agencies in the United States. Canadian agencies follow the United States' listing.

State Housing Finance Agencies

Alabama Housing Finance Authority, P.O. Box 230909, Montgomery, AL 36123-0909. Tel: 334-244-9200; Fax: 334-244-9214; TTY: 334-271-6785; Toll Free: 800-325-2432; www.ahfa.com. Programs:

- Federal HOME Investment Partnerships Program provides loans and grants for multifamily housing development, acquisition and rehabilitation. Builders and developers may apply for multifamily mortgage revenue bond financing. The Alabama multifamily loan consortium provides additional funding. Low-income housing tax credits are available.

- Below-market interest rate loans, down payment assistance, and closing cost assistance are available to first-time home buyers.

Alaska Housing Finance Corporation, P.O. Box 101020, Anchorage, AK 99510-1020. Tel: 907-338-6100; Fax: 907-338-9218; www.ahfc.state.ak.us. Programs:

- Multifamily loan purchase program for five units or more with individuals, partnerships, joint ventures, and profit/nonprofit corporations as eligible borrowers; the Whole Loan Program provides 100 percent of finance amount; terms up to 30 years; loan proceeds may be used to acquire, refinance, moderately rehabilitate multifamily properties.

- Many other residential loan programs including mobile homes.

- Grants for a variety of real estate projects as defined by the state.

- Residential single-family, log-cabin, and other home loan programs. Down payment assistance and closing cost assistance are available to first-time home buyers.

Arizona Department of Housing/Arizona Housing Finance Authority. 1700 Washington, Suite 210, Phoenix, AZ 85007. Tel: 602-771-1000; Fax: 602-771-1002; TTY: 602-771-1001; www.housingaz.com. Programs:

- Private Activity Bonds financing is available for the development of rental housing in a rural or urban area.

- The State Housing Fund Program helps finance the development of qualified affordable rental properties. All financing is provided in the form of a loan.

- Home for Arizonans Program offers first-time home-buyers mortgage financing; down payment, and closing cost assistance; federal tax credits for individuals.

- Depending on the borrower's income level, offers up to 15 percent of the purchase price (or appraisal, whichever is less) for down payment and closing cost assistance.

Arkansas Development Finance Authority, 423 Main Street, Suite 500, Little Rock, AR 72201. Tel: 501-682-5900; Fax: 501-682-5859; www.state.ar.us/adfa. Programs:

- Tax-exempt multifamily housing bonds provide below-market-rate mortgages to developers who agree to set rents that are affordable to low- to moderate-income families. Low income housing tax credit is available to builders and developers of apartments for low-income families.

- Federal HOME Program funds may be used for rehabilitation of multifamily and single-family housing. Funds may also be used for new construction and addition of new units to existing properties.

- HomeToOwn (Mortgage Revenue Bond Program) offers low-interest rate loans to low- and moderate-income first-time home buyers. Down payment assistance is available.

California Housing Finance Agency, P.O. Box 4034, Sacramento, CA 95812. Tel: 916-322-3991; Fax: 916-324-8640; www.calhfa.ca.gov. Programs:

- Multifamily programs provide permanent financing for the acquisition, rehabilitation, and preservation or new construction of rental housing that includes affordable rents for low- and moderate-income families and individuals. Permanent loans, special-needs financing, tax-exempt bridge loans, predevelopment loans, preservation acquisition loans, HUD Section 202 refinancing program, and construction loans are available to qualifying developers, builders, and investors.

- Homeownership mortgage loan program is designed to enhance affordability and homeownership in the form of 30-year below-market fixed-rate loans up to 100 percent loan-to-value.

- Several mortgage loan programs with down payment assistance are available to home buyers/home owners. These include affordable housing, housing assistance, extra-credit teacher home purchase program, high-cost area home purchase assistance program, stand-alone down payment assistance program, and home choice program.

Colorado Housing and Finance Authority, 1981 Blake Street, Denver, CO 80202. Tel: 303-297-2432; Fax: 303-297-7305; TTY: 303-297-7305; www.colohfa.org. Programs:

- Offers various loans for acquisition, rehabilitation, new construction, and refinance of rental housing sponsored by private for-profit, non-profit, and public housing developers. Housing can be independent apartments or may be designed to serve group living needs of special populations.

- Loan products include construction/predevelopment, permanent loan financing, preservation lending.

- Offers many solutions and programs to get individuals and families their home, including 30-year fixed-rate mortgages, optional second mortgage for down payment and closing costs, free home-buyer education classes, and a network of qualified, experienced lending partners ready to help home buyers.

Connecticut Housing Finance Authority, 999 West Street, Rocky Hill, CT 06067-4005. Tel: 860-721-9501; Fax: 860-257-8614; www.chfa.org. Programs:

- Financing for creation of new or rehabilitated affordable multifamily units. Construction-to-permanent, or permanent "takeout" financing for multifamily housing. first mortgage loans for multifamily units with interest rates at or below conventional rates. Loan terms of up to 40 years for multifamily housing.

- Nonrecourse financing is offered on multifamily loans.

- Single-family home-buyer programs include Home Buyer Mortgage Program, Down Payment Assistance Program, Smart Move Second Mortgage Program, Police Homeownership Program, Military Homeownership Program, Section 8 Housing Choice Voucher Homeownership Program, and Rehabilitation Mortgage Loan Program.

Delaware State Housing Authority, 18 The Green, Dover, DE 19901-3612. Tel: 302-739-4263; Fax: 302-739-2415; TTY: 302-739-7428; www.2.state.de .us/dsha. Programs:

- Loans are available to investors, developers, local governments, and nonprofit organizations to develop affordable housing.

- The Housing Development Fund provides financing to create or rehabilitate affordable housing, or offer unique housing programs for low- or moderate-income persons.

- Multifamily Mortgage Revenue Bond Program issues bonds to finance new construction or rehabilitation of multifamily housing for low-income individuals and families.

- The Housing Capacity Building Program provides a range of assistance including capacity building grants.

- Low-interest mortgages, down payment assistance, and closing cost assistance are available to first-time home buyers.

District of Columbia Housing Finance Agency, 815 Florida Avenue NW, Washington, DC 20001. Tel: 202-777-1600; Fax: 202-986-6705; www .dchfa.org. Programs:

- Low-interest loans are available to housing developers through taxable and tax-exempt bond financing. Funds are intended to build and rehabilitate affordable and mixed-income housing in Washington.

- McKinney Act Loans can be used to finance the acquisition, predevelopment, and rehabilitation costs associated with a housing development. The loans are for organizations that may lack the financial resources to pay for the initial costs of planning and undertaking an affordable housing initiative.

- Below-market-rate mortgage financing, down payment assistance, and closing cost assistance are available for first-time home buyers. Acquisition/Rehabilitation Program Loans are offered to individuals looking to purchase and remodel a house.

Florida Housing Finance Corporation, 227 N Bronough Street Suite 5000, Tallahassee, FL 32301. Tel: 850-488-4197; Fax: 850-488-9809; www .floridahousing.org. Programs:

- The State Apartment Incentive Loan Program (SAIL) provides low-interest loans to affordable housing developers. These loans are available to individuals, public entities, for-profit and not-for-profit organizations for construction or rehabilitation of affordable multifamily housing.

- A number of homeownership programs are offered for first-time home buyers, low-income families and individuals, and people with special needs. Down payment assistance and closing cost assistance are available for first-time home buyers.

Georgia Housing and Finance Authority, 60 Executive Park South, NE, Atlanta, GA 30329-2231. Tel: 404-679-4940; Fax: 404-679-4844; www.dca .state.ga.us. Programs:

- Financing is available for for-profit and not-for-profit developers for the construction and/or renovation of affordable multifamily rental units.
- The Georgia Dream Homeownership Program makes purchasing a home easier for low- to moderate-income families and individuals by offering fixed, low-interest mortgage loans. Down-payment and closing-cost assistance is also offered to eligible borrowers.

Housing and Community Development Corporation of Hawaii, 677 Queen Street, Suite 300, Honolulu, HI 96813-5112. Tel: 808-587-0680; Fax: 808-587-3416; www.hcdch.hawaii.gov. Programs:

- The Hula Mae Multifamily Program promotes the development and rehabilitation of existing rental housing projects through the mortgage revenue bond financing, interim and/or permanent, at rates below market interest rates. Both for-profit and not-for-profit entities are eligible to apply for funding.
- Below-market interest rate mortgages, down payment, and closing cost assistance are available.

Idaho Housing and Finance Association, P.O. Box 7899, Boise, ID 83707-1899. Tel: 208-331-4889; Fax: 208-331-4804; TTY: 800-545-1833; www.ihfa.org. Programs:

- Affordable housing programs offering construction loans, subordinated financing, housing tax credits, and other benefits for developers.
- First-time home-buyer program offers excellent assistance for families and individuals seeking their first home. Offers grants for some home-related activities, such as home repair.

Louisiana Housing Finance Agency, 2415 Quail Drive, Baton Rouge, LA 70808. Tel: 225-763-8700; Fax: 225-763-8710; www.lhfa.state.la.us. Programs:

- HOME Program loans and grants provide permanent financing to for-profit companies and nonprofit organizations for development of low- and very-low income rental housing. Projects may receive subordinate, deferred mortgage loans payable on resale, refinancing, or default. Tax-exempt bond financing is available for developers and builders. The Affordable Housing Trust Fund provides loans and grants for acquisition, development, and preservation of low-income rental housing, group homes, and manufactured housing cooperatives. Low-income housing tax credits are available.

- Other programs include HOME/MRB Program Loans, Low-Rate Program Loans, MRB Assisted Program Loans, Rural Housing Development Loans, and down payment and closing cost assistance.

Maine State Housing Authority, 353 Water Street, Augusta, ME 04330-4633. Tel: 207-626-4600; Fax: 207-626-4678; TTY: 800-452-4603; www.mainehousing.org. Programs:

- Rental Loan Program offers loans to for-profit and nonprofit developers of large scale affordable apartment buildings. Predevelopment Loan Program provides interest-free loans to nonprofit borrowers for predevelopment costs of developing affordable housing. Low-income housing tax credits are available.

- First-time home-buyer loans with below-market interest rates, down payment/closing cost loans, and home improvement loans. Loan guarantees and mortgage insurance are available.

Maryland Department of Housing and Community Development, 100 Community Place, Crownsville, MD 21032-2023. Tel: 410-514-7001; Fax: 410-987-4070; 800-756-0119; Toll Free TTY: 410-514-7531; www.dhcd.state.md.us. Programs:

- Several loan programs are available for developers of affordable multifamily housing. Low-income housing tax credits are available, as are federal HOME Program loans and grants. Operating Assistance Grants, Capacity Building Grants, and Production Grants are awarded to nonprofits to develop and rehabilitate affordable housing. The Partnership Rental Housing Program makes loans of up to $75,000 per unit for rental housing. Bond financing is also available. The Affordable Housing Trust offers grants to create, preserve, and promote affordable housing.

- The CDA Maryland Mortgage Program provides low-interest mortgage loans to eligible home buyers in low- to moderate-income households. The Downpayment and Settlement Expense Loan Program offers 0 percent deferred loans up to $3,000 for down payment and settlement costs to low- and moderate- income home buyers.

MassHousing, One Beacon Street, Boston, MA 02108. Tel: 617-854-1000; Fax:617-854-1029;TTY:617-854-1025;www.masshousing.com.Programs:

- Tax-exempt bond financing, bridge loans, and low-income housing tax credits are available to builders and developers of rental housing. Construction and rehabilitation loans are also available for development of affordable single-family homes.
- Offers several first-time home-buyer programs with Low-Interest, Low- and No-Down Payment Mortgages. Down payment and closing cost assistance is available.

Michigan State Housing Development Authority, P.O. Box 30044, Lansing, MI 48909-7544. Tel: 517-373-8370; Fax: 517-335-4797; TTY: 800-382-4568; www.michigan.gov/mshda. Programs:

- HOME Team Advantage Program provides tax-exempt loans along with federal HOME Program loans and grants for rental housing developers and investors with projects in nonurban areas. Loans are also available for acquisition and preservation of affordable housing. Through the TEAM Program, tax-exempt financing is available for development of low- and moderate-income households.
- First-time home-buyer loans with below-market interest rates, down payment/closing cost loans, and home improvement loans.

Minnesota Housing Finance Agency, 400 Sibley Street, Suite 300, Saint Paul, MN 55101-1938. Tel: 651-296-7608; Fax: 651-296-8139; www.mhfa .state.mn.us. Programs:

- Deferred loans, grants, amortized first mortgage loans, housing tax credits, and operating subsidies are available to for-profit businesses and nonprofit organizations developing multifamily housing. Loans can be applied to new construction, rehabilitation, and other development costs.

- First-time home-buyer loans with below-market interest rates, down payment/closing cost loans, and home improvement loans.

Mississippi Home Corporation, P.O. Box 23369, Jackson, MS 39225-3369. Tel: 601-718-4642; Fax: 601-718-4643; www.mshomecorp.com. Programs:

- The Housing Tax Credit provides a tax credit or reduction each year for 10 years for owners and investors in affordable-income rental housing. The credit is based on the costs of development and the number of units. Fifteen-year fixed-rate permanent loan funds are available to developers completing construction through the Financial Institutions Housing Opportunity Pool. These loans pay off construction loans and have amortization periods of 20 to 30 years. The Affordable Housing Development Fund provides financing to developers of low-income housing.

- The Home Run Mortgage Program offers loans to low- and moderate-income first-time home buyers; down payment and closing cost assistance are available.

Missouri Housing Development Commission, 4625 Lindell Boulevard, Suite 300, St. Louis, MO 63108-3729. Tel: 816-759-6600; Fax: 816-759-6828; TTY: 816-759-6839; www.mhdc.com. Programs:

- Housing Trust Fund provides funding for acquisition and/or rehabilitation or new construction of rental housing for very low-income families, rental assistance, emergency housing aid, and home repair. HOME Program provides loans and grants for low-income housing development. Low-income housing tax credits are available for multifamily housing. The Affordable Housing Assistance Program offers tax credits to businesses, nonprofits, and individuals for constructing or rehabilitating affordable housing.

- Low-interest rate loans are available to first-time home buyers, as well as 6 percent down payment and closing cost grants, and home repair grants up to $20,000.

Montana Board of Housing/Housing Division, 301 South Park Avenue, Helena, MT 59601-6282. Tel: 406-841-2840; Fax: 406-841-2841; www .housing.mt.gov. Programs:

- HOME Program provides loans and grants for low-income housing development. Low-income housing tax credits are available for multifamily housing acquisition, construction and rehabilitation.
- Single-family homeownership program provides low-interest mortgage loans for first-time home buyers.

Nebraska Investment Finance Authority, 1230 O Street, Suite 200, Lincoln, NE 68508-1423. Tel: 402-434-3900; Fax: 402-434-3921; TTY: 800-833-7352; www.nifa.org. Programs:

- Loans are available to developers under the Bar-None program and to nonprofit housing development groups and others under the NebHi-RED program. Low-income housing tax credits, multifamily bond financing and loan guarantees are also available.
- Low-interest financing is available to qualified first-time home buyers for manufactured homes built under the Bar-None housing program. A lease-to-own program assists low-income families in achieving homeownership. Home Buyer Assistance Program provides down payment and closing cost assistance.

Nevada Housing Division, 1802 N. Carson Street, Suite 154, Carson City, NV 89701. Tel: 775-687-4258; Fax: 775-687-4040; Fax: 702-486-7220; Fax: 702-486-7226; www.nvhousing.state.nv.us. Programs:

- Multifamily Project Bond Financing Program provides loans for housing sponsors and developers. The HOME Program provides loans and grants to promote the purchase, rental, and rehabilitation of eligible multifamily properties. Funding is available for acquisition, new construction, reconstruction, moderate or substantial rehabilitation, site improvements, conversion, demolition, and certain soft costs.
- Low-income housing tax credits are available.
- Below-market interest rate mortgages, down payment, and closing cost assistance are available.

New Hampshire Housing Finance Authority, P.O. Box 5087, Manchester, NH 03108-5087. Tel: 603-472-8623; Fax: 603-472-8501; TTY: 603-472-2089; www.nhhfa.org. Programs:

- HOME Program loans and grants provide permanent financing to for-profit companies and nonprofit organizations for development of low- and very low-income rental housing. Projects may receive subordinate, deferred mortgage loans payable on resale, refinancing, or default. Tax-exempt bond financing is available for developers and builders. Affordable Housing Trust Fund provides loans and grants for acquisition, development, and preservation of low-income rental housing, group homes, and manufactured housing cooperatives. Low-income housing tax credits are available.
- Single-Family Mortgage Program provides first-time home buyers with below-market interest rate loans; Special Homeownership Program provides mortgages for households with special needs; down payment and closing cost assistance is available.

New Jersey Housing and Mortgage Finance Agency, P.O. Box 18550, Trenton, NJ 08650-2085. Tel: 609-278-7400; Fax: 609-278-1754; www.nj-hmfa.com. Programs:

- Multifamily Rental Financing program provides loans to nonprofit and for-profit developers for mortgage, construction, rehabilitation, and preservation of housing for low- and moderate-income families and individuals. Turnkey Construction Loan program provides up to 90 percent of the financing needed for certain types of housing. Developers and sponsors may be eligible for low-income housing tax credits.

- The Home Express program provides a streamlined application process for developers in need of loan subsidies.

- The Small Rental Project Loan Program offers loans for renovation and construction of 5 to 25-unit buildings.

- Several home-buyer programs are available, including down payment and closing cost assistance, below-market rate mortgages for first-time buyers, special loans for police and fire fighter families, and loans for renovation and rehabilitation. A 100 percent financing option is available for preapproved new or rehabilitated single-family housing developments and for certain newly constructed units.

New Mexico Mortgage Finance Authority, 344 4th Street, SW, Albuquerque, NM 87102-3206. Tel: 505-843-6880; Fax: 505-243-3289; www .housingnm.org. Programs:

- Developer programs provide funding for affordable multifamily and single-family housing—including rehabilitation and construction—carried out by private for-profit, not-for-profit and public housing developers. Short-term development loans, loan guarantees and Federal HOME Program loans and grants are also available.

- Provides a variety of assistance to first-time home buyers of low to moderate income, such as below-market interest rate loans, closing cost assistance and down payment assistance.

New York City Housing Development Corporation, 110 William Street, 10th Floor New York, NY 10038-3901. Tel: 212-227-5500; Fax: 212-227-6865; www.nychdc.org. Programs:

- The Housing Development Corporation is a mortgage lender for affordable, multifamily housing. It works directly with housing developers and other mortgage lenders to structure low-cost mortgage loans for many different types of affordable housing.

- Programs are available for low-income, middle-income, and mixed-income housing.

New York State Division of Housing and Community Renewal, Hampton Plaza, 38-40 State Street, Albany, NY 12207-2804. Tel: 518-473-8384; Fax: 518-473-9462; www.dhcr.state.ny.us. Programs:

- Manages approximately 15 different programs, which provide loans to builders and others for development of affordable housing, low-income housing, rural housing, and preservation and rehabilitation
- Assists renters and home buyers in finding affordable housing.

New York State Housing Finance Agency/State of New York Mortgage Agency, 641 Lexington Avenue, 4th Floor, New York, NY 10022-4503. Tel: 212-688-4000; Fax: 212-872-0789; www.nyhomes.org. Programs:

- Proceeds of tax-exempt bonds are used to provide low-cost loans to private and not-for-profit developers. Projects may also be eligible for Low Income Housing Tax Credits and subsidy loans. The All Affordable Program encourages the development of new or rehabilitated multifamily rental housing for low-income families through a variety of funding channels. Loans are provided for development of manufactured home parks and senior housing facilities.
- Through the New York State Affordable Housing Corporation, loans and grants are provided for new construction, acquisition and rehabilitation, and home improvement projects.
- The Construction Incentive Program provides 100 percent financing to builders and other eligible parties for new construction of one- and two-family homes.
- Down payment assistance, closing cost assistance, and below-market interest rate mortgages available. Additional programs available for first-time home buyers and low-income home buyers.

North Carolina Housing Finance Agency, P.O. Box 28066, Raleigh, NC 27611. Tel: 919-877-5700; Fax: 919-877-5701; www.nchfa.com. Programs:

- State housing credits, low-interest developer and investor loans, rental production program loans, multifamily tax-exempt bond financing, rehabilitation, and preservation loans.

- Most are available to for-profits and nonprofit organizations.
- Low-interest first-time home-buyer mortgage, down payment assistance, and closing cost assistance.

North Dakota Housing Finance Agency, P.O. Box 1535, Bismarck, ND 58502. Tel: 701-328-8080; Fax: 701-328-8090; TTY: 800-366-6888; www.ndhfa.org. Programs:

- Housing tax credits and reduced interest rates on loans available to for-profit developers and nonprofit organizations.
- Down payment assistance, closing cost assistance, rehabilitation funding, and low-interest rate home mortgage loans.

Ohio Housing Finance Agency, 57 East Main Street, Columbus, OH 43215. Tel: 614-466-7970; Fax: 614-995-1951; TTY: 614-466-1940; www.ohiohome.org. Programs:

- For developers and investors: Affordable Housing Tax Credits; HOME Program funding; Housing Trust funds available for new construction rental or homeownership units, conversion of nonresidential structures into rental or homeownership, acquisition and/or rehabilitation; multifamily bond financing.
- Home owner rehabilitation loans, loan guarantees, mortgage insurance, mortgage assistance, and down payment assistance.

Oklahoma Housing Finance Agency, 100 Northwest 63rd, Suite 200, Oklahoma City, OK 73116-8250. Tel: 405-848-1144; Fax: 405-840-1109; TTY: 405-848-7471; www.ohfa.org. Programs:

- HOME Program provides loans and grants for low-income housing development; Housing Trust Funds help finance new construction of rental or homeownership units. Additional programs: loans for conversion of nonresidential structures into rental or homeownership; acquisition and rehabilitation loans; rural housing funding; and multifamily bond financing.
- OHFA Advantage program provides below-market interest rates, down payment, and closing cost assistance for families.

Oregon Housing and Community Services, P.O. Box 14508, Salem, OR 97309-0409. Tel: 503-986-2000; Fax: 503-986-2020; www.ohcs.oregon.gov. Programs:

- Loan guarantee program promotes financing of new housing construction, acquisition, or rehabilitation. Lease guarantees are available to sponsors and leasing companies for assistance in financing housing for low- and very low-income families. Predevelopment loans, rural rehabilitation financing, and bond financing available.

- Single-family homeownership loan programs and vouchers; down payment and closing cost assistance; rehabilitation and home improvement loans.

Pennsylvania Housing Finance Agency, 211 N. Front Street, Harrisburg, PA 17101. Tel: 717-780-3800; Fax: 717-780-3905; TTY: 717-780-1869; www.phfa.org. Programs:

- Financing available to project sponsors of affordable rental housing; additional programs include federal HOME funding, housing tax credits, and bond financing for residential rental facilities.

- Homestead Second Mortgage Program and Keystone Loan Program assist first-time home buyers and others. Down payment assistance and home improvement loans are also available.

Rhode Island Housing and Mortgage Finance Corporation, 44 Washington Street, Providence, RI 02903. Tel: 401-751-5566; Fax: 401-457-1136; TTY: 401-427-9799; www.rihousing.com. Programs:

- Short- and long-term construction loans, bridge loans, first mortgages, deferred-payment second mortgages, federal low-income housing tax credits, and HOME Program grants and low-interest loans. Property types include everything from single-family houses to apartments to assisted living and other special needs housing.

- Low-interest mortgages for first-time home-buyers; down payment assistance grants equal to 3 percent of the loan.

South Carolina State Housing Finance and Development Authority, 300-C Outlet Pointe Boulevard, Columbia, SC 29210. Tel: 803-896-9005; Fax: 803-253-7698; www.schousing.com. Programs:

- Multifamily tax-exempt bond financing is offered to investors, developers, and rehabbers. HOME investment partnership promotes development of affordable housing by loans to developers.
- Single-family Homeownership Programs provide below-market interest rates to new home buyers.

South Dakota Housing Development Authority, P.O. Box 1237, Pierre, SD 57501-1237. Tel: 605-773-3181; Fax: 605-773-5154; www.sdhda.org. Programs:

- Provides housing tax credits to developers to build and rehabilitate housing for low-income households. HOME investment partnership promotes development of affordable housing; additional programs offer loans for rural site development.
- First-time home-buyer loans and down payment assistance programs.

Tennessee Housing Development Agency, 404 James Robertson Parkway, Suite 1114, Nashville, TN 37243-0900. Tel: 615-741-2400; Fax: 615-741-9634; www.tennessee.gov/thda. Programs:

- Tax-exempt bond financing available for multifamily housing development; low-income housing tax credit for owners and investors in low-income rental housing. HOME Program loans and grants to nonprofit organizations and local agencies.
- Down payment assistance; low-interest mortgages for low- and moderate-income home buyers.

Texas Department of Housing and Community Affairs, P.O. Box 13941, Austin, TX 78711. Tel: 512-475-3800; Fax: 512-472-8526; www.tdhca.state.tx.us. Programs:

- A wide array of programs administered by Texas state agencies focus on expanding and maintaining the supply of decent, affordable housing. Most programs provide loans or grants to individuals and organizations interested in developing affordable housing. Multifamily bond financing program assists developers.

- Home-buyer assistance, owner-occupied housing assistance, rental housing set-asides, down payment assistance, and housing tax credits are available.

Utah Housing Corporation, 2479 South Lake Park Boulevard, West Valley City, UT 84120. Tel: 801-902-8200; Fax: 801-359-1701; www.utah-housingcorp.org. Programs:

- The Low-Income Housing Tax Credit and the Multifamily Bonding programs are the most often utilized sources of financing for developers of affordable rental projects.
- Low-interest first-time home-buyer programs available.

Vermont Housing Finance Agency, P.O. Box 408, Burlington, VT 05402-0408. Tel: 802-864-5743; Fax: 802-864-5746; www.vhfa.org. Programs:

- Low-interest construction and permanent mortgage financing for development and preservation of affordable rental housing is available to for-profit businesses and nonprofit entities. Ten types of rental housing properties are eligible.
- Homeownership programs offered through participating lenders. MOVE program offers flexible down payment requirements and qualifying guidelines for borrowers based on credit history. Under the HOUSE program, home buyers team with a nonprofit housing group in exchange for home financing.

Virginia Housing Development Authority, 601 South Belvidere Street, Richmond, VA 23220. Tel: 804-782-1986; Fax: 804-783-6704; TTY: 804-783-6705. Toll Free: 800-968-7837; www.vhda.com. Programs:

- Four types of multifamily loan programs available to builders and developers, including tax-exempt bond financing for low-income housing, taxable bonds for new projects, below market interest rates, and housing for special needs populations.

- Several first-time home-buyer programs, including conventional fixed, FHA insured, interest only, and step rate loans are available.

Washington State Housing Finance Commission, 1000 Second Avenue, Suite 2700 Seattle, WA 98104. Tel: 206-464-7139; Fax: 206-587-5113; www.wshfc.org. Programs:

- Under the multifamily housing program for for-profit developers, tax-exempt bond money can be used for construction, rehabilitation, acquisition, and predevelopment costs of residential rental projects. Financing is also available to nonprofit organizations for multifamily housing and facilities such as schools.
- Down payment assistance; programs offering low rate and fee options for first mortgage.

West Virginia Housing Development Fund, 814 Virginia Street East, Charleston, WV 25301. Tel: 304-345-6475; Fax: 304-340-9943; Toll Free: 800-933-9840; TTY: 304-345-5728; www.wvhdf.com. Programs:

- Development financing programs for builders and developers provide financing for construction and land development; a rental unit development program offers leveraged development loans, rehabilitation loans, construction loan incentives, and Low-Income Housing Tax Credits.
- For single-family homes: Single-Family Bond Program, Secondary Market Program, Refinancing Program, Closing Cost and Down Payment Assistance Loans, Employer Assisted Loan Program, Housing Emergency Loan Program.

Wisconsin Housing and Economic Development Authority, P.O. Box 1728, Madison, WI 53701. Tel: 608-266-7981; Fax: 608-261-5928; www.wheda.com. Programs:

- Tax credits and tax-exempt bond financing fund real estate development and provide loans for construction, acquisition, and rehabilitation of affordable multifamily rental housing. Additionally, construction loans, rental housing accessibility loans, and HOME Program loans and grants are available.

- Home-buyer programs offer down payment assistance and lines of credit for future home repairs. A housing grant program awards grants for providing housing for groups with special needs, such as low-income or elderly persons.

Wyoming Community Development Authority, 155 North Beech Street, Casper, WY 82601-1907. Tel: 307-265-0603; Fax: 307-266-5414; www.wyomingcda.com. Programs:

- Through the HOME Investment Partnerships Program, private developers and nonprofit organizations can apply for funding for development of safe, affordable housing for low- and very-low-income households. Funds may be used for rental housing production and home rehabilitation.

- Standard home-buyer program for low-income and moderate-income first-time home buyers; down payment assistance; loans for buying and rehabbing substandard houses; mortgage loans for newly built homes; and incentives for employers to make home loans to employees.

Canadian Mortgage Funding Assistance

Some Canadians are unaware of the Canadian Mortgage and Housing Commission (CMHC). The CMHC is a government agency providing mortgage loan insurance to ensure the availability of housing funding to Canadians. CMHC states that it reduces the down payment needed to buy a home to 10 percent of the purchase price, or 5 percent for first-time home buyers.

CMHC funding is used widely throughout Canada and can be obtained from any CMHC-approved lender. Besides providing mortgage assistance. CMHC also supplies housing information to the public. Full information on the many programs CMHC provides can be obtained at:

Canadian Mortgage and Housing Corporation (CMGC)
Suite 200, Royal Insurance Building
28 Cumberland Street North
Thunder Bay, Ontario P7A 4K9
Canada
Tel: 807-343-2010; Fax: 807-345-0696
Mailing Address: P.O. Box 2026, Thunder Bay, Ontario P7B 5E7, Canada.

U.S. Government Loan Help

The U.S. Government, through the Department of Housing and Urban Development (HUD), Veterans' Administration (VA) and the Farm Service Agency (FSA) has numerous programs to guarantee real estate loans for both multi- and single-family homes of many types. These guarantees can be a great help to you.

You'll find these three agencies listed in the government section of your local telephone book. You can reach these agencies on the Internet at: www.hud.gov; www.va.gov; www.fsa.gov.

HUD has a number of loan guarantees, including:

- Section 221(d) Low/moderate income housing.
- Section 203(k) Rehabilitation housing.
- Section 203(b) Single-family homes.
- Section 203(i) Outlying-area single-family homes.
- Title 1 Manufactured homes.

The VA has some assumable loans. And the VA sometimes has auctions of foreclosed homes with excellent financing terms.

Likewise, the FSA has a number of useful programs for rural housing. Its FSA 502 program deserves your attention, as does its 504b program for home repair.

Your Key Ideas for Little-Known Money Sources

❏ **State, and city, loan sources** can be valuable suppliers of money for your income real estate wealth building.

❏ **Both multifamily and single-family money sources** are available from most state housing agencies.

❏ **The Canadian government** offers loan guarantees for Canadian citizens needing help in buying a home.

❏ **Several U.S. Government departments,** namely HUD, VA, and FSA have excellent loan guarantee programs, plus other income real estate assistance.

 **CHAPTER 9**

100 Percent Financing Is Alive and Well Today

100 PERCENT FINANCING IS A SIMPLE AND PROVEN METHOD IN WHICH YOU borrow ALL the money you need to take over ownership of an income producing real estate property. You do NOT have to use any of your own money to purchase the property. And you do NOT have to take any money out of your personal, or business, savings accounts to buy the income property.

Since many people ask me searching questions about 100 percent financing, I want, as your author, to be sure we're all "on the same page" about the techniques of 100 percent financing of income real estate. So we'll describe it a bit more.

Understand Today's 100 Percent Financing

Here's a real-life example to show you how 100 percent financing might work for you. This is a typical situation you could meet:

An income property is for sale for $100,000. A 90 percent first mortgage is available for $0.90 \times \$100,000 = \$90,000$. So you need 10 percent, or $10,000, for the down payment on the property. If you can borrow the $10,000 down payment you will have 100 percent financing because your two loans = $90,000 + $10,000 = $100,000 which *equal the price of the property. So you have financed 100 percent of your purchase.*

This real-life example brings out several important points about 100 percent financing. These points are:

- **You almost always need** two, or more, loans on an income property to obtain 100 percent real estate financing.
- **The first mortgage,** which can range from 75 percent to 95 percent of the purchase price of the property, is usually relatively easy to obtain because the income property itself is the collateral for the loan.
- **When you can borrow** the full down payment for the income property, you are able to secure 100 percent financing for the income real estate.
- **You do not take any money** out of your savings to buy the property on which you're getting 100 percent financing.

100 Percent Financing Can Work Fast for You

Here's a letter from a lady subscriber to our *International Wealth Success* newsletter telling how she acquired some $1 million in income real estate in less than one year on borrowed money:

> "You started me on income real estate. Last week I found a 'don't wanter'—a property the owners wanted to get rid of. We had just bought a foreclosure from a bank. I got a private investor to put up the money for 30 days, including the fix-up costs, after which I would refinance it. While there I noticed a lawn sign down the street. I jotted down the telephone number that was on the sign and called. I had a good conversation with the seller and he suggested we meet. When we met he brought along his lady business partner who was the investor in the property. She had to go north (this is Florida) and he did not want to run the property without her because there are

> 19 properties with a total of 29 rental units. Most of the rental units have positive cash flows. They invited me to take all of the properties and units—which I did. So I spent two days of writing 'Agreements for Deed' with 'O' down. The seller takes a payment to include the mortgage now and the portion he has in equity. Now all I do is start collecting rents and making payments. The positive cash flow is about $2,000 per month. I am an instant landlord! My portfolio of 19 properties totals almost $800,000. Two days' worth of work from one phone call on a 'ratty' looking lawn sign. This should be an inspiration to BWBs to make telephone calls on those lawn signs, especially if the sign looks weather beaten!" —Florida

Reading this letter gives you several real-life key pointers that can help you build your riches in real estate. These pointers are.

- **Follow your instincts** when looking for real estate bargains. This lady says a weather-beaten sign can lead to interesting results—and it did.

- **Don't be afraid to meet** with motivated sellers. You may find a don't wanter—a property a seller does not want—and is ready to sell at a low price.

- **Look for zero-down deals.** You may find them in the most unlikely places. In this letter it was behind a ratty lawn sign.

- **Never buy without being sure** you'll get a Positive Cash Flow (PCF)—in this case $2,000 per month after paying all expenses, and mortgages.

- **Be willing to cooperate** with the seller on details of your transaction. Doing so can put big bucks into your pocket.

- **Go-getters find 100 percent financing** because they actively look for it. You must be willing to look in every place in your area where 100 percent financing may be available. When you look you learn.

And when you learn you have the chance of the 100 percent financing that can lead to your ownership of $1 million in real estate in one year, in your spare time. The lady who wrote the letter earlier reached this goal in a lot less than one year!

Know the Important Facts about 100 Percent Financing

Keep these important facts about 100 percent financing in mind at all times:

- **100 percent financing** DOES work—every day of the week.
- **100 percent financing** CAN work—if you work at it.
- **100 percent financing** is one of the smartest ways for you to get started in income real estate.
- **100 percent financing** is the lever that gets Beginning Wealth Builders (BWBs) into income real estate even though he or she may have poor credit, or no credit, or a recent bankruptcy.
- **100 percent financing** may be the only way a beginner can get into income real estate investing, especially if he or she has big credit-card debt, low, or no, income and little hope of a bright future on a job, or in a business other than real estate.

Your First Steps to 100 Percent Financing

There are dozens of ways for you to get 100 percent financing today. Let's first look at the most direct ways you can get 100 percent financing now.

Use the 80/20 Product

Talk to mortgage bankers today and some will say: "Use the 80/20 product." And just what is the 80/20 product? The 80/20 product is:

A loan for an income property that provides an 80 percent long-term first mortgage (typically 30 years) and a 20 percent Down Payment loan that is called a Home Equity Loan *(HEL) for the balance of the price of the property. Lenders that want to move mortgage money into the market offer such loans around the country. Why? It helps them get money out on good properties that are rising in value as time passes. So the collateral for their money becomes worth more as time passes. In the previous example for the $100,000 property, the first mortgage would be 80 percent of the purchase price, or $80,000. Then your down payment Home Equity Loan would be $20,000, or 20 percent of the purchase price. Thus, you have the 80/20 product!*

Help Mortgage Bankers Lend More Money

Most mortgage bankers want to lend more money on income properties. Why? Because their largest income is derived from mortgage loans they make on good properties. So to get more money out into the real estate loan marketplace, mortgage bankers will make 100 percent loans. Thus, here are portions of two typical ads recently run by mortgage bankers in the real estate section of a large national newspaper:

The second ad says:

At my company, IWS, Inc., we specialize in searching for such lenders, evaluating them, assembling the loan data in a logical format, and then publishing the list for BWB real estate investors. With each lender we provide the name, address, and telephone number. This information is omitted from the previous ads because the data may change during the long life of this book.

Since you now know how anxious mortgage bankers are to put their money to work in good real estate loans, you can start applying for 100 percent financing in your area. Be sure to follow earlier recommendations in this book, namely:

- **Deal only** with lenders who make your type of loan.
- **Prepare** a neat Loan Application.

- **Type** your Loan Application throughout.
- **Don't hassle** the lender for an answer; be patient.
- **Accept a lender's offer;** get the loan; then refinance.
- **Don't worry about a high interest rate** if you can pay all loans on the property and have a PCF every month.

Have Your Seller Finance the Down Payment

An anxious seller will help you buy his or her property with 100 percent financing if he or she believes, you will run the business profitably. So how, and why, does a seller become anxious? Here are a number of common reasons for seller anxiety:

- **The property has been on the market** a long time and the seller is worried that it won't "move"—sell. "The lawn sign is weather beaten."
- **The seller has a time commitment** to go elsewhere—job transfer, close on another property, pay off a loan with some of the proceeds from the sale, and so on.
- **External pressures on the seller**—a divorce settlement, an estate sale, a desire to move to another climate, and so on—are pushing him or her into a quick sale.
- **"Ownership fatigue"**—the seller is "burned out," "tired," "had it up to here" with a property and "just wants out," as you'll frequently hear.
- **Career change**—the seller wants to leave single-family homes to invest in multifamily units. Or the seller wants to go from residential properties to office buildings, industrial units, commercial suites, or shopping malls.

Winning the Property from a Motivated Seller

Any of these reasons can be a "foot in the door" for you acquiring income real estate that can make you wealthy. So take these easy steps when you find a motivated seller:

1. **Figure out why the seller is anxious.** Most sellers will give you clues when you talk to them about the property. Remarks like "I've had it," or "I have to get into a warmer climate; this cold weather is 'killing me,'" will help you understand why the seller wants to get out in a hurry.

2. **"Play" to the seller's emotions.** That is, be understanding about a seller "having had it," or "hating the cold weather." By being understanding and sympathetic with the seller you build a friendship bridge that could get you the 100 percent financing you seek.

3. **Figure out how you might improve the cash flow** from the property without offending the seller or giving large rent increases to long-term tenants. By increasing the cash flow you indirectly tell the seller that you'll be better able to repay any loans made to you on the property.

4. **Try to have the seller finance your purchase of the property.** Why? Because:
   - **Seller financing** is much faster than other types of financing.
   - **Seller financing** often skips a credit check and credit history review, so it does not show up on your Credit Report.
   - **Seller financing** can be at a lower rate than currently charged by big lenders.
   - **Seller financing** may not be recorded; this gives you greater freedom for future loans.
   - **Seller financing** is often the best deal for BWBs anywhere.

5. **Become your seller's "helper"** to allow him or her to achieve his or her stated goal while allowing you to get the property you want with 100 percent financing. Set up a "Win-Win" situation in which the seller is the big winner but you also come out a quiet—but successful—winner, too! Result? Two happy people with you on your way to your real estate fortune!

Look Into Government Sales of Property

A number of government agencies may have—on occasion—100 percent financing for properties they want to get off their books. These agencies include:

- Farm Service Agency.
- FHA—Federal Housing Administration.
- Internal Revenue Service.
- Veterans Administration.

In addition, your large local city, and the state in which it is located, may also have agencies offering properties for sale with 100 percent financing. You'll find such agencies listed in your local telephone book on the Government Pages. To deal with any agencies—federal or state—take these easy steps:

1. **Contact the agency** by phone, postal mail, or e-mail. Tell the agency you're interested in getting information on their property sales. This will be sent to you free of charge.

2. **Review the information** you receive. With some agencies you might receive information on both real estate and other property offered for sale—such as seized autos, boats, aircraft, clothing, jewelry, and so on. You'll probably pass over these items because they do not enhance your real estate career.

3. **Choose the real estate properties** that interest you. Attend an auction that is being held to sell real estate of this type. Unless there's a property you "just must have," attend as a spectator eager to "learn the ropes." Watch what goes on. Take notes about bidding procedures, prices paid, type of property purchased, and the kinds of people who buy—speculators, builders, rehabbers, and so on. Bring yourself "up to speed" on the way auction properties are bought. Make notes on any properties that are not sold at the auction because bidders aren't interested in buying them. These properties could make you rich.

4. **Follow up and check to see if there are any "post auction" properties available.** Such properties are the ones that did not sell at the auction. Why? There could be many different reasons, such as:
   - **Poor condition**—buyers often seek pristine properties that don't require much work.
   - **Unattractive location**—this can turn buyers away.
   - **Too small,** too big, too far away, and so on.

While these negatives may turn away some buyers, you can deal with them if you get 100 percent financing because with no cash input you have lots of room to convert a negative to a positive. For most BWBs the post auction buys are a gold mine of opportunity. Find out who to contact for post auction data on unsold properties.

5. **Contact the post auction data source.** This person is probably charged with "dumping the property" as fast as possible. You can help the "dumper" do his or her job quickly and efficiently by taking over the unit with 100 percent financing. Sometimes the agency seller will even pay the closing costs to make it easier for a buyer to obtain the property. And the seller will often have his or her attorney act as your attorney so you have no legal costs. It's always wise, of course, to hire an independent attorney to look over the papers before you sign any. This will protect you from mistakes that might be made during the rush to "get the properties off the books."

6. **Use your 100 percent financed property to build your wealth.** Take over the property from the agency and:
   • **Rent it out** for a monthly income if this is in your wealth plan for yourself. Or: **Flip the property** for an immediate profit on the sale.

The whole key for you is to use your 100 percent financing as the first step to acquiring $1 million in real estate in one year in your spare time. Thus:

• **With rental real estate** you use the equity (ownership) you have in the property as collateral for a loan to buy more income property, aiming at reaching your total goal of $1 million, or more.

• **With flipping of properties** you use the cash profit you receive from the sale to buy larger properties to reach your total goal.

Buy Undervalued Properties and Get 100 Percent Financing

You can get 100 percent financing of income property by "doing your homework" early. Here's what you can do for quick results using undervalued property:

- **Choose an area** of a city, town, or state you want to buy property in.
- **Become a "mini-expert"** on this area by studying what are called the "comps" or "comparables" for the area. This means you study the prices for various size properties sold in the area. Do this by getting info from local real estate agents, from the county records, and so on. Get to know what a two-bedroom home sells for, a three-bedroom, and so on. Or the selling price of a small 10,000 square feet office building, and so on.
- **Look for undervalued properties** in the area. Such properties might need some minor exterior cosmetic work. Or they may not be fully rented and you can work to find suitable tenants quickly.
- **Estimate—using the "comps"**—what the property will be worth after you have the cosmetic or rental work done. Your fixed-up value should be 25 percent more than what you plan to pay for the property.
- **Plan on buying,** fixing, and then refinancing the property quickly after you acquire it.
- **Activate your down payment strategy** using the following down-payment loan technique.

Get a Down-Payment Loan Guarantee

Some BWBs have trouble borrowing the down payment for an undervalued property for which they need 100 percent financing. Friends, relatives, and other people they approach to borrow the down payment money are reluctant to part with funds they have in the bank, in a 401(k), or other savings account. If you need a guarantee for a down payment loan you can overcome such reluctance described earlier in this way:

- **Ask the person** you're seeking money from to guarantee (cosign) with you on a loan for the down payment.
- **Tell your guarantor** that he or she need not supply even one penny—all you're asking for is their signature on a piece of paper.
- **Give your loan guarantor** a written promise to repay the down payment loan within two months after you receive his or her guarantee.
- **Use your loan guarantee** to borrow the down payment for the property.

- **Acquire the property;** do some minor fix up, as detailed previously, using local contractors for the work.
- **Have the property reappraised** at the higher value.
- **Refinance the property** at the higher value.
- **Use the excess cash** you get from refinancing to pay off the down payment loan and as seed money for the down payment on your next property. Thus, you have 100 percent financing of your first property and you're on your way to acquiring your second property the same way.

Now let's look at an actual set of numbers to see how this might work for you. We'll use a property underpriced at $100,000 in an area where similar properties sell for $140,000, and up. Here are your numbers:

Price: $100,000

Down payment: 20 percent, or $20,000

Fix up cosmetics: $5,000

Sale price after fix up: $142,000

Your gross profit after you sell the fixed up property = $142,000 − $100,000 = $42,000

Repayment of the down-payment loan = $20,000

Your net after repaying the down payment = $42,000 − $20,000 = $22,000

Fee to your loan guarantor @ 10 percent of loan = $2,000

Net to you after paying cosigner = $20,000 − $2,000 = $18,000

Other costs of the sale (cosmetic fix up, interest, legal) = $6,000

Your Net Profit = $18,000 − $6,000 = $12,000

You can use your net profit of $12,000 as the down payment on other income properties. By using this plan, or a similar one, you can soon acquire enough properties to reach your goal of $1 million in one year in your free time.

Fifteen More Ways to Get 100 Percent Financing for Real Estate

One of the most frequently asked questions about real estate is: "How, and where, can I get 100 percent financing for the income real estate I want to buy or flip?" Following are 15 more ways you can get 100 percent finance for income real estate.

But before giving you these methods we want you to understand, again, what is meant by 100 percent financing. It is:

- **You borrow** the down payment from one lender—typically 10 percent to 25 percent of the purchase price—$10,000 to $25,000—on a $100,000 purchase price for an income property.
- **You get a long-term mortgage** for 15 to 30 years for the balance of the purchase price—$90,000 or $75,000—for this project from another lender—usually a traditional real estate mortgage lender. You will usually have two lenders with 100 percent financing, unless you use a Private Lender that may make a 100 percent loan to you, depending on your income property project and its future promise.
- **You usually will have little trouble** getting the long-term mortgage because the property is the collateral for it.
- **Your challenge,** then, is to get the down payment loan you need to buy the income property of your choice.

Now here are 15 more ways for you to get 100 percent financing for the income real estate you want to buy:

1. **Use credit-card lines** of credit—3 lines @ $10,000 each = $30,000.
2. **Get a personal signature loan**—such loans go up to $50,000.
3. **Take an equity loan** on other property you currently own.
4. **Have the seller issue** you a purchase-money (PM) mortgage for the down payment on the income property you want to buy.
5. **Let the seller take out** a loan for the down payment; you assume responsibility for paying off the loan and make the payments.

6. **Borrow actively traded stocks** or bonds and use them as collateral for your down payment loan.

7. **Get a second mortgage** on the property and use this as your down payment.

8. **Buy the property** using a Lease-Option with zero down and part of your monthly lease payment being used for your down payment.

9. **Use a government program** (federal, state, or city) offering property with zero down payment.

10. **Look for repossessed** and nonperforming-loan properties offered to you at zero down payment by banks and other mortgage lenders.

11. **Finance the income property at its market value** with the purchase price at a lower value; use the difference for your down payment.

12. **Assume the existing long-term mortgage** on the property and have the seller take a second mortgage from you for your down payment.

13. **Get a mortgage** from a Private Lender for 100 percent of the property value.

14. **Use a Hard-Money Lender** for a 100 percent loan—such lenders may be very aggressive on solid property deals.

15. **Refinance other property** you own to get the down payment money you seek. Use part, or all of the proceeds, for your down payment.

Where Can I Use 100 Percent Financing?

Now that you know how, and where, to get your 100 percent financing, your next question, logically, is "Where can I use 100 percent financing to acquire $1 million in real estate in one year in my free time?" There are dozens of types of properties you can use 100 percent financing for. Here are some of them:

- **Single-family homes** of many types are available with 100 percent financing. And these homes need not be "starter" (first-home) types. They can be almost any type of home you might choose to own for income, or residential, purposes.

- **Multifamily homes** (apartment houses, garden apartments, townhouses, etc.) can be financed with 100 percent borrowed money.

And you can have a PCF with such properties even though you acquire them with none of your own money. Some larger multifamily properties can provide a gross income of more than $250,000 per year, before expenses.

- **Unusual properties—such as islands**—are sometimes available with 100 percent financing. Why? Because it takes a certain type of person to be attracted to such properties. You must have a kinship with the water and marine life to appreciate island living. Yet you can earn a large income from summer rentals of island properties that can rise in value as time passes. And the longer you own an island property, the higher—in general—will its summer rental cost rise. So you have a double reward—a rise in the property value and a rise in its rental income. Few other businesses offer you such advantages.

- **View-type properties** are another unusual type of real estate that can be available with 100 percent financing. Thus, you may have city, water, land, mountain, or a combination of any of these views. And a view property is almost always easy to rent or sell. Why? Because people love to glance out their window and see a familiar landscape, bay, mountain, and so on.

- **International properties**—those in another country—can make you rich sooner than you might imagine. Real estate is booming throughout the world. And you can get in on this boom if you plan your future carefully and become familiar with international real estate investing. More and more overseas lenders are into real estate, making property loans easier for you to get.

- **Student housing** is expanding as the population grows and more young people enroll in colleges throughout the country. You can get 100 percent financing for such properties because the cash flow from student rents and Internet services leased to occupants is predictable. Your cash flow projections can show prospective lenders how you can pay for the mortgage on the property.

- **Motels and hotels** can be a steady source of income for you when you operate them on an absentee basis. And the earnings from such properties are predictable and can pay off your mortgage in record time. Thus, 100 percent financing can allow you to acquire such properties while enabling them to pay for themselves and give you a monthly PCF.

Four Secrets to Getting 100 Percent Financing for Any Type of Property

You can improve your chances for getting the 100 percent financing by taking these four easy steps:

1. **Get the Income and Expense Statement** for the property you want to acquire. Or construct an Income and Expense Statement for a property you plan to build, or rehab.

2. **Prepare a Cash Flow Statement** showing how the income from the property can pay for all expenses, plus your long-term mortgage (15 to 30 years), and your down-payment loan. You must have a PCF from every property after paying all expenses.

3. **Present your Cash Flow Statement** to a Second Mortgage Lender, Private Lender, Real Estate Investors, or other money sources to convince them to make your down payment loan. The long-term mortgage seldom is a problem because the real estate collateralizes it.

4. **Keep applying at suitable lenders** until you get your down-payment loan. I'll be happy to help you find suitable lenders if you're a subscriber to both my newsletters, described at the back of this book. *REMEMBER: It takes just ONE lender to fund your down-payment loan.* Once you have your first property you're on your way to acquiring $1 million in real estate in one year in your free time.

Down-Payment Grants Can Help You Get 100 Percent Financing

A down-payment grant gives you the money you need to buy either a single-family or multifamily property. The grant can be either for your personal residence or for an income property. And the grant immediately gives you 100 percent financing, the subject of this chapter.

At present there are several organizations making such grants. As your author I will be happy to supply the names of such organizations for your area if you're a subscriber to both my newsletters, described at the back of this book. Since each area requires research for the latest name, address, and telephone number, I've had to omit them from this book. Further, with so many areas in all 50 states, the space required could fill several books of this size.

Just remember: *A grant is money you NEVER have to repay, if you use it to buy real estate!* So your down-payment grant will truly give you 100 percent financing of an income property. Can you ask for anything more? You will get what the title of this chapter promises you!

Your Key Ideas for 100 Percent Financing of Real Estate

❑ **100 percent financing** is a simple and proven method in which you borrow ALL the money you need to take over an income-producing property.
❑ **You almost always need** at least two loans to obtain an income producing property with 100 percent financing—the down-payment loan and the long-term mortgage loan.
❑ **100 percent financing can work fast for you.** Thus, one reader obtained $800,000 worth of real estate in two days with zero cash down.
❑ **Never be afraid to meet motivated sellers.** Your life can be changed for the better in just minutes when you take over an income property for zero cash down.
❑ **Keep looking for zero-down deals.** Looking costs you almost nothing but can bring you a fortune sooner than you think.
❑ **Use the 80/20 product.** It's popular today in many parts of the country for new construction, and for existing properties. This product gives you 100 percent financing in just moments.
❑ **Search for lenders advertising "100 percent financing."** There are plenty of them out there. All you have to do is find one in your area.

❏ **Seller financing** can be a quick, short way to 100 percent financing when you've exhausted other options.

❏ **Motivated sellers** may be able to provide the financing you need, especially if their property has been on the market for six months, or longer.

❏ **Government sales** of foreclosed properties can be a lucrative source of zero-down properties for you.

❏ **Buy undervalued properties** and your chances of getting 100 percent financing are stronger than with traditional purchases.

❏ **Get a down-payment loan guarantee** and you increase your 100 percent financing chances enormously. Try it and see for yourself!

❏ **Down-payment grants** are available for both single-family and multifamily homes. Check your area for their availability after getting the source from your author.

CHAPTER 10

Use Property Appreciation to Build Your Real Estate Wealth

INCOME REAL ESTATE USUALLY RISES IN VALUE AS TIME PASSES. WHY? Because the components of income real estate, namely:

- Land.
- Labor.
- Materials.

increase in cost as time passes. So the longer you own income real estate, the higher—in general—will its price rise. This price rise gives you an opportunity to earn a profit by selling your real estate at a higher price than you paid for it. In this chapter, we show you how to do this while acquiring $1 million in real estate in your free time on borrowed money in one year.

Eleven Easy Steps to Building Wealth through Property Appreciation

Here's an easy way for you to earn big money from the natural appreciation that occurs with most real estate. Once you learn how to use these steps we'll take you through actual ways you can use them in real-life situations.

Here are your 11 steps:

1. **Obtain the increase in price (appreciation) data for an area** you want to invest in. You can get this free from local real estate brokers, from newspapers serving the area, from your local Apartment Owners Association, and from the city and county tax records that often give the purchase and sale price of real estate.

2. **Express the price increase in percentage and in dollars** or whatever other monetary system you're using—euros, pesos, francs, and so on. Your most important number is the percentage—5 percent, 10 percent, 15 percent, and so on. Why? Because with a known price for a property you can project your potential profit.

3. **List the types of properties having the largest percentage and dollar** appreciation. Thus, they might be single-family units, 2 family, 10 family, and so on.

4. **Choose the type of property having the highest percentage increase** as the kind you'll invest in. Remember: You're in this for the profit you'll earn when you eventually sell the property. Keep your profit objective in mind at all times!

5. **Look for such properties in your area.** Use the Sunday papers, local real estate brokers, the Apartment Owners Association. (If there are no such properties locally, check out nearby cities and towns—or distant ones. Use these methods on those properties.)

6. **Get the price, the income, the expenses, and the down payment** for the type of property you've chosen.

7. **Project the potential appreciation** for one year, two years, three years, and so on. See the following examples for the appreciation in several real-life properties.

8. **Estimate the price you can sell the property at** in one year, two years, three years, and so on. Decide if the potential profit is worth your time. That is, will you earn $100 per hour, $500 per hour, and so on, for the estimated time you'll spend looking for,

negotiating for, buying, and reselling the property? Only you can decide if the effort is worth your time!

9. **Negotiate to buy the selected property** at the lowest down payment you can get. Remember: The lower your cost, the higher your potential profit!

10. **Buy the property.** Have cosmetic repairs made. Get the property fully rented with three months' security deposit for each unit. Put the property on the market at a price that gives you your targeted profit.

11. **Sell the appreciated property** at the price you set. Go on to your next profitable appreciation deal!

Now we'll show you a number of real-life deals in which these steps are used. This info could put big money into your pocket in a short time.

Go the Preconstruction Route to Your Wealth

With the rapid growth in two-income families seeking "places in the sun" for relaxation or year-round living you'll find:

- **Major increases** in high-rise condo construction.
- **Ocean-front properties** in great demand nationwide.
- **Builders anxious to sell** their units before construction starts.
- **Attractive financing terms** with built-in long-term mortgages.
- **Other waterfront properties** (rivers, lakes, bays) also in strong demand almost everywhere around the country.
- **Double-digit value increases** annually in some areas.

To cash in on these opportunities, many Beginning Wealth Builder (BWB) income real estate entrepreneurs are going the "preconstruction route" to their wealth. Here's how you too, can cash in on these wealth opportunities.

We'll assume you're interested in buying an ocean-front preconstruction one-bedroom condo that you'll hold until its price increases to a level that gives you a suitable profit—say at least 25 percent in one year.

The method given here will work equally well for any other type of property you want to buy and profit from its appreciation—that is, its rise in value. But before we give you the steps to take, let's take a look at the property you plan to buy.

Purchase the Best Property You Can

You request a sales brochure from the condo builder. This brochure describes a new ocean front building on the La Jolla coast, in California. The brochure shows you a corner apartment on the 10th floor that you've chosen. "Your" apartment's living-room windows look westward onto the Pacific Ocean and south to the Mission Bay, California, shipping inlet.

Looking westward, you can see the large cruise ships headed toward the inlet. Further out to sea, jetliners crisscross the sky, headed to Asia or South America. Looking downward you can see the ocean beach. Closer in is the building's swimming pool. Adults and children frolic in the waves and in the pool.

The condo building you're looking at is interesting because:

- **The first eight floors** will be a hotel.
- **The remaining 12 floors** will be condo apartments.
- **The hotel management** will rent your condo apartment when you're not using it, if you want them to do so.
- **The possibility of renting your condo** apartment when you're not using it assures you that you'll be able to earn some money from it.

The price of the ocean front one-bedroom condo you've picked is $800,000. A $10,000 preconstruction deposit is required. After 12 months elapse, another $70,000 will be required of you.

Construction will take 18 months. After checking comparable one-bedroom condos in the area, you see they've risen in price from a low of 32 percent in one year to a high of 76 percent in one year. Using an intermediate rise in value of 54 percent, your $800,000 condo would be worth $800,000 × 1.54 = $1,232,000. This takes your breath away!

Being a careful person, you write out some "worst case" numbers:

Value with no appreciation in 1 year = $800,000

Value with 10 percent appreciation in 1 year = $880,000

Value with 20 percent appreciation in 1 year = $960,000

Value with 25 percent appreciation in 1 year = $1,000,000

Deciding that the risk for yourself is not too great, you take a $10,000 cash advance on two credit cards, $5,000 on each, and make a deposit on the condo apartment. Then you sit back and wait for construction to start.

Use the "High-Yield Strategic Appreciation Method" Anywhere

I can just hear you saying: "I'm from Illinois. I don't want to go to California to invest." Or, "I'm from Ontario, Canada. I'd rather invest in western Canada than in California. So what method should I use?"

My answer is that you use the High-Yield Strategic Appreciation Method I'm about to give you. Why? Because this method works equally well in:

- **Fort Lauderdale, Florida,** overlooking the Atlantic Ocean.
- **Chicago, Illinois,** overlooking Lake Michigan.
- **New Orleans, Louisiana,** overlooking the Mississippi River.
- **Almost any coastline city** or town overlooking a body of water— ocean, lake, river, reservoir, creek, and so on.

Using this income property appreciation method, you take proven steps to your real estate success. How do I know? Hundreds of BWBs who attend my seminars in Manhattan, thousands who read my books and newsletters, report they've made preconstruction profits using my special

High-Yield Strategic Appreciation Method. Here's the Method in easy-to-follow steps that you'll have fun with while you build your wealth.

Step-by-Step to Preconstruction Wealth

To build your income real estate wealth in preconstruction purchase and resale, take these easy steps, starting right now:

1. **Decide what area you want to invest in.** This could be locally, in the sun belt, in ski vacation areas, or even in popular overseas locations.

2. **Get data on the construction activity** in your area of choice. Do this by checking local Sunday newspaper ads in the Real Estate section. You can also go on the Internet and get info from real estate brokers in the area.

3. **Call, write, fax, or e-mail new-construction companies.** Ask for their free brochures on the properties that interest you. Study these brochures carefully, comparing prices, down payment required, location, views, nearness to shopping, religious facilities, transportation, restaurants, parks, schools, rental possibilities, and so on.

4. **Pick one unit you believe has promise** of strong price appreciation based on the factors listed in Item 3. Get full data on the "Ernest Money Down Payment Deposit" required.

5. **Estimate what you can sell your unit for** at the finish of construction. You can do this by comparing earlier builder selling prices for units in the area and the sales price people paid at the finish of construction. Local real estate brokers have this info and will be glad to give it to you free. Since construction of high-rise condos normally takes about 18 months, you have this time frame to work with.

6. **Negotiate with the seller** for the lowest Ernest Money Deposit you can get. Why? Because this money will be in the builder's hands during construction and will not be earning interest for you. The loss of this interest will be one of your costs of doing business. So you want to keep it as low as possible to conserve your cash.

7. **Make your Earnest Money Down Payment Deposit** using borrowed money. Know, in advance, how you'll repay this borrowed money! DO NOT RUSH INTO A DEAL LIKE THIS WITHOUT KNOWING HOW YOU'LL REPAY YOUR LOAN. Why? Because your down payment will not be earning money for you. So the repayment funds must come from another source—such as your salary, or income from other properties you own.

8. **Watch your condo property every week,** on a set day, such as Sunday. Do this by contacting the builder by e-mail, on the Internet, by phone, fax, or postal mail. Ask for the current price of one-bedroom ocean-view units. If your property is like many others you'll see a gradual increase in price as construction progresses. Typically, the price jump will be $5,000 1 month after construction starts. A few months later, the price will rise by $10,000, or $15,000. And by the time 12 months have passed, you may see a 25 percent, or more, rise in price. When this happens you know your investment is safe.

9. **Decide when you'll sell your condo unit** for a profit. Be sure to have the advice of a competent accountant before selling. Why? Because your income tax could be a lot different, depending on how long you hold the property before selling.

10. **Follow the example given earlier in this chapter** to figure your potential profit before you sell. Don't sell until you're sure you can earn the profit you've projected for your property.

11. **Never sell your real estate property** without the full guidance of a competent real estate attorney. YOU MUST HAVE A COMPETENT REAL ESTATE ATTORNEY EVERY STEP OF THE WAY IN YOUR SALE.

Preconstruction Sales Can Build Your Real Estate Wealth

In my position as director of a large full-service lender making hundreds of loans a year, I see lots of preconstruction profits. And as the author of a number of successful real estate books, readers regularly report to me the profits they earn from preconstruction sales.

Then I get further backing when attendees at my real estate seminars in Manhattan tell the audience:

> "Preconstruction financing really works! I bought two condos for $25,000 down and I walked away with $50,000 in profit a few months later!"
>
> Or, "I really wanted the townhouse in San Diego when I put a small deposit on it before the builder started work on it. But six months later an anxious buyer offered me $60,000 more than I was going to pay for it. I couldn't refuse—$60,000 is more than I earn in one year!"

Use In-Place Real Estate as Your Wealth Source

In-place real estate consists of existing buildings and homes you acquire at low cost and sell at a higher price. With preconstruction—remember—the property does not yet exist when you acquire it.

Existing property can be seen, can be inspected, can be tested for undesirable paint, and so on. So you know—in general—what you're buying. Your challenge is to:

Buy Low—Sell High!

Your next question is: "How, and where, can I buy low and sell high?" There are two primary sources of low-priced properties:

- **Foreclosure sales** of various types.
- **Motivated sellers** seeking to get out of property ownership fast.

Let's take a look at foreclosure sales first. Then we'll show you how, and where, to find motivated sellers.

Foreclosure Sales for Your Future Success

Foreclosure sales occur when a property owner has not made the required payment on his or her mortgage or real estate taxes. The lender, municipal authority, or federal government, decides that the property must be sold to satisfy (that is, pay) the mortgage or tax debt. There are three types of foreclosure sales you can use:

1. **Buy directly from the owner** before the official foreclosure occurs, but after there has been notice that a foreclosure will occur sometime in the future if the existing debt is not paid within a stated time period.
2. **Buy at the official auction** on the courthouse steps or at the federal government facility when the property is sold to the highest bidder to repay the debt(s) owed on it.
3. **Buy from the lender** in a postauction sale a property that was not sold at the auction.

Let's look at each of these ways of obtaining good properties at 25 percent to 50 percent off the going market price.

Buy Directly from the Owner

Municipal authorities list properties on which they have sent a default notice. You can find such listings in your local city or County Courthouse. Each listing gives data on the property—owner's name, property address, how much is owed, and to whom. With this info in hand you can:

- **Visit the owner** personally in the property.
- **Make an offer** to assume the debt from the owner.
- **Allow the owner to stay** in the property for a monthly rental fee.
- **Offer to sell the property** to the owner after a stated time period— one year, two years, and so on, at a stated price that gives you a profit.
- **Sell the house** after the stated time period if the owner does not buy it.

Let's see how this might work with an actual property you discover is about to be foreclosed.

Foreclosure of Mountain View Property

Here are the steps you take to buy a foreclosure property before the actual foreclosure steps begin:

1. **You check your local County Courthouse records** and find that a mountain retreat type home is about to go into foreclosure. Its owner is a local businessman whose business sales have been lagging for the past several years. He, his wife, and three children reside in the home.

2. **Visiting the property** you find it nestled on a plateau in local hills. The home has gorgeous views of wooded landscapes of nearby mountains and valleys through a 270-degree angle. A brook traces a glistening curving white path down the side of the mountain opposite the living room windows of the house.

3. **The property is valued at $680,000** by local realtors. A $575,000 mortgage exists on the property and the owner is three months behind on his payments, or $10,500.

4. **You agree with the owner to assume responsibility** for the $575,000 mortgage and to rent the house to the owner for $1,000 per month for one year. He saves $2,500 per month.

5. **At the end of one year** you will sell the house to the owner for $800,000. The owner agrees to all these terms because he wants to hold on to his beautiful mountain home. You pay the $10,500 arrears on the mortgage (which you get from your credit-card line of credit). It's WIN-WIN for both of you!

6. **If the owner cannot buy the house after one year,** you are free to sell it on the open market.

7. **The owner gladly accepts all your terms because by doing so he can stay in his home.** Further, he has the chance to buy it back from you. After 11 months you find that the property is valued by local realtors at $780,000.

"This real-life example sounds great," you say. "But, what are the negatives?" you ask. There are several, namely:

- **Dealing with the owner** can be very painful for you. Why? Because the owner is facing eviction from his or her home. That can be a gut-wrenching experience for anyone.

- **Working out the deal** can take time because you have to get an appraisal of the current value of the property, determine the existing mortgage balance, negotiate a deal with the owner as to the monthly rent, and set a price for the eventual resale to the owner.

- **Supervising the property** during the time interval you've negotiated can be time-consuming. Why? Because if a person has gone into default once, there is a strong likelihood that he or she will do it again in the future. So you must watch the deal every day of the week!

- **Guiding you every step of the way,** you must have a highly competent real estate attorney so all the paperwork is properly prepared. This will cost you some money. But every penny you spend on competent legal guidance is worth many dollars. *You must have good legal advice on every real estate transaction!*

Take a Look at Your Results

At the end of 12 months you look over your account books and your real estate records. Here's what you see. You have two options—(1) Sell the property on the open market; (2) Sell the property to the former owner for the agreed-on price of $800,000. Your numbers show:

- **Mortgage payments made** = $42,000 (rounded, includes real estate taxes and insurance). Or, 12 months × $3,500/month = $42,000.

- **Increase in house value** = $780,000 − $680,000 = $100,000.

- **Actual value increase,** based on the mortgage you assumed = $780,000 − $575,000 mortgage = $205,000.

- **Net cash to you** before closing costs = $205,000 − $42,000 − $10,500 = $152,500.

- **Estimated closing costs** for sale @ 4 percent of sales price of $780,000 = $32,000 (rounded up).

- **Net cash to you** if you sell without a real estate broker = $152,500 − $32,000 = $120,500. Or you earned $120,500/12 = $10,042 per month, with no rent payments.

- **If you sold to the owner** after one year at $800,000, your profit would be $800,000 − $575,000 mortgage − $42,000 − $10,500 = $172,500, with no rent. (Your profit would actually be somewhat higher because of mortgage principal reduction and any rent you received from your tenant.)

- **Monthly profit** = $172,500/12 = $14,375. By selling to the owner you would avoid the 4 percent closing costs. No real estate broker commission would be involved, either.

- **Your monthly profit is higher** when you sell to the owner. And you also have the satisfaction of helping the owner keep his home without disrupting his family life. This could be worth more than the monthly profit you earn!

Buy Foreclosed Properties at Auctions

The second way you can buy foreclosed properties is at auctions on the courthouse steps. When you're just starting your real estate career I suggest that you avoid such auctions. Why? Because:

- **At auctions you're competing with professionals** who know the properties for sale, including the property pluses and minuses.

- **You usually are not allowed to inspect a property** before the auction. Hence, you're buying an unknown. For a beginner this could be a disaster.

- **Auctioneers demand cash** shortly after you win an auction bid on a property; coming up with the cash could be a problem for beginners because the payment must be made by Certified or Banker's check.

- **To protect yourself,** you should have a title search made before you bid on a property. Why? Because if there are liens against the property you—as buyer—become the "happy" owner of those liens. You'll have to pay them off to obtain clear title to the property. This could really put you in a hole financially and negate any possible profit you might make on later sale of the property.

For these, and many other reasons, I suggest you skip property auctions at the start of your real estate career. Once you have some experience with properties and their care and sale, you can explore auctions and the profit potential they may have for you.

Post-Auction Properties Could Be Your Best Choice

When a property doesn't sell at an auction it reverts (goes back) to the lender or the taxing authority that foreclosed on it. These properties are called REOs for *Real Estate Owned.* Lenders and tax agencies don't want to own real estate they repossessed! So what do they do? Most of these organizations:

- **Advertise the property** for sale at a reduced price.
- **Offering—in some cases**—to pay the closing costs.
- **Giving 100 percent financing** when the property doesn't sell quickly.
- **Handling all the details of the sale,** including title search, environmental inspection, payment of overdue taxes, and so on.
- **Allowing you to get started** with lower-cost properties in a safe and controlled way that can seldom go wrong.

"So," you say, "how can I get started buying REOs I can sell for a profit?" Here are your easy steps to take:

1. **Look in your telephone book** *Yellow Pages* under "Banks" to locate potential local real estate lenders having REOs.
2. **Contact the bank by phone.** Ask for the Mortgage Department. Tell the person you're talking to that you're interested in buying postauction REOs.

3. **Don't be put off if you're told** the bank doesn't have any REOs. This is a defensive answer because banks and other real estate lenders dislike admitting that they made a bad loan—that is, a loan that went into default, requiring foreclosure on the property. It's embarrassing

4. **Continue calling** banks, credit unions, insurance companies, and other real estate lenders until you find postauction REOs.

5. **Be prepared to be told** that a bank farms out its REOs to local real estate brokers. If you're told this, get the names and addresses of the real estate brokers and contact them. Tell the broker you're interested in buying REOs at bargain prices.

6. **Have the broker or bank send you a list** of available REOs. Drive by each REO to see its external appearance. Ask to be shown through those properties that interest you from an investment standpoint.

7. **Get info on local rentals** and what your selected properties would rent for BEFORE making any offer on a property. You MUST have a Positive Cash Flow (PCF) on EVERY property you invest in, even when you expect appreciation in value to provide your major profit. Why? Because if a negative-cash-flow property doesn't sell as quickly as you plan, you will have to "feed" it with income from other sources. This can lead to major financial problems for you.

8. **Take over REOs that promise to provide a good profit** when you sell them, usually after some cosmetic improvements. Its best to have this work done by a competent contractor. If you try to do such work the time you spend at it may detract from your business activities of finding new, profitable REOs.

9. **Continue building your REO profits** until you reach the income level you seek. In some REO situations your $1 million in acquisitions in one year will be a "rolling" investment. By that I mean you will have acquired that much value in 12 months but you may have sold some of the properties for a quick profit during the year.

Yes, REOs can build your wealth in low-cost properties much faster than the auction route. Further, REOs are better suited to beginners. Once you've bought and sold some REO properties, you can try the auction route to wealth. Just look at this letter that I received while writing this chapter:

> "Please share this with your readers. Since beginning as a member of IWS and leveraging its resources, we have created a portfolio of $3.5 million with no money down (in about 5 months)—generating close to $10,000 monthly cash flow. It consists of single-family homes, duplexes and quads. We are now aggressively looking to move into bigger, more profitable multifamily and commercial units. Your publications and your telephone advice have added tremendous value, and we are happy to have you a part of our team."
>
> —Virginia

Twelve More Ways to Find Low-Cost Properties

To make appreciation work for you, you must buy low-cost properties and wait for them to appreciate while you help them rise faster in value by making selected improvements. Good advice from real estate millionaires is given in the saying:

Buy the worst house in the best neighborhood and improve the house while it grows in value. You can expand this saying to include condos, multifamily units, and other real estate.

Now here are 12 ways for you to find low-cost properties. Each takes some doing on your part. But—good friend—the doing is worth the effort. It can help you acquire $1 million in real estate in one year in your spare time, on borrowed money! So:

1. **Look for property being sold** because the owner(s) have marital problems. The spats have become so intense that both "just want out." Result: They sell to you at a price well below the market value "just to get out, and away."

2. **Look for property offered** by an owner who's being transferred to another location by an employer that does not take responsibility

for the employee's property sale. The seller will often sell at less than the market value because he or she may have bought another property at his or her new job location and has to get there fast.

3. **Look for property offered** for sale by a seller who's being constantly harassed by someone to whom he or she owes money—a government agency, such as the IRS; credit-card issuer, bank, credit union, real-estate tax authority, and so on. Such a person often decides to get rid of all their bills by selling their last remaining asset (real estate) to clean up all their debts, once and for all. Result? They offer the property cheap—just to get out! You get the property and they're no longer hounded by their creditors. It's a win-win situation for both of you.

4. **Look for laid-off, downsized, reduced-force sellers** who have to raise cash quickly because they have little, or no, savings. So they want to sell rapidly because their property is the only substantial asset they have. Autos, boats, mopeds, and so on, rarely have significant value in these circumstances. Such sellers need cash to tide them over until they find their next job. You can help them by buying their property at a below-market price—quickly.

5. **Look for sick, maimed, handicapped owners** who must sell their property because it is beyond their physical capabilities to handle it at this stage of their lives. While it may seem cruel to buy from such people, you are actually helping them to move on to a better lifestyle in a more comfortable property. Such people will often sell at a reduced price because they want to go to a different location (dryer, warmer, etc.) where they will be happier and more comfortable. They want to sell fast so they can do what the doctor ordered.

6. **Look for property that's been on the market six months,** or longer. The seller is getting worried because the property hasn't sold while others around it have sold in much less time. So the seller reduces the price drastically to encourage you to buy it quickly! Which I'm sure you will if it helps you reach your million-dollar goal in one year!

7. **Look for estate sales** where the survivors (often the children of the deceased) don't want to have anything to do with real estate.

All they want is the money from the sale so they can do their "thing"—which isn't real estate! Their only desire is to get the money and run! You satisfy this desire by buying at a reduced price, allowing you to profit from appreciation of the property after you take title to it.

8. **Look for sellers who are squabbling** with neighbors, the local school system, the town board over a planned improvement, the tax authority over a big rate increase, zoning change, and so on. Frustrated, the seller wants out—fast. Such festering problems can give you the property at a real bargain price—which is your goal! And I'm sure you'll avoid getting into the same squabbles the former owner did.

9. **Look for sellers who are suddenly impacted by worries** over pending inflation, depression, rising energy (gas, oil) prices, and so on. Some people will be so obsessed with such possibilities that they decide to sell their property quickly—to get their money while they can. You come along and pay their under-market price so they can get away from the cause of their worries! They "cash-out" and are happy. So, too, are you, with the bargain deal you negotiated.

10. **Look for sellers who want to sell out quickly** so they can buy another property, a business, a boat, an airplane—whatever turns them on. Such people are so gripped with their new love that they want to have it yesterday. They can't even wait until tomorrow. They must have it NOW! You buy their property at a bargain price so they can "dance" with their new love today! Again, a win-win situation for both you and the seller.

11. **Look for sellers who are "burned out"** dealing with tenants, repairs, renting vacant apartments, and so on. Then an "earth-shaking" incident in their lives leads to the "I've had it" attitude. So the owner decides to sell—fast. When the decision to sell is made, the owner can barely get out fast enough—even a day seems too long. Result: You pick up a bargain property at an excellent price giving you plenty of "room" for appreciation to take over.

12. **Look for older owners (80 and up)** who want to move north, south, east, or west and "smell the roses." Such owners may bond with you when you demonstrate that you're ambitious, honest,

hardworking, and have exciting plans for the future of their beloved properties. Some of our readers have worked out zero-down deals with owner financing of such properties being sold by older owners. You can share in the future appreciation of these properties without putting up much, or sometimes, any, money.

So now you have 12 more ways to find properties with high appreciation potential. Use any, or all, of these ways and watch your acquisitions grow to the million-dollar level, in one year, or less!

 ## Your Key Ideas for Building Wealth with Property Appreciation

❑ **Real Estate appreciates** in value because the price of land, labor, and materials increases as time passes.
❑ **Buy preconstruction properties** and their price is likely to increase because of the rise in costs as construction proceeds.
❑ **Scenic-view properties**—oceans, bays, lakes, mountains—often rise significantly in value during, and after, construction.
❑ **Buy the best property** you can. It is almost always likely to rise in value—appreciate—as time passes. You almost can't go wrong!
❑ **Use the High-Yield Strategic Appreciation Method** anywhere and you have a good chance of earning a large return on your real estate investment.
❑ **You can buy foreclosure properties** three different ways: From the owner before foreclosure; at auction after foreclosure; from the lender after the foreclosure auction.
❑ **REOs** bought at postauction may often be your best foreclosure purchase.
❑ **To get the highest appreciation** from a property you buy, use any of the dozen methods given you in this chapter.

CHAPTER 11

Use a Wraparound Mortgage to Acquire the Income Real Estate You Seek

YOU CAN USE A *WRAPAROUND MORTGAGE* (OFTEN SHORTENED TO *WRAP* BY real estate professionals) to acquire $1 million in real estate in one year in your free time on borrowed money. To do so, you should understand:

- **What** a wraparound mortgage is.
- **Why** you should consider using a wraparound mortgage.
- **Where** a wraparound mortgage can best be used.
- **When** you should use a wraparound mortgage.
- **How to** use a wraparound mortgage.

Now let's look at each of these ideas and see how you can use it.

What Is a Wraparound Mortgage?

A wraparound mortgage is a loan using real estate as collateral that has these features:

- **The wrap loan is a new loan** on a property that already has a first mortgage on it.
- **The interest rate on the first mortgage** is usually lower than going rates in the area for first mortgages.
- **The wrap loan helps you buy** the income property with a small down payment, or no down payment at all.
- **The wrap loan enables you to make** just one payment per month that covers both the existing first mortgage and your new loan.
- **The wrap loan avoids the stigma** that sometimes accompanies a second mortgage, even though the wrap loan is—in essence—a second mortgage.

Example of a Wraparound Mortgage

You, we'll say, want to buy an eight-unit garden apartment house in a lovely area.

The garden apartment house is priced at $275,000. Annual income from the apartment rentals and a laundry room in the basement is $47,000. The annual expenses before mortgage payments total $19,000. This leaves $47,000 − $19,000 = $28,000 per year to pay for the loans you take to buy this garden apartment house.

A down payment of $25,000 is required by the seller. There is a $100,000 first mortgage at 5.75 percent existing on the property. If you buy this well-cared-for garden apartment house you will assume the first mortgage, if you would like to keep it on the property.

You know you can borrow the $25,000 down payment from your credit-card lines of credit. To do so you'll use several credit cards. This means you can acquire ownership of this desirable garden apartment house on zero cash out of your pocket.

Inspecting your prospective purchase you find the garden apartment is in good condition. Little maintenance will be needed when you take it over.

Checking local lenders you find you can get a wraparound mortgage for $250,000 at 6 percent interest for 30 years. Now you "work the numbers."

Working the Numbers for Your Wrap Loan

You can work the numbers for your wrap loan using any of the readily available mortgage interest tables. Or you can do it on the Internet at various loan sites. Lastly, as a subscriber to one of my newsletters, you can fax, e-mail, or postal mail me the numbers and I'll work them for you free of charge. Here's how they'll work for this garden apartment house:

Annual income before nondebt service = $47,000

Annual expenses before debt service = $19,000

Net annual income before debt service = $28,000

Debt Service

Monthly payment on wraparound loan of $250,000 @ 6 percent for 30 years = $1,500

Monthly payment on $25,000 down payment credit-card loan @ 12 percent interest = $556 for a 5-year (60-month) personal loan

Total monthly debt service = $2,056

Monthly positive cash flow = ($28,000/12) − $2,056 = $277.33

Monthly positive cash flow after credit-card loan payoff = $277.33 plus $556 = $833.33

"So," you say, "I take out $275,000 in loans to make $277.33 per month. Does that make any sense? Isn't it very risky?"

The answers, good friend of mine are:

- **Does it make any sense?** Yes, if you want to acquire $1 million in real estate in one year on borrowed money.

- **You are, after all getting a return** of $277.33 per month on *borrowed money—none of the money you put up comes from your bank account.*

- **Is it risky?** Yes, *IT IS RISKY.* But when you're starting your career, risk is almost always necessary, especially when your capital is limited, or nonexistent.

Now for more details on your wrap loan for the eight-unit garden apartment house described earlier.

- **When you make** your $1,500-per-month payment on your $250,000 wrap loan, your lender pays $584.00 of that on the $100,000 existing 5.75 percent loan on the property.

- **Your total monthly payments** of $2,056 come from the monthly rents you receive for the eight units in the garden apartment house. So no money comes out of your pocket.

- **As time passes** you will probably be able to raise the rents, increasing your monthly Positive Cash Flow (PCF).

- **Your equity (ownership) in the property** increases with every monthly payment you make on your wrap loan. Why? Because you're paying down both mortgages (the $100,000 and the $150,000, along with your down payment loan).

Why You Should Use Wraparound Mortgages

The wrap mortgage offers you many excellent advantages. As a Beginning Wealth Builder (BWB) you should know why wraparound mortgages offer you so many advantages. Here are a number of these advantages you can use in acquiring $1 million in real estate in one year on borrowed money:

- **The title of the property comes to you** when you buy with a wrap loan. This is extremely important to you because you really own the property—it's not like buying on contract where you really don't yet own the property.

- **You can get a wrap loan from** either a traditional mortgage lender or from the seller of the property. Usually, though, your wrap comes from a traditional lender.

- **The existing loan on the property is not "disturbed"**—that is, there is no title search on it, no closing costs, and so on. As a loan, it just "stays where it is."

- **Lenders like wrap loans** because they earn a higher return from such loans. Hence, lenders may be more willing to make you a wrap loan than a traditional mortgage loan.

- **A wrap loan is good for you** when second mortgage loan rates are high. Why? Because the interest rate on a wrap loan is usually less than on a second mortgage loan.

- **Most wrap loans can usually be made faster** than a conventional mortgage loan. This can save you time in your acquisition of the property.

- **You may be able to negotiate a balloon payment** on a wrap loan. This means you pay interest only for a stated period—often 10 years, after which the entire amount becomes due. During the 10-year period your monthly payments are lower, giving you a larger PCF. And, after 10 years, you may be able to renegotiate the mortgage. Or you may have sold the property at a high profit before the 10 years passed!

- **While a wrap loan is a junior mortgage** (usually a second mortgage), it is not thought of in the usual negative terms associated with a second mortgage. Hence, a wrap loan is often more acceptable to both buyer and seller.

- **The wrap lender loans** only the difference between the price less the down payment, less the first mortgage. For the garden apartment house earlier this would be: $275,000 price – $25,000 down payment – $100,000 existing First mortgage = $150,000. Hence, the wrap lender's cash outlay is less but the lender is receiving interest, and payments, on a larger amount. Lenders love this scenario!

- **Getting a wrap loan may allow you to complete a deal** when conventional financing is not available. Lenders like wrap loans because the very fact that there's an existing first mortgage on a property means that the property was strong enough to support a loan from another lender. The earlier loan affirms a lender's decision to do a wrap. (Lenders think alike and look to other lenders to affirm their decisions.)

- **Think of a wraparound mortgage** as one loan on top of another with the top loan being larger, dollar-wise, than the lower loan.

Once you have this idea in your mind you will be able to work effortlessly with wrap loans!

Negotiate to Keep Your Wrap Payment Low

You can—if you put your negotiating "cap" on—get a lower monthly payment on your wrap loan. How?

Ask for a balloon wrap loan with a 10-year term.

Let's take a look at how this will increase your income from the garden apartment house earlier. Here are the numbers:

- **With a 10-year balloon loan** you'll pay $0.06 \times \$250,000 = \$15,000$ per year in interest. This interest is fully tax-deductible to your real estate business.

- **Your monthly payment** to the wrap lender will be $\$15,000/12 = \$1,250$, compared to \$1,500 you'll pay on a fully amortized (paid off) loan.

- **Thus, your PCF income rises** by \$250 per month (= \$1,500 − \$1,250), giving a total monthly PCF of $\$277.33 + \$250 = \$527.33$, or \$6,327.96, compared to \$3,327.96 with an amortizing loan.

When to Use a Wraparound Mortgage

You should consider using a wraparound mortgage whenever you have the following conditions in your real estate wealth building:

- **The property you want to buy** is priced a bit beyond your means but it has enough income to pay all its loans and still have a PCF.

- **The property you want to buy** has an existing first mortgage that you can assume and which will be comfortably paid by the monthly PCF.

- **The property you want to buy** is in reasonably good condition and will not need extensive maintenance when you take it over.

- **The property you want to buy** will give you a bigger jump in your real estate holdings using a wrap than you could get with conventional financing.

Where to Use a Wraparound Mortgage

Consider using a wraparound mortgage when you have any of the following conditions in your real estate wealth building:

- **Your credit score is not the highest,** but you're working on increasing it and getting into the 700+ FICO range.
- **You've been turned down by banks** when you applied for conventional mortgage financing.
- **You want to take a "giant step" forward** and get a really big property quickly.
- **You do not want to "buy on contract"** because this really doesn't give you the ownership you want.

How to Use a Wraparound Mortgage

The previous example shows you the essence of wraparound mortgages. Don't let the name frighten you! I'm here to help you get, and use, a wrap for your deal, whenever you need me. I like to have you be a subscriber to one of my newsletters because it gives you my thinking every month of the year. That puts us on the same wavelength. To use a wraparound mortgage:

- **Go to lenders who like wraps.** A bank that has lots of postauction foreclosure properties will usually be happy to work with you to do a zero-down wrap loan to get properties off its books. And, good friend of mine, most banks do—at some time during the year—wind up with too many postauction properties in their inventory!
- **The Veterans' Administration may use wrap loans** to sell properties in foreclosure. The existing mortgage remains as is, without the "due-on-sale" clause coming into play. So look for VA properties locally. You may be able to acquire them quickly, often with zero cash down.

- **If there is ever the so-called "bubble burst" in real estate,** you will be able to acquire excellent properties using a wraparound mortgage. So the bubble burst will really benefit you, not penalize you!
- **Use a wrap loan every time there's an existing first mortgage** you can assume or use with a "subject to" agreement prepared by your attorney, while getting a PCF from the property. *Never buy with a Negative Cash Flow!*

Your Key Ideas for Using Wraparound Mortgages

❏ **Wraparound mortgages** can help get you properties that could not be financed using conventional mortgages.

❏ **Wraparound mortgages** are junior loans (second mortgage) but they are generally looked on more favorably than seconds.

❏ **Wraparound mortgages** may be obtainable with a lower credit score than conventional mortgages.

❏ **Wraparound mortgages** are liked by lenders because the overall interest income can be higher.

❏ **Wraparound mortgages** are popular with banks having excess postauction foreclosure inventories and with some federal agencies.

❏ **Wraparound mortgages** can give you the opportunity to acquire zero-down income properties.

CHAPTER 12

Bringing It All Together— Acquiring $1 Million of Income Real Estate in One Year Using Borrowed Money in Your Free Time

You now know you want to acquire $1 million of income real estate in one year in your free time using borrowed money. Here's exactly how to achieve your financial goal, using the methods you learned earlier in this book.

Your Real-Life Schedule to Income Property Wealth

And—as you know—your author, Ty Hicks—is your friend and is ready to help in every way I can. So let's get started, here and now. Your easy steps are:

1. **Decide what type of real estate you want to own:** (a) single-family homes (SFHs); (b) multifamily homes (MFHs), apartment houses; commercial property (CP), such as small office buildings, strip malls, and so on.
2. **Select an area in which you'd like to own property.** At the start you'll usually find that your local area is best for you. But if prices are too high locally, you may have to look for property in areas

away from you. Try to limit your travel time to one hour, or less, by car, when you invest at a distance.

3. **Contact real estate brokers, banks, mortgage lenders,** and others selling property in the area you've selected. Also read the newspapers and magazines serving the area. Focus on the type of property you want to own to reach your real estate goal of $1 million in income property in one year.

4. **Set up a plan for acquiring your chosen properties.** Use these guidelines:

What You'll Need with Single-Family Homes

10 SFH @ $100,000 each = $1,000,000—about one property per month.

5 SFH @ $200,000 each = $1,000,000—one property every other month.

3 SFH @ $350,000 each = $1,050,000—one property every quarter.

What You'll Need with Multifamily Homes

3 MFH @ $350,000 each = $1,050,000—one property every quarter.

2 MFH @ $500,000 each = $1,000,000—one property every six months.

What You'll Need with Commercial Property

3 CPs @ $350,000 each = $1,050,000—one property every quarter.

2 CPs @ $500,000 each = $1,000,000—one property every six months.

5. **Prepare a schedule for acquiring the type of property you've chosen.** You can, of course, invest in more than one type of property at the start. But I suggest that you focus on just one type. Why? Because you have a greater chance of success by concentrating on just one type of property. After you get some experience you can expand to other types.

6. **Use the following schedule as a guide for your own schedule.** To help show you how the schedule can work for you I've worked it out for acquiring five single-family homes at $200,000 each in one year. You can use the schedule and steps for any other type of property you choose to invest in.

Warning

This schedule is given to you only as **an example.** Your situation may be completely different from what is given here. Thus, your prices may be higher, or lower. And your closing times may be faster or slower. Your schedule is only an **EXAMPLE** of what might occur. So if your prices are higher, or lower; or if your times are faster, or slower, that's what it is. Please don't call me to tell me that your prices are $1,000 higher, or lower, and therefore the schedule is not accurate! The schedule is a guide for you. Use it as is to earn money and reach your goal. Or tear it apart and rebuild it to suit your needs! (Just be sure to send me a copy of your better version!)

Real Estate Acquisition Schedule

Month No.	Check Off Date When Done	Action to Be Taken
1	_____	**Contact local real estate brokers** to find an SFH in the $200,000 price range. Visit each property. Get data on: (a) Asking price; (b) Down payment; (c) Financing available from seller; (d) Available mortgage-lender financing; (e) Income potential from each property and probable Positive Cash Flow (PCF) after paying all loans and expenses. **Make an offer on the property** if the PCF is suitable. Acquire the property using borrowed money for the down payment as described in earlier chapters of this book. Rent the property; be certain to obtain a three-month Rent Security Deposit on your first income SFH.

(continued)

Month No.	Check Off Date When Done	Action to Be Taken
2	_____	**Get your first income property in good financial condition.** Have an accountant set up an account book for your SFH property. Make careful entries of all income and expense items. **Start looking for your second SFH.** Try to get a property having about the same price, or a bit higher, so you're targeted on your goal of $1 million worth of income real estate in one year on borrowed money.
3	_____	**Acquire your second SFH** for $200,000+ using your first SFH as collateral for an equity loan for the down payment on SFH #2. Follow the same steps as you did in Month #1. Get a three-month Rent Security Deposit.
4	_____	**Devote Month #4** to getting SFH #2 in good financial condition with a PCF from your rental income. You now have six months of Rent Security Deposits that could amount to $12,000 with a $2,000-per-month rent for each property.
5	_____	**Find SFH #3 by contacting** your earlier helpers—real estate brokers, mortgage lenders, banks, and so on. See if you can get a bank foreclosure or other reduced-price SFH having your target $200,000 market value for a lower price. Why? Because with ownership of two SFHs you have "clout" in the market and may be able to build your holdings faster to reach your $1 million goal sooner.

Month No.	Check Off Date When Done	Action to Be Taken
6	_____	**Acquire SFH #3** using borrowed money in the form of an equity loan against either, or both, of your two existing homes. Spend the remainder of the month getting SFH #3 rented and earning the rental income you seek. Get a three-month Rent Security Deposit if you buy through conventional sellers or through a foreclosure seller. Why? The deposit protects you from unreliable tenants. If a prospective tenant can pay you a three-month Rent Security Deposit, he or she is usually a reliable person.
7	_____	**Take a month off!** You're 60 percent on the way to your $1 million goal. A month of relaxing will help recharge your mind and get you ready for the next two SFHs you'll acquire. Besides, "You're entitled to a bit of normal living, for a change!"
8	_____	**Acquire SFH #4.** Again, use the sources you've dealt with earlier for leads on good properties available for you. Or look in the areas of your first three SFHs for similar properties that might be available. Make bids on those that are available if you can negotiate a suitable price and down payment. The numbers, of course, must give you a monthly PCF, plus your three-month Rent Security Deposit.
9	_____	**Use Month 9 to get SFH #4 in shape** to earn the income you seek from it. This may mean you have some cosmetic work done on it to improve its appearance and *(continued)*

Month No.	Check Off Date When Done	Action to Be Taken
		its livability. And count your Rent Security Deposit cash. With a $2,000-per-month average rental you will have $6,000 per SFH × 4 SFH = $24,000. That's a nice cash cushion to have on hand!
10	_____	**Look for, and acquire, SFH #5** at a price in the $200,000 range. As soon as you buy it you will be the proud owner of more than $1 million in income real estate, in just about one year. Collect your three-month Rent Security Deposit. This will raise your Cash on Hand (what I call COH) to $30,000! True, you had to work hard to achieve this level of property ownership. But you now probably have more money than you ever had before. And your assets ($1 million+ in income real estate) are probably more than you ever had in your life. And it really wasn't that difficult to get to where you are!
11	_____	**Use this month to get SFH #5** in good condition, both financially and structurally. Bring all your properties up to a high level of cleanliness, safety, attractiveness, and your wealth will increase while you sleep!
12	_____	**Take the month off! You deserve it!** And while you're enjoying your free time with a gross rental income of five SFHs @ $2,000-per-month = $10,000/month, or $120,000/year, start thinking about your next five SFHs. Or consider other types of real estate for which you might conduct the same kind of wealth-building plan.

Summary of Your First-Year Holdings

Property #	Current Value
SFH #1	$205,000
SFH #2	$201,000
SFH #3	$200,000
SFH #4	$200,500
SFH #5	$200,000
Your Total Holdings	$1,006,500

You have achieved your goal and you're ready to go to the next level in your real estate wealth building plan!

Further, you now have a basic Real Estate Acquisition Schedule you know works and which you can use for a variety of income properties. Typical properties you can use this Schedule for are:

- **Multifamily**—such as apartment houses.
- **Commercial**—stores, bowling alleys, supermarkets.
- **Mixed-use buildings**—stores and residential apartments.
- **Office buildings**—both small and large structures.
- **Self-storage** facilities.
- **Industrial buildings** for manufacturing and warehousing.
- **Assisted-living facilities**—nursing homes, rehab centers, and so on.
- **Automotive**—gas stations, garages, parking lots.
- **Motels** and hotels.
- **Shopping malls,** strip malls, mini-malls.

Building Real-Life Single-Family Home Assets and Income

Here's a recent letter from a reader showing how you can build SFH assets and income in your spare time to achieve your goal of $1 million in real estate in one year on borrowed money. With his letter this reader

submitted a schedule of his investments that resembles the one we suggested previously. This reader and newsletter subscriber writes:

> "My wife and I have been investing in Single-Family
> Homes for the last 2.5 years. We have $2 million in
> assets, approximately $1.2 million in equity, and
> $900,000 in finance. We have been very successful in
> what we have been doing. Our monthly income is $14,337
> and the monthly profit is $6,331. The weekly net clear
> income is $1,582.78. We have a plan where we buy a
> house, lease-option the house, sell it to the renter after 18
> to 36 months per lease-option agreement, taking the
> excess cash of approximately $30,000 to $50,000 from
> each house sold and buying two or three more houses and
> doing the same thing over and over again. We have pur-
> chased all our houses through bank repossessions (bank
> repos for short), HUD, VA, and asset companies using our
> real estate agent in town. We have purchased approxi-
> mately 18 homes. We fix them up ($5,000 to $20,000
> each) with our own money and now the bank's money,
> then we lease-option them to first-time buyers, divorcees,
> bankruptcy-declarers, and slow-pay people. We also fix-up
> and sell a house every once in a while. We developed our
> own Lease Option Contract that protects both the buyer
> and ourselves. We are now thinking of buying 10 to 30
> houses for only Section 8 rentals. A management company
> would operate all these Section 8 houses for us."
>
> —Indiana

Getting the Best Results from Your Schedule

The Schedule form you have now is a good starting point for your Real
Estate Acquisition Plan. Just remember: You can add to the form, sub-
tract from it, double its size, and so on. All that really matters is that the
form you develop works for you! Your focus thoughts for this chapter are
the following steps in maximizing results in your wealth building.

To get the best results from your Schedule, use these helpful pointers before you start:

1. **Settle on the type of property you'll acquire.** At the start it's best to focus on just one type of property. After you have your first $1 million in income real estate holdings you can consider branching out to other types of property. At the start, FOCUS!

2. **Get your long-term financing sources lined up.** Know from whom you can get your long-term mortgage. Focus on trying for a 30-year fixed-rate mortgage. Why? Your monthly payments will be smaller and they will not change because your interest rate is fixed. There's comfort in knowing how much you'll have to pay each month. Use government sources available to you—either from the federal government or your state government. These sources are covered in Chapter 9 of this book. Be sure NOT to overlook your state government real estate loans. These can be important sources of long-term financing for you at competitive rates.

    For example, the California Housing Finance Agency offers a variety of loan programs for single-family homes, multifamily homes, and so on. Loan types include bridge, permanent, predevelopment, construction, down-payment assistance, and so on. You should check out such programs for your state because by not doing so you may be overlooking many attractive loan offers available to you. Some state programs even offer properties for sale that you might obtain at attractive prices. And some states even offer mortgage insurance that can help you get the long-term funding you seek.

3. **Arrange for your down-payment loan as early as possible.** Your whole key to income real estate success is in getting your first income property. And the secret of getting that property is having the down payment available before you buy. Use the many hints given to you earlier in this book to get your down payment money.

4. **Find the income property that's right for you.** Never accept a property you're not happy with. Why? You'll only have trouble with it from day one. Find what you want, even if it takes longer than your Schedule shows. Getting the right start is extremely important, especially for beginners. And, as you know, your author—

Ty Hicks—is ready to help you when you have a question. As you know, I help my newsletter readers first; then I help other readers in the sequence they ask for assistance. But subscribers always get their answers first—and fast!

5. **Have the advice of a competent real estate attorney** BEFORE you sign any contracts or other documents to buy the property. I cannot emphasize too strongly to you the need for competent legal advice in all your real estate transactions. Without an attorney you can run into serious problems. And I don't want that to happen to you!

6. **Buy your first income property** AFTER you've analyzed the numbers—price, income, expenses, and down payment of the property. I'll be happy to analyze these numbers for you completely free of charge if you're a two-year, or longer, subscriber to one of my newsletters. See the back of this book for full info on them.

Go Where the Future Profits Are in Real Estate

Real estate is one of the most exciting businesses in the world. Why do I say this? Because I am in the business as an advisor and lender, and I see—almost daily—the exciting changes taking place in real estate. You can be part of these changes and use them to earn future profits for yourself. Here are important changes that can put big real estate bucks into your bank account if you work them into your Wealth Schedule:

1. **Baby boomer retirement homes** will zoom in value and cost in the sun-belt areas—Florida, Arizona, California. So, too, will sports areas—skiing, golfing, swimming, sailing, and so on—as Baby Boomers try to stay young by being active. Buy homes, land, or other properties in these areas and watch them sky rocket in price and value.

2. **Mortgage cashout specialist:** In this role you help mortgage buyers find home owners who want to sell the mortgage they took as a portion, or all, of the down payment on a house when they sold it. For example, say a home seller accepted a $25,000 five-year second mortgage when she sold the house two years ago. After receiving payments for 24 months, she is faced with paying the college

tuition for her eldest child. She wants to "cash out of the mortgage" so she'll have money to pay for the college tuition. You find
her through small ads you run in local newspapers. To help her get
immediate cash for her mortgage you put her in touch with a
mortgage buyer. You earn a fee from the mortgage buyer for
bringing the mortgage to him or her. If the seller's current balance
on the mortgage is $22,000, she will be paid about $14,300 cash
for it. The buyer waits out the remaining 36 months and receives
$22,000 from the monthly payments. Hence, the mortgage buyer's
profit is $22,000 − $14,300 = $7,700. You, meanwhile, are working
in real estate as a Mortgage Cashout Consultant, learning a lot
about real estate while earning a nice commission. The usual commission you're paid is 4 percent of the cashout amount, or 0.04 ×
$14,300 = $570. No real estate license is usually required to act as a
Mortgage Cashout Broker. *Success Tip for You:* Get as much information about this business as you can, before starting it.

3. **Hard-money Loan Finders** will earn big commissions from deals
   they fund for a variety of properties—multifamily residences, hotels, motels, and so on. Big-money deals will always be with us as
   the cost of land, labor, and materials rise. Learn how to handle such
   deals in your spare time and your commissions can be enormous!

4. **Tax lien purchase and use.** You can often get control of excellent
   properties by buying—at very low cost—the tax lien that exists
   on the property. In effect, you're paying the back taxes on the
   property and gaining control of it. If the owner does not pay you
   the amount you paid on the back taxes, plus interest (and possibly penalties) within a stated period of time (often up to one
   year, or longer), the property becomes yours. Once you own the
   property you can sell it, rehab it (if necessary) for rental, or reside in it yourself. The choice is yours. Yet your investment can
   be very small, compared to the value of the property. And your
   tax lien purchase can be done on borrowed money! To learn
   about tax lien sales and/or auctions in your area, contact by
   phone, e-mail, postal mail, or in person, your local County
   Courthouse. You'll be given full information completely free of
   charge.

5. **Fast-turn properties** can build your wealth quickly. A fast-turn property is one in which you use borrowed money for a quick down payment and sell your acquisition within days of its purchase. You might even have a simultaneous closing in which you buy, and sell, a property in one hour, or less—at a profit. To do such deals takes planning because you must know how you'll sell before you buy. Your author will be happy to evaluate any fast-turn deals you're contemplating. See the last paragraph of this chapter for data on how to contact him.

6. **Outlying-district bargains.** Many of my readers who live in "hot" real estate areas—California, New York City, Chicago, and so on—complain that "they're priced out of the market" by the high local prices. This can be true. But try looking 50 to 100 miles outside your local area. You'll often find jewel properties at less than half the price in your area. And many times the properties offered for sale are owned by older people who want "out" fast. You can negotiate a favorable deal to gain control of valuable properties at a low price, on borrowed money. True, you have to travel to see, inspect, and close on such properties. But once you own them you can have a local management firm collect rents, supervise maintenance, find new tenants, and so on. Twelve such properties in the $80,000 price range will give you your $1 million in real estate in one year on borrowed money. Buy out-of-town Sunday newspapers and search their real estate listings. You'll be delighted with what you see. And when you see an ad saying: "0 down, 0 closing cost" I'm sure you'll say, "That Ty Hicks IS right! I didn't believe it when I read his book, but there are such properties available!"

7. **Probate properties.** When a property owner dies and leaves his or her real estate to survivors, the house, building, factory, and so on is called a *probate property.* Often the survivors have goals in life that do not include real estate. You can help such people by buying their property quickly—at a price below the market value. Why would such people sell at a discount? Because they seek a speedy relief from the burden of caring for the property. Giving them the

"out" is worth a reduced price because they get what they want (relief), plus some money. A good place to find probate properties is through your local newspaper obituary columns. When you find the obit of a real estate owner, contact the family and tell them you'd like to talk to the executor about buying the real estate. You'll be rewarded with an open channel to potentially valuable real estate at a low price!

8. **Get control of land in the path of development.** Most cities expand outward from their center at the rate of about one mile per year. Your key to using this fact is to determine in which direction a city is expanding, north, south, east, west, or a combination of two directions. You determine the expansion direction by:
   - **Looking for** planned super-store openings in the area.
   - **Looking for** housing permits issued by the city.
   - **Looking for** new school construction being planned.
   - **Looking for** new transportation routes or facilities being planned for an area.
   - **Looking for** airport, train station, bus stop plans.

   Data such as these will help you project the direction of future development in an area. Once you know the probable direction, get control—by options or down payments—of land in the path of development. Then just wait for developers to come to you to beg you to sell them your land! *Just remember: Keep your price high; if your price is refused because it's too high, time is on your side. The next buyer will probably pay your asking price, or more!*

9. **Work with the Federal Deposit Insurance Corporation (FDIC),** buying real estate assets from them. The FDIC sells a wide variety of real estate, including properties in the affordable housing program. A list of properties available for sale is updated weekly on the FDIC Internet site, www.fdic.gov/buying/owned. Here are Frequently Asked Questions (FAQ) from the FDIC web site that give you an excellent insight to this important source of affordable real estate. In this display of FAQs I changed the question numbers to letters so there would be no confusion with the text of the book you are reading. Please note Question F, concerning

seller financing. The answer to this question states that "seller financing may be available to qualified buyers for properties with a minimum purchase price of $500,000, or more." Two such properties would fulfill your goal for this book!

FDIC REAL ESTATE FAQ

A. How should I use this listing of properties?
This listing of Real Estate is intended to provide interested parties with preliminary information only. This list is not a solicitation of offers and does not constitute an offer to sell. The information is provided for the purpose of inviting further inquiry and has been obtained from sources we believe to be reliable.

B. I am interested in a few properties off the current listing. How do I find out more information relating to those properties?
Each property will have a contact name and phone number. The contact name will either be an individual from an FDIC office or an individual associated with the sales initiative (e.g., Auction Company, Real Estate Broker). If a Property Information Package (PIP) has been prepared on a particular property, it can be obtained from this individual.

C. How often is the listing of properties updated?
It is the FDIC's intent to update the listing of properties by close of business each Monday. Therefore, with the volatile nature of the real estate business, it is important to contact the individual associated with a particular property to find out if the property is still available since the last update.

D. What is the condition of properties sold from FDIC?
All properties are sold in an "AS IS" condition. The FDIC makes no guarantee, warranty, or representation, expressed or implied as to the location, quality, kind, character, size, description, or fitness for any use or purpose, now or hereafter.

E. How is the Listed Price established?
Listed prices are established by a variety of factors which may include independent appraisals, brokers' opinion of value and current market conditions. All prices are subject to change without notice.

F. Is seller financing available on the properties?

Seller financing may be available to qualified buyers on residential properties with a minimum purchase price of $500,000 or those sold as affordable housing and on all commercial and land properties, regardless of price. Specific sale terms and conditions can be obtained from the individual assigned to market the property.

G. Once an offer is submitted on a property, how is my offer evaluated?

A number of criteria are considered when evaluating offers from prospective purchasers. These include, but are not limited to, net funds received after deducting brokerage commissions and sale expenses, and payment terms considered in light of the applicant's credit worthiness and ability to perform. The FDIC reserves the right to accept, reject or counter any submitted offer. While reviewing such offers, the FDIC further reserves the right to continue its sales efforts, including responding to any inquires or offers to purchase the property.

H. How can I have my name added to the FDIC Real Estate Mailing List?

The FDIC does not maintain a mailing list of those interested in purchasing real estate as the Corporation sees the Internet as the most efficient method to communicate its current property listings in a timely fashion. Auctions and Sealed Bid Sales announcements will both appear on the Internet, under the *Real Estate Sales Announcements,* and be advertised in local and regional newspapers.

If you have questions concerning FDIC property sales that are not answered on the Internet, please feel free to call our Service Centers:

Office	Phone
Field Operations Branch	800-568-9161
1910 Pacific Avenue	
Dallas, TX 75201	

10. **Do a condo conversion of a multifamily rental property:** A number of multifamily rental property owners are converting their individual units to condominiums, selling each unit at an excellent profit. Take a 10-unit multifamily property that might sell for $1 million based on its rental income. This same multiunit apartment house could bring a total of $1.8 million if each of the 10 apartments was sold as a condo for $180,000. In today's market the $180,000 price is low in many areas. *Success Tips for You:* (a) Don't try this strategy unless you have experience in condo conversions, or have a trusted partner with the know-how. It takes lots of real estate experience to succeed in such conversions. (b) Another new development in condo real estate is the condo buys, or leases, a passenger automobile and sublets the car to condo owners for one month at a time. This is popular in vacation areas (such as Florida and Arizona). Having the auto available on a sublet allows the condo owner to fly to his or her apartment and not worry about having a car available for use during the time he or she stays in the condo apartment.

11. **Employ energy conservation in both multi- and single-family buildings:** "Green" buildings are becoming more popular. Such buildings use less energy for heating and cooling. And they conserve water use. When newly built, or rehabbed, they use materials requiring less energy for manufacture. As the owner of such a building you can charge a higher rent because you are more in tune with today's energy usage. *Success Tip for You:* You may be able to get grants from federal, state, or city agencies to pay for "green" rehabbing of a building you currently own.

12. **Install digital wiring and wireless services for multiunit buildings:** The computer, and the Internet, are almost everywhere in our lives. If you can provide digital wiring services and wireless Internet for multiunit buildings you can attract a wealthier group of tenants willing to pay you higher rents for your apartments. And if you own college student housing, you have no choice today but to provide these services to your tenants. You can, however, charge each student for the service you provide. *Success Tip for You:* Have digital and wireless services designed and installed by a

competent professional. Don't try to do it yourself unless you're an experienced electronics installer!

13. **Get to know foreclosure sources in your area** and start working with them. Becoming a competent foreclosure buyer takes time and experience. Devote 15 minutes a day to local foreclosures and in a few months you'll become a mini-expert on your area. Do dry runs, pretending you're buying a specific property. Then follow what happens to it by going to the public records in your County Courthouse. See what price the property sells for. Compare that price to what you estimated the property would sell for. Build your know-how as time passes. When you feel confident that you can make a profit on a property, invest in it. But don't do this until you've studied foreclosure methods and procedures and feel you know enough to risk your time and money!

14. **If you're a first-time home property buyer with less than perfect credit,** consider using the help offered by the Neighborhood Assistance Corporation of America (NACA for short). As a participant you can buy a residential single- or multifamily property in which you plan to reside for no down payment, zero closing costs, zero fees, and a lower interest rate than the going rate in the area of your purchase. The Neighborhood Assistance Corporation of America is an excellent organization that will have you follow their 10-step purchase procedure. It's a solid educational route that you'll travel when you work with NACA. And you'll be a much better informed real estate investor/owner when you buy your first property, which can be a multifamily building if that's the type of property you wish to own. And, in most cases, you'll save money when you use NACA help in buying your first property.

15. **Consider owning a specialty building** if you're a professionally trained person—such as a medical doctor, dentist, accountant, engineer, attorney, and so on. There's an increasing market for small- and medium-size professional buildings of many types. You can house your offices in the building while renting additional space to other professionals. The rents will supplement your professional income. And the depreciation on the building will usually shelter all, or most of, the rental income. Meanwhile,

the value of your professional building will usually rise every year you own it. Some professionals eventually earn more from the appreciation of their building when they sell it than they did from the professional work they did in the in their office in the structure!

16. **Use Section 8 rent voucher payments whenever you can.** With Section 8 rent payments you receive a federal government check each month for each apartment in your building covered by this program. So you never have to worry about your tenant not paying his or her rent. And if you want to sell, or flip, your building, you will find that having Section 8 tenants will usually increase your sales price. In most cities there is a waiting list of Section 8 tenants seeking a suitable apartment. Hence, you can reduce your vacancies to zero when you have apartments suitable for Section 8 tenants. You can find the bedroom square footage, bathroom number, and other requirements for Section 8 housing on the www.hud.gov web site. In some areas of the country you will be paid a hefty cash bonus if you rent your vacant apartment to a Section 8 tenant. These bonuses can go as high as $10,000 for an eight-member family. Above this family number you receive $1,000 for each additional family member you allow to reside in the apartment. Bonuses such as these can go directly to your bottom profit line, increasing your annual rental income every time you rent to a Section 8 tenant. On a monthly rental basis, for example, your *Contract Rent*—the amount you charge your tenant might be $1,134.00. Your *Section 8 Housing Assistance Payment* paid directly to you by the U.S. Government might be $1,114.00. The difference, or $20 per month, is paid to you by your tenant. So you see that nearly 100 percent of your rent payment is made by the government.

17. **Check the properties in your area available from the VA** (Veterans' Administration). Data from the VA states: The VA sells mostly single-family properties that are acquired as a result of foreclosures on VA guaranteed loans. These homes are sold through the facilities of 46 regional offices. Property listings for most homes

are available on the Internet at www.va.gov, or by direct mail. Regional offices whose Internet sites are not fully functional issue sales listings in local newspapers. Offers to purchase VA acquired properties must be submitted on VA forms. These forms can be obtained free on the Internet or from regional VA offices. And your regional office, once you contact it, will provide data on any additional local addenda that might be needed. The first VA form you need is No. 26-6705, Offer to Purchase and Contract of Sale.

18. **Use real estate ratios to evaluate potential properties** and check your progress toward acquiring $1 million in real estate in one year on borrowed money in your free time. True, your real estate ratios do involve some math. And if math turns you off, I can tell you this:

- **Ratio math** is simple—just multiplication and division.
- **Ratio math** is delightful because it tells you how much money you can earn!
- **Ratio math** will guide you, in just a few seconds, to money-making properties for your million-dollar fortune building.

So let's look at a few simple ratios you can almost do in your head that can lead you to the amount of money you want—$500,000, $1 million, $2 million, and so on. Your first real estate ratio is:

GROSS RENT MULTIPLIER

To find the Gross Rent Multiplier (GRM) for a property you're considering buying, do this simple calculation:

$$GRM = \frac{\text{Price of the Property, \$}}{\text{Gross Rent Income per Year, \$}}$$

For example, if you're thinking of buying a property priced at $500,000 and the annual rent income is $100,000, your GRM is:

$$GRM = \frac{\$5000,000}{\$100,000} = 5.0$$

For residential income properties, the typical GRM ranges between 3 and 12. For this property the GRM = 5. A GRM ratio of between 4 and 7 usually means that you can have a good PCF, after paying all expenses, including the loan payments for buying the property with 100 percent financing. So before buying any residential income property, figure its GRM. If it is between 4 and 7, you probably have a winner on your hands!

GROSS INCOME REQUIRED

You can use your GRM to figure the Gross Income Required (GIR) to show a PCF for a property. Thus,

$$GIR = \frac{Price\ of\ Property}{GRM}$$

For the preceeding property,

$$GIR = \frac{\$500,000}{5} = \$100,000$$

MONTHLY RENT MULTIPLIER (MRM)

Some Beginning Wealth Builders (BWBs) use what's called the "One Percent Rule." This rule says: "The monthly rent for a residential income property should be 1 percent of the price you pay for the property." Thus, for the $500,000 property considered earlier, the monthly rent should be 0.01 × $500,000 = $5,000. The rents for this property are $100,000 per year/12 months = $8,333. Thus, the rents exceed the suggested amount, meaning that this is a good buy for you! Another way of expressing the 1 percent rule is to say that the market value of an income property is 100 times its monthly rent income. For this property, 100 × $8,333 = $833,300. Again, this is a good buy for you. You can turn this ratio around and say Monthly rent needed = Market Price/100. For this property, the Monthly rent needed = $500,000/100 = $5,000. Again, we have a good buy here! Another important number, obtained after using these ratios is PCF, sometimes called Net Spendable Income (NSI). Your PCF is the money you have after paying ALL expenses and ALL loans associated with an income property.

LOAN-TO-VALUE RATIO

For this $500,000 property having a $400,000 first mortgage, the Loan-to-Value (LTV) ratio, defined as

$$LTV = \frac{\text{First Mortgage Loan, \$}}{\text{Property Selling Price, \$}}$$

is = $400,000/$500,000 = 0.80. Your annual mortgage payment with a 7.5 percent 30-year mortgage of $400,000 = $33,552 per year. With a $100,000 down payment loan for five years at 10 percent interest, your annual payment will be $25,500. Last, with annual nondebt expenses (taxes, insurance, electric), of $29,800, you will have an annual PCF of $11,148. This is a nice return when you remember that this multifamily residential property is paying for itself!

19. **Don't overlook commercial property** as a way to acquire $1 million in one year in your spare time on borrowed money. Commercial property includes office building, shopping malls, hotels, motels, and so on. Why do I suggest commercial properties to you as a way to build your million-dollar holdings in one year? For several good reasons, namely:
    - **Most BWBs seek residential properties.** Hence, there is less competition for you when you're seeking commercial property.
    - **When your commercial property is fully rented** your PCF can be much higher than with the same size residential property.
    - **You can often buy bank-held commercial properties** at a much lower price (sometimes zero cash) quickly because banks are

afraid of the complications of renting such buildings and want to get them off their books fast.

- **Tax law allows you to do a 1031 exchange** of commercial property with less hassles than with residential property, deferring income tax you might be slated to pay on the gain on the exchange. You might say that the 1031 rule was written for commercial property. For this reason it's easier for you to use it for such property. You must, of course, have a qualified Certified Public Accountant (CPA) advise you on the tax aspects of your 1031 exchange. Don't try to "Do It Yourself" (DIY) because you might run into problems that will trip you up!

- **Commercial properties allow you to have every weekend off.** Why? Because almost all offices are closed on the weekend. So you're not expected to be around on Saturday or Sunday. Result? You can spend time with your family, doing what you enjoy.

- **A major anchor tenant in a shopping mall** can be your collateral for all sorts of loans for your commercial property. The lease from a major anchor tenant "is gold" because the tenant's credit rating almost becomes yours. So when you approach a lender they "see," standing at your side, your major anchor tenant. Your creditworthiness zooms, in the lender's eyes. It's almost impossible to refuse your loan request when you have such collateral at your side! You're a "hero" in the lender's eyes. So you can get the loan you seek, no matter how low a credit score you may personally have.

- **You can write a net, net, net lease** (also called a triple-net lease) for your commercial tenants so they pay all taxes, insurance, utilities (electric, gas, etc.), repairs, and so on on their space. This saves you bundles of money and increases your profit from every square foot of space you lease to your business tenants.

- **Commercial tenants are usually easier to deal with** than residential tenants because the space is occupied by business people. As such, business people understand what it takes to have a repair made, how employees can be less than reliable at times, and so on. So when a requested service is rendered later than expected, the business tenant is more understanding and less likely to complain abusively.

20. **Make use of Operating Leverage whenever you can.** Operating Leverage is the increase in PCF you obtain when your income from rents and other sources—laundry, locker rental, and so on—increase by the same, or a similar, percentage amount. Thus, if your gross rental income is $50,000 per year and expenses before debt service are $20,000, your Net Operating Income = $50,000 − $20,000 = $30,000. A 5 percent increase in both income and expenses yields these results: New gross income = $52,500; New expenses = $21,000; New Net Operating Income = $52,500 − $21,000 = $31,500. With a fixed debt service of $11,000 per year, your PCF goes from $30,000 − $11,000 = $19,000 per year, to $31,500 − $11,000 = $20,500, an increase of nearly 8 percent! So work at improving your Operating Leverage in every way you can because it will put more money into your pocket every month of the year! And that, after all, is why you're in real estate—to earn a larger income than you might in any other business you chose.

21. **Get preapproval of your down-payment and long-term mortgage loans** before you find the property you want to buy. Why? Because preapproval shortens your closing time, allowing you to start earning rental or flipping income sooner. Remember: A dollar today is more valuable than a dollar in the future! It's called the time-value of money. You can get your down-payment preapproval by getting credit-card lines of credit in advance, or by applying for, and getting a personal loan that you don't take until you find a suitable property. For your long-term first mortgage you speak to a suitable lender and negotiate an amount, term, and tentative rate of interest, based on your probable needs. Being preapproved can get you more attention and better service from real estate brokers because they know "you're in the money!" Some will ask you for a letter showing that you've been preapproved for the long-term first mortgage.

22. **Use the Internet in your real estate wealth building.** The Internet is here to stay and you can use it to build your $1 million in real estate holdings faster than you might think. You can use the Internet even if you don't have a computer, or your computer

skills are nonexistent. How? As a two-year or longer subscriber to one of my newsletters described at the back of this book, my staff will do—free of charge—all kinds of computer real estate searches for you for your real estate. Thus, they will do what I recommend you use the computer for in your real estate work, namely to:

- **Find** suitable properties
- **Get full data** on each property—price, income, expenses, down payment.
- **Search for,** and find, suitable financing for a property you want to buy.
- **Locate data on comparable properties** so you can compare prices.
- **Send much of the paperwork** back and forth between yourself and the seller, the lender, and the attorneys handling the sale.
- **Research building violations** in properties you plan to buy, using the data supplied free of charge by large cities having a violation database for potential property buyers. Thus, New York City has a violation database you can reach via the Internet to check a building you plan to buy. Other large cities near you may have similar databases you can check with your computer and the Internet. Such violation information can be valuable to you when you're negotiating a purchase price. The seller should give you a generous allowance (reduction in the purchase price) for all violations you have to pay a mechanic to correct so the building is in compliance with all local regulations. Never agree to buy a building unless the seller corrects ALL violations before the sale is closed, or gives you a monetary allowance to have the violations corrected.

The Internet can save you many hours in the purchase of the properties you want to buy. And even if you've never sat in front of a computer screen you can use my computers, just by telling my staff what type of property you're looking for, the price range you're contemplating, the cash down payment you can afford (if any), and your target income from the property. With this information in hand in written form, my staff will search for suitable properties and send you the information they gather any way you want—postal mail, fax, e-mail. Our staff can even find housing violations for you on the Internet in those cities that publish such infractions on their web site. Just ask for our Internet service when you subscribe to one of our newsletters listed at the back of this book.

 ## Your Key Ideas for Real Estate Future Success

To conclude this chapter, and this book, the following Key Ideas summarize why real estate is probably the best investment you'll ever make:

❏ **The population of the world is increasing** every year. More housing is needed everywhere. So you have a built-in demand for neat, clean properties.

❏ **Land values are rising** because people seek more homes to live in, both in cities and outside cities.

❏ **Being a borrowed-money business,** real estate allows you almost unlimited creativity in arranging, and financing deals for yourself.

❏ **Real estate offers** tax shelters to most investors, such as yourself, because mortgage interest, real estate taxes, and property improvements are, in general, deductible.

❏ **The market value of well-kept real estate** usually increases as time passes. If you build (or have a builder build for you) an income property, the finished property is usually worth 25 percent to 35 percent more than it cost to build, when it is finished.

❏ **An almost instant profit of 25 percent to 35 percent in a short time** (often just a year or two) is usually better than you can achieve in most businesses you'll find anywhere. And this profit is usually earned on borrowed money!

❏ **Finished real estate usually rises in value** as time passes. So you might say that with real estate "Older is better!" Most other built items—autos, trucks, airplanes, ships, and so on—DECLINE in value as time passes! Again, real estate usually RISES in value.

❏ **Cash flow from income real estate also usually rises** as time passes. Thus, rents for income properties (apartment houses, stores, factories, office buildings) generally rise with the passage of time. So you have an unbeatable combination: Your income producer (the building) is going UP in value while the income it produces (RENTS) are also RISING! Your ROI—Return on Investment—is probably higher in real estate than in almost any other business.

❏ **Mortgage payments you make** to repay the money you borrowed to pay for the real estate that's rising in value while paying you a higher income, increases your equity (ownership) of your property every month. It's a WIN-WIN deal for you!

❏ **Time is usually on your side in real estate.** The longer you own a property, the higher (usually) will be its value, and the larger its income paid to you. And almost all costs you pay to improve your property to produce a larger income for yourself are tax deductible! And you do all this with Other People's Money (OPM)! That's why real estate is so great for you.

❏ **Last, a down-turn in real estate** is not "the end of the world!" Instead, a downturn is an opportunity for you to acquire more property at bargain prices. So don't let the "doomer and gloomer" set get you down! Lower prices offer you the chance to build your real estate holdings (called your *portfolio*) so you reach your $1 million goal sooner. Real estate may rise and fall slightly in value. But the land rarely goes away and the inherent value of most real estate remains forever! Keep that in mind when you begin to worry about a minor (or major) correction in real estate values.

❏ **If you want to contact me** you can reach me any of the following ways: Telephone: 516-766-5850 from 8 A.M. to 10 P.M. New York time; Fax: 516-766-5919, 24/7; e-mail: TYGHICKS@AOL.COM, 24/7; on my web site www.iws-inc.com; postal mail: Ty Hicks, IWS, Inc., P.O. Box 186, Merrick, NY 11566-0186.

APPENDIX

Useful Real Estate Books, Reports, Training Courses, and Newsletters for Beginning and Experienced Wealth Builders

You CAN BUILD YOUR REAL ESTATE RICHES ON BORROWED MONEY FASTER! How? By getting more know-how about real estate. As has often been said—"Knowledge is power!" And as Ralph Waldo Emerson said, "Only an inventor knows how to borrow and every person is, or should be, an inventor!"

Here are a number of sources of real estate techniques you'll find helpful, and profitable.

Real Estate Investment and Management Books

The following books are available from John Wiley & Sons, Inc., 111 River Street, Hoboken, NJ 07030. Telephone: 201-748-6000. Books listed here range from beginner's guides to helpful dictionaries and comprehensive references.

Achenbach—*Goldmining in Foreclosure Properties,* paperback, $24.95.

Albrecht—*Buying a Home When You're Single,* paperback, $14.95.

Arnold—*The Arnold Encyclopedia of Real Estate,* paperback, $360.00.

Berges—*The Complete Guide to Buying and Selling Apartment Buildings,* paperback, $29.95.

Berges—*The Complete Guide to Flipping Properties,* paperback, $19.95.

Boiron—*Commercial Real Estate Investing in Canada,* $125.00.

Boroson and Austin—*The Home Buyer's Inspection Guide,* paperback, $19.95.

Carey and Carey—*Going Going Gone! Auctioning Your Home for Top Dollar,* paperback, $16.95.

Cummings—*The Tax-Free Exchange Loophole: How Real Estate Investors Can Profit from the 1031 Exchange,* $34.95.

deRoos—*52 Homes in 52 Weeks: Acquire Your Real Estate Fortune Today,* $16.95.

Edmunds—*Retire on the House: Using Real Estate to Secure Your Retirement,* $18.95.

Eldred—*The Complete Guide to Second Homes for Vacations, Retirement, and Investment,* paperback, $16.95.

Eldred—*The 106 Common Mistakes Homebuyers Make and How to Avoid Them,* paperback, $16.05.

Eldred—*Trump University Real Estate 101: Building Wealth with Real Estate Investments,* $21.95.

Finkel—*The Real Estate Fast Track: How to Create $5,000 to $50,000 Per Month Real Estate Cash Flow,* $19.95.

Haight—*The Real Estate Investment Handbook,* $69.95.

Irwin and Ganz—*The 90 Second Lawyer Guide to Buying Real Estate,* paperback, $19.95.

Kahr—*Real Estate Market Valuation and Analysis,* $70.00.

Larsen—*Core Concepts of Real Estate Practices and Principles,* paperback, $51.95.

Lucier—*How to Make Money with Real Estate Options: Low-Cost, Low-Risk, High-Profit Strategies for Controlling Undervalued Property . . . Without the Burdens of Ownership,* $24.95.

Lumley—*Challenge Your Taxes: Homeowners Guide to Reducing Property Taxes,* paperback, $16.95.

Lumley—*Five Magic Paths to Making a Fortune in Real Estate,* paperback, $16.95.

Masters—*How to Make Money in Commercial Real Estate: For the Small Investor,* $40.00.

Molloy—*The Complete Home Buyer's Bible,* hardcover, $29.95.

Shemin—*Unlimited Riches: Making Your Fortune in Real Estate Investing,* paperback, $16.95.

Siegel and Hartman—*Dictionary of Real Estate,* paperback, $24.95.

Real Estate Self-Study Success Kits, Books, Reports, and Newsletters

The following success kits, books, reports, and newsletters are available from the publishing company of which Tyler G. Hicks is president. To obtain any of these publications, send a check or money order to the following address. You can call the following phone number to order by credit card. You can also order on the Internet or by fax:

International Wealth Success, Inc. (IWS, Inc.), P.O. Box 186, Merrick NY 11566-0186. Order on the Internet at: www.IWS-Inc. com. Order directly by telephone using a credit card at 516-766-5850. You can fax your orders 24/7 to 516-766-5919.

Success Kits

Single-Family Home Riches Kit by Tyler G. Hicks covers earning money from single-family homes (SFHs) by owning them and renting them out, flipping them, leasing them to Section 8 tenants, and so on. Topics include: 10 ways to get your SFH on zero cash using OPM—Other People's Money, where to find big cash-flow properties, how to buy low and sell high today, when—and where—to get zero-down finance, getting hard-money loans today, investing with no risk to your money, easy ways to make big flipping profits, fast financing methods for real estate start-up, getting started with poor—or no—credit. Includes four big bonuses—*Home Buying Guide, Getting the Best Mortgage, Handbook of Adjustable-Rate Mortgages,* and *The TY Hicks Fast Financing Methods for Real Estate Start-Up and Expansion.* **$150, 500 pages, 8.5 × 11 inches, paperback.**

Fast Financing of Your Real Estate Fortune Success Kit shows you how to raise money for real estate deals. You can move ahead faster if you can finance your real estate quickly and easily. This Kit concentrates on getting the money you need for your real estate deals. The Kit gives you more than 2,000 lenders of real estate money all over the United States. It includes Private Lenders who may consider your real estate deal. And the Kit shows you how, and where, to find deals that return a big income to you but are easier to finance than you might think. **$99.50, 7 Speed-Read Books, 523 pages, 8.5 × 11 inches, paperback.**

Financial Broker/Finder/Business Broker/Business Consultant Kit shows you how to start your own private business as a Financial Broker/Finder/Business Broker/Consultant. As a Financial Broker you find business or real estate money for companies or individuals and you are paid a fee after the loan is obtained by your client. As a Finder you are paid a fee for finding things (real estate, money, raw materials, etc.) for firms or people. As a Business Broker you help in the buying or selling of a business—again for a fee. This big Kit shows you how to collect fees for the work you do for your clients. The Kit also contains typical agreements used in the business, tells you what fees to charge, gives you a prewritten news release to get free publicity for your business, and four colorful membership certificates (each 8 × 10 inches). **$99.50, 12 Speed-Read Books, 485 pages, 8.5 × 11 inches, paperback, four membership cards.**

Foreclosures and Other Distressed Properties Kit shows you—with six audio cassette tapes and a comprehensive manual—how and where to find, and buy, foreclosed and other distressed properties of all types. Gives names, addresses, and other data about agencies offering foreclosed properties—often at bargain prices. Presents forms giving examples of actual foreclosure documents and paperwork. Shows how to evaluate properties you're considering buying. **$53.95, 150+ pages, 8.5 × 11 inches, paperback, six cassette audio tapes.**

How to Build Your Real Estate Fortune Today in a Real Estate Investment Trust Kit shows you how to start a REIT to finance any type of real estate you want to invest in to earn money from. Gives you the exact steps to take to raise money from either private or public sources. Today's REITs raise millions for almost every type of real estate used by human beings—multifamily residential (apartment houses), factories, marinas, hotels, motels, shopping malls, nursing homes, hospitals, and so on. REITs can own these types of properties, lend on them (issue mortgages), or make a combination of these investments. Written by Tyler G. Hicks. **$100, 150+ pages, 8.5 × 11 inches, paperback.**

Low-Cost Real Estate Loan Getters Kit shows the user how to get real estate loans for either a client or for themselves. Lists hundreds of active real estate lenders seeking to make first and/or junior mortgage loans for a variety of property types. Loan amounts range from a few thousand dollars to many millions, depending on the property, its location, and value. Presents typical application and agreement forms for use in securing real estate loans. No license is required to obtain loans for oneself using the data in this Kit. This big Kit provides step-by-step guidance for obtaining the real estate loan, or loans, of the user's choice. Written by Tyler G. Hicks. **$100, 150+ pages, 8.5 × 11 inches, paperback.**

Real Estate Riches Success Kit shows you how to make big money in real estate as an income property owner, a mortgage broker, mortgage banker, real estate investment trust operator, mortgage money broker, raw land investor, and industrial property owner. This is a general Kit covering many key aspects of real estate ownership, financing, and investment. Includes numerous financing sources for your real estate wealth building. The Kit also covers how to buy real estate for the lowest price. (Down payments of no cash can sometimes be arranged.) And the Kit also shows how to run your real estate for the biggest profits. Written by Tyler G. Hicks. **$99.50, 6 Speed-Read Books, 446 pages, 8.5 × 11 inches, paperback.**

Mega-Money Methods Kit covers the raising of large amounts of money (multimillions) for real estate and business projects of all types. Some of these projects may be offshore in overseas countries. The Kit shows how to prepare Loan Packages for very large loans, where to get financing for such loans, what fees to charge after the loan is obtained, plus much more. Using this Kit, the Beginning Wealth Builder (BWB) should be able to prepare effective loan requests for large amounts of money for viable projects. The Kit also gives a list of offshore lenders for big real estate and business projects. Written by Tyler G. Hicks. **$100, 200+ pages, 8.5 × 11 inches, paperback.**

Loans by Phone Kit shows you how and where to get real estate, business, and personal loans by telephone. With just 32 words and 15 seconds of time you can determine if a lender is interested in the loan you seek for yourself or for someone who is your client—if you're working as a Loan Broker or a Finder. This Kit gives you hundreds of telephone lenders. About half have toll-free 800 or similar numbers, meaning that your call is free of long-distance charges. Typical agreement forms are also included in the Kit. Written by Tyler G. Hicks. **$100, 150+ pages, 8.5 × 11 inches, paperback.**

Zero-Cash Success Techniques Kit shows you how to get started in income real estate or in your own business venture with no cash of your own. This big Kit includes a special book by Ty Hicks titled *Zero Cash Takeovers of Real Estate and Business,* plus a 58-minute audio cassette tape by him titled *Small Business Financing.* In the tape Ty talks to you, telling you how you can get started in income real estate or in your own business without cash and with few credit checks. **$99.50, 7 Speed-Read Books, 876 pages, 8.5 × 11 inches, paperback, 58-minute audio cassette tape.**

Multifamily Home and Small Office Building Riches Kit shows beginning and experienced real estate wealth builders how to acquire multifamily properties (apartment houses, garden- and townhouse multifamily units, and small office buildings) and operate them profitably. This big Kit shows where to get the money to buy multifamily properties, what to do to get started on zero cash, when is the best time to start building your real estate fortune in multifamily units, which multifamily properties can build your real estate fortune the fastest. Covers loans, grants, lines of credit, and other smart ways to finance these "cash cows." Details seller financing, equity loans, Section 8 bonuses, and more than 3,000+ lenders for multifamily properties. Includes four valuable bonuses on Private Lenders, real estate foreclosure documents, free weekly sales data, and lenders for large multifamily projects. Written by Tyler G. Hicks. **$150.00, 5 Speed-Read Books, 504 pages, 8.5 × 11 inches, paperback.**

Private Loan Money and Funding Kit shows how and where to find private money for real estate of all kinds. More than 150 Private Lenderare described in detail, giving their name, address, telephone and fax numbers, web site (if any), and details on their lending parameters—amounts loaned, types of projects funded, geographic preferences (if any), and lending guidelines important to borrowers. Other topics presented include successful loan packaging for better approval results, unique financing techniques you can use to secure your real estate loans, numerous ways to find private money for your real estate deals. Includes four bonus items. Written by Tyler G. Hicks and other authors. **$100, 5 Speed Read Books, 716 pages, 8.5 × 11 inches, paperback.**

Real Estate Books

Comprehensive Loan Sources for Business and Real Estate gives hundreds of lender's names, addresses, telephone numbers, and types of loans made. **$25, 136 pages, 8.5 × 11 inches, paperback.**

Directory of 2,500 Active Real Estate Lenders lists 2,500 names, addresses, and telephone numbers of direct lenders or sources of information on possible lenders for real estate of many types. Lists lenders nationwide for a variety of real estate projects—from single-family homes to multiunit residential buildings. **$25, 197 pages, 8.5 × 11 inches, paperback.**

Diversified Loan Sources for Business and Real Estate gives hundreds of lender's names, addresses, telephone numbers, and lending guidelines for business and real estate loans of many different types. **$25, 136 pages, 8.5 × 11 inches, paperback.**

How Anyone Can Prosper and Get Wealthy Trading Country Land by Frank Moss shows how to acquire wealth and have fun trading in country land. Covers supply and demand, starting your own home-based spare-time moneymaking business buying and selling woodlands, estimating value, time/distance analysis, plus much more. Using this book, a person can get started in this lucrative part of today's real estate market. **$21.50, 100+ pages, 8.5 × 11 inches, paperback.**

How to Be a Second Mortgage Loan Broker by Richard Brisky gives complete details on how to set up your office, find clients, locate lenders, negotiate with clients and lenders, what fees to charge, how to comply with any licensing laws in your area of business, what files to keep, plus much more. Using this book, a person can get started in this lucrative aspect of today's real estate market. **$25, 100 pages, 8.5 × 11 inches, paperback.**

How to Create Your Own Real Estate Fortune by Jens Nielsen covers investment opportunities in real estate, leveraging, depreciation, tax rules, remodeling your purchases, buy-and-leaseback, understanding your financing, plus much more. **$17.50, 117 pages, 8.5 × 11 inches, paperback.**

Rapid Real Estate and Business Loan-Getting Methods by Tyler G. Hicks, gives innovative techniques to get loans, ways in which real estate can make you rich, getting free of the "9-to-5 grind," new steps to getting venture capital, smart-money ways to get loans, plus many other ideas for real estate and business financing. **$25, 96 pages, 8.5 × 11 inches, paperback.**

How to Make Your Fortune in Real Estate Second Mortgages by Tyler G. Hicks covers Second Mortgages, how a Second Mortgage finder works, registering your firm, running ads, finding capital, expanding the business, Limited Partnerships, plus much more. **$17.50, 100 pages, 8.5 × 11 inches, paperback.**

How to Borrow Your Way to Real Estate Riches Using Government Sources, compiled by Tyler G. Hicks, lists numerous mortgage loans and guarantees, loan purposes, amounts, terms, financing charges, types of structures financed, loan-to-value ratio, special factors, plus much more. **$17.50, 88 pages, 8.5 × 11 inches, paperback.**

Computer Services

IWS Computer Specialist will conduct a comprehensive personalized Internet search for you for real estate properties you would like to own, obtaining their price, down payment, income and expense data, comparable sales prices, potential lenders you can work with, loan applications, loan submission, and so on. Fifty hours of Internet time will be available to you. **$150.**

Real Estate Reports

Here are eight real estate reports on various aspects of property financing. Each report is 8.5 × 11 inches and presents essential information on getting money for the real estate transaction detailed in the report.

Neighborhood and Convenience Shopping Center Loan Package, Report M-1. Example of a typical successful Loan Package. **$12.50, 40 pages.**

Downtown Office Building Loan Package, M-2. Example of a successful Loan Package for an office building. **$12.50, 24 pages.**

Single-Family Home Foreclosure Business Plan, M-3. Shows how money could be raised to buy single-family home foreclosures and rent them out or resell them for a profit. **$12.50, 24 pages.**

Single-Family Home Income Property Business Plan, M-4. Shows how money could be made by owning a string of single-family homes that you rent to tenants for a profit. **$12.50, 24 pages.**

High-Rise Apartment-Building Loan Package and Business Plan, M-5. Presents a comprehensive Loan Package and Business Plan for the financing and operation of a multifamily apartment building. **$12.50, 24 pages.**

Refinancing Proposal for a Multifamily Apartment House, M-6. Shows how a large apartment house can be refinanced to enhance its competitive position in its marketplace. **$12.50, 61 pages.**

FHA Multifamily Building Loan Package and Business Plan, M-7. Shows a typical Loan Package and Business Plan that complies with Agency requirements. **$12.50, 24 pages.**

Offering Circular for Real Estate Mortgage Company, M-8. Real-life example of an Offering Circular used to raise money for an actual mortgage company formed by a BWB. **$12.50, 50 pages.**

Newsletters

International Wealth Success, Ty Hicks' monthly newsletter published 12 times a year. This 16-page newsletter covers loan and grant sources, real estate opportunities, business opportunities, import-export, mail order, and a variety of other topics on earning money in your own business. Every one-year, or longer, subscriber can run one free 60-word (or less) classified ad, or a one-inch display ad free of charge in the newsletter each month. Ads can be for Money Wanted, Business Opportunities, or Money Available. The newsletter has worldwide circulation, giving readers and advertisers extremely broad coverage. Started in January 1967, the newsletter has been published continuously every month since that date. **$24 per year, 16 pages plus additional inserts, 8.5 × 11 inches.**

Money Watch Bulletin, gives a monthly coverage of 100+ active lenders for real estate, business and personal use. The newsletter gives the lender's name, address, telephone number. In some cases the lender's funding guidelines are also given, along with other helpful information about the lender. All lender names were obtained during the past two weeks; the data is therefore right up to date. In addition, lender's names are supplied on self-stick labels on an occasional basis. Also covers venture capital, accounts receivable financing, government mortgage guarantees, overseas and Canadian lenders. Institutions listed include banks, mortgage brokers, credit unions, Private Lenders, and so on. **$95 per year, 12 issues, 20 pages, 8.5 × 11 inches.**

Index